Reducing Crime

Wiley Series in

The Psychology of Crime, Policing and Law

Series Editors

Graham Davies   and   **Ray Bull**

University of Leicester, UK   *University of Leicester, UK*

The Wiley series in the Psychology of Crime, Policing and Law publishes concise and integrative reviews on important emerging areas of contemporary research. The purpose of the series is not merely to present research findings in a clear and readable form, but also to bring out their implications for both practice and policy. In this way, it is hoped the series will not only be useful to psychologists but also to all those concerned with crime detection and prevention, policing, and the judicial process. Current titles of interest in the series include:

Offender Profiling: Theory, Research and Practice
Edited by Janet L. Jackson and Debra A. Bekerian

Psychology, Law and Eyewitness Testimony
Peter B. Ainsworth

Detecting Lies and Deceit: The Psychology of Lying and the
Implications for Professional Practice
Aldert Vrij

Children's Testimony: A Handbook of Psychological Research and Forensic Practice
Edited by Helen L. Westcott, Graham M. Davies and Ray H.C. Bull

Stalking and Psychosexual Obsession: Psychological Perspectives for Prevention, Policing
and Treatment
Edited by Julian Boon and Lorraine Sheridan

The Psychology of Interrogations and Confessions: A Handbook
Gisli H. Gudjonsson

Terrorists, Victims and Society:
Psychological Perspectives on Terrorism and its Consequences
Edited by Andrew Silke

Reducing Crime:
The Effectiveness of Criminal Justice Interventions
Edited by Amanda E. Perry, Cynthia McDougall and David P. Farrington

Reducing Crime

The Effectiveness of Criminal Justice Interventions

Edited by

Amanda E. Perry
University of York, UK

Cynthia McDougall
University of York, UK

and

David P. Farrington
University of Cambridge, UK

John Wiley & Sons, Ltd

Other Wiley Editorial Offices

John Wiley & Sons Inc., 111 River Street, Hoboken, NJ 07030, USA

Jossey-Bass, 989 Market Street, San Francisco, CA 94103-1741, USA

Wiley-VCH Verlag GmbH, Boschstr. 12, D-69469 Weinheim, Germany

John Wiley & Sons Australia Ltd, 42 McDougall Street, Milton, Queensland 4064, Australia

John Wiley & Sons (Asia) Pte Ltd, 2 Clementi Loop #02-01, Jin Xing Distripark,
Singapore 129809

John Wiley & Sons Canada Ltd, 22 Worcester Road, Etobicoke, Ontario, Canada M9W 1L1

Wiley also publishes its books in a variety of electronic formats. Some content that appears in
print may not be available in electronic books.

Library of Congress Cataloging-in-Publication Data

Reducing crime : the effectiveness of criminal justice interventions /
    edited by Amanda E. Perry, Cynthia McDougall, and David P. Farrington.
        p.   cm. — (Wiley series in psychology of crime, policing, and law)
    Includes bibliographical references and index.
    ISBN-13: 978-0-470-02373-0 (cloth)
    ISBN-10: 0-470-02373-2 (cloth)
    ISBN-13: 978-0-470-02374-7 (pbk. : alk. paper)
    ISBN-10 0-470-02374-0 (pbk. : alk. paper)
        1. Crime prevention—Great Britain—Evaluation.   2. Criminal justice,
Administration of—Great Britain—Evaluation.   3. Criminology—Great
Britain.   4. Evaluation research (Social action programs)—Great Britain.
I. Perry-Kessaris, Amanda E.   II. McDougall, Cynthia.   III. Farrington, David P.
IV. Wiley series in psychology of crime, policing, and law.
HV7431 .R443   2006
364.4—dc22   2005013735

British Library Cataloguing in Publication Data

A catalogue record for this book is available from the British Library

ISBN-13 978-0-470-02373-0 (hbk)   978-0-470-02374-7 (pbk)
ISBN-10 0-470-02373-2 (hbk)   0-470-02374-0 (pbk)

Typeset in 10/12pt Century Schoolbook by TechBooks, New Delhi, India
Printed and bound in Great Britain by TJ International Ltd, Padstow, Cornwall, UK
This book is printed on acid-free paper responsibly manufactured from sustainable forestry
in which at least two trees are planted for each one used for paper production.

Contents

About the Editors

Amanda E. Perry is a forensic psychologist working as a research fellow for the Centre for Criminal Justice Economics and Psychology at the University of York. Amanda has worked in academia, healthcare and forensic settings. Her specialist areas of interest are: systematic review and evaluation of research methodology, screening and assessment for suicide and self-harm risk in offenders, and mental-health services. She has published systematic reviews for the Cochrane and Campbell collaborations on drug treatment for offenders and the effectiveness of screening and assessment tools for offenders, and is a guest lecturer for the MSc in Applied Forensic Psychology course at the University of York.

Cynthia McDougall, OBE, is professor and director of the MSc in Applied Forensic Psychology at the University of York, and co-director of the university's Centre for Criminal Justice Economics and Psychology. She has wide practical and research experience in crime-related issues, having worked as a probation officer in the community and as a psychologist in prisons, as head of psychology for prison and probation services. She is a chartered forensic psychologist, a consultant psychologist to the Durham probation area and a member of HM Prison Service Close Supervision Centres Advisory Group.

David P. Farrington, OBE, is professor of psychological criminology at the Institute of Criminology, Cambridge University. He is also co-chair of the Campbell Collaboration Crime and Justice Group, a member of the board of directors of the International Society of Criminology, and joint editor of *Cambridge Studies in Criminology* and the journal *Criminal Behaviour and Mental Health*. His major research interest is in the longitudinal survey of delinquency and crime, and he is director of the Cambridge Study in Delinquent Development, a prospective longitudinal survey of more than 400 London males between the ages of 8 and 48. In addition to more than 360 published papers on criminological and psychological topics, he has published 41 books, monographs and government publications, one of which (*Understanding and Controlling Crime*, 1986) won the prize for distinguished scholarship of the American Sociological Association criminology section.

List of Contributors

Trevor Bennett is professor and director of the Centre for Criminology, University of Glamorgan, Wales.

Mia Debidin works as a principal research officer at the Department for Research Development and Statistics, Home Office, UK.

David P. Farrington is professor of psychological criminology at the Institute of Criminology, University of Cambridge.

Caroline Friendship is principal practitioner with the Barnet Youth Offending Team, London.

Carol Hedderman is professor of criminology at the University of Leicester.

Mike Hough is professor and director of the Institute for Criminal Policy Research, King's College London.

Cynthia McDougall is professor and co-director of the Centre for Criminal Justice Economics and Psychology, University of York.

Mary McMurran is senior research fellow at the School of Psychology, Cardiff University, and consultant clinical and forensic psychologist, Llanarth Court Hospital, Rhaglan, Wales.

Amanda E. Perry is research fellow in psychology at the Centre for Criminal Justice Economics and Psychology, University of York.

Lawrence W. Sherman is Albert M. Greenfield Professor of Human Relations in the Department of Sociology, and director of the Jerry Lee Center of Criminology, University of Pennsylvania, USA.

Raymond Swaray is lecturer in economics at the Business School, University of Hull.

Brandon C. Welsh is assistant professor in the Department of Criminal Justice, University of Massachusetts, Lowell, USA.

Series Preface

The Wiley Series in the Psychology of Crime, Policing and Law publishes both single-author and edited reviews of emerging areas of contemporary research. The purpose of this series is not merely to present research findings in a clear and readable form, but also to bring out their implications for both practice and policy. The series will be useful not only to psychologists, but also to all those concerned with crime detection and prevention, policing and the judicial process.

How can crime be reduced in contemporary society? This is a question all of us have pondered, but answers remain elusive. As I write, a General Election is in full swing and the airwaves are choked with politicians peddling simplistic nostrums for our sometimes venal and violent society with a certainty that belies experience. If there were simple answers to deterring crime, they would surely have been discovered by now. The bleak pessimism of the 1960s and 1970s of the last century, that 'nothing works', has given way to a more cautiously positive view that certain interventions work with particular categories of offenders and offences: 'What works and for whom?' The current book summarises a systematic review of more than a hundred studies conducted in the UK, which have set out to assess the effectiveness of interventions by local authorities, the police and the courts designed to reduce and deter crime. It is based on a survey of the available literature originally commissioned by the Home Office in its search for an evidence-based policy towards offenders and offending. It uses the methodology of the Cochrane Collaboration to weed out all but the best-designed and controlled studies, so that any policy pointers are well founded. Comparisons are drawn between the findings of UK research and those of similar research conducted in North America and elsewhere in Europe.

The book has been edited by Amanda E. Perry, Cynthia McDougall and David P. Farrington. Amanda E. Perry is a research fellow at the Centre for Criminal Justice Economics and Psychology at the University of York. The centre was founded precisely to pursue the kinds of policy-driven research epitomised by the current volume. Professor Cynthia McDougall came to

York as the founding director of the centre after a distinguished career at the Home Office, where she headed psychology for the prison service and, later, the probation service for nine years. Professor David P. Farrington is a professor of psychological criminology at the University of Cambridge; he is the UK's leading forensic psychologist and one of the pioneers of the international movement to understand crime and criminality in objective and scientific terms.

The distinguished editors have attracted major researchers from forensic psychology and criminology to examine different facets of the problem of crime reduction. The principal issues examined are alcohol and drug treatment, courts and sentencing, probation and prison intervention, the use of closed-circuit television (CCTV), improved street lighting and other interventions designed to reduce burglary through such measures as the introduction of neighbourhood watch schemes or 'hardening' vulnerable housing through the fitting of modern security devices. The research appears to confirm that mundane but effective measures such as fitting window locks to the nation's housing estates have as important a role in deterring crime as the costly technologies associated with CCTV surveillance. True to past form, no magic formula emerges from this distillation of the best UK-based research on crime reduction, but some promising leads emerge and gaps in our knowledge are effectively highlighted, as are the methodological lessons to be learned if better and more reliable research is to be carried out in the future.

Reducing Crime deserves to be read, not merely by politicians and policy makers, but by all those who seek to understand crime and criminal behaviour. They include, inevitably, academics and students, but also probation officers, judges and the new generation of police officers, who often have degrees in criminology or psychology. As Professor Lawrence W. Sherman notes in his Foreword to this book, this systematic review represents a milestone in British criminal justice research and deserves to be widely read and influential in policy and practice, whichever political party is in power.

GRAHAM M. DAVIES
University of Leicester

Foreword

This book is a major milestone in British criminology. It provides, by far, the most systematic scholarly assessment of the effects of very costly efforts to prevent crime. The fact that so much money has been spent on so little evidence is nothing new to crime prevention, or even to fields such as agriculture or medicine with more evidence already in hand. What is new is the rising commitment among a small network of British social scientists to remedy the situation.

The influence of this book may become most evident throughout the next generation of British criminologists. Far too many students from previous generations have been taught nothing, or worse, about efforts to reduce bias in assessing the effects of interventions. What can be worse than nothing is the message that it is impossible to reduce bias, or that it doesn't matter because the available methods are ineffective. They have also been taught, for example, that it is better to analyse the results of programmes for people (or communities) who have completed their intended treatments, rather than to group all those randomly assigned to an intention to treat. These and other fallacies of graduate education in social sciences have left the British people with a truly short supply of independent evaluators of expensive programmes.

This book offers a very welcome antidote to such disinformation about systematic evaluations, as well as about systematic reviews. It is an excellent British application of the emerging principles of the Campbell Collaboration's Crime and Justice Group (co-chaired by one of the editors of this volume, Professor David P. Farrington), which is completing a growing number of systematic and international reviews of the effectiveness of crime and justice programmes (www.aic.gov.au/campbellcj/). It is a primary British companion for members of the Academy of Experimental Criminology (www.crim.upenn.edu/aec/) and its new *Journal of Experimental Criminology*. Used in conjunction with specific policy evaluation questions, it can provide compelling examples and clear explanations of preferred research designs.

All areas of science have room for debate, and one may certainly wish to debate the editors and contributors to this volume on certain points. One claim, for example, is that neighbourhoods cannot be randomly assigned to different treatments, when in fact they can be and have been. A 2003 Rockefeller Foundation meeting on random assignment of large social units yielded many ideas and much support for the idea that major advances in knowledge about social programmes must come from the use of such units of analysis as entire schools, housing estates or basic command units of police agencies. A commitment by the British government to support random assignment on that scale would help to answer questions that indeed cannot be answered at the individual level—as in the general deterrent effects of such specific reformation strategies as restorative justice, or the community effects of changes in licensing laws for serving alcohol.

Unlike much previous British literature on the effectiveness of crime prevention, this book provides a constructive platform for debate. Using it to improve, rather than abandon efforts to generalise externally valid conclusions about programme effects could save British taxpayers a great deal of money. And it could also prevent a great deal of crime.

Lawrence W. Sherman
Director, Jerry Lee Center of Criminology
and
Albert M. Greenfield Professor of Human Relations,
University of Pennsylvania

Acknowledgements

The research on which this book is based was supported by funding from the UK Home Office.

Many people have contributed to the original research and to the making of this book. Thanks are due to the research staff: Tracy Murphy, Rochelle Harris and Hedinn Bjornnson for their involvement in the original research project, searching and reviewing the identified literature, and to the administrative support of Judith Jackson and Matt McGovern for the production of the original report. Finally, to Jim McConalogue and Zoe Neale who have assisted with the editorial process for the current book.

DISCLAIMER

CHAPTER 1

Reducing Crime

CYNTHIA MCDOUGALL, AMANDA E. PERRY AND DAVID P. FARRINGTON

BACKGROUND

This book had as its starting point a systematic review of criminal justice interventions aimed at reducing crime in the UK. The *UK review* was initiated to fill a gap in the current literature on the effectiveness of criminal justice interventions specifically relating to the UK. Its inspiration came from three sources: first, the UK Government's commitment to basing policy development on research evidence; second, the concurrent enthusiasm of practitioners for research knowledge; and third, from the influential publications by Sherman et al. (1997) on *Preventing Crime: What Works, What Doesn't, What's Promising*, and Sherman, Farrington, Welsh and MacKenzie (2002) on *Evidence-Based Crime Prevention*, reviewing research conducted in the US and internationally.

HM Home Office initially sponsored the systematic review and the findings are presented throughout this book. The UK studies are part of a programme that had three main aims: (i) to summarise the UK research evidence on reducing crime; (ii) to identify the gaps in research knowledge; and (iii) to stimulate research to fill these gaps. It was a similar process to that initiated by the US National Institute of Justice that led to the original Sherman et al. (1997) publication. This review of UK effectiveness studies is seen as complementary to the Sherman et al. (1997; 2002) publications, but also has some notable differences. The *UK review* has included only those studies that specifically reported on actual crime, self-reported crime or reconviction data. The latter constraint has resulted in the exclusion of a number of UK studies in the field of, for example, early

Reducing Crime: The Effectiveness of Criminal Justice Interventions.
Edited by A. E. Perry, C. McDougall and D. P. Farrington. © 2006 John Wiley & Sons, Ltd.

childhood and school interventions, that have used as outcome measures, risk factors for crime, such as antisocial behaviour or truancy, rather than offence data. In addition, the *UK review* concentrates on the economic evaluations reported in the studies, focusing not only on what works with whom, but also at what cost. Therefore, the range of studies included in the review differs in some respects from that of Sherman et al. (1997; 2002). A similarity, however, is that recognised experts have been invited to update and comment on the systematic review findings, and to place them within a wider context of international research and policy development in their area of expertise.

Despite the slight difference in focus, we have recognised the value of the clear and practical framework adopted by Sherman et al. (1997; 2002). The *UK review* has followed their example by allocating studies to the categories of *What Works, What Doesn't, What's Promising, What's Unknown*, using their strict quality criteria for allocation to those categories. Where appropriate we have indicated the related supporting evidence in international research.

It will be noted that, in the original *UK review*, only a small number of UK studies found their way into the *What Works* category, despite the fact that inclusion in this category only required positive results from two well-conducted studies. This, in our view, makes the case for examining separately the research-evidence base of UK studies, but within the context of international research findings, so that gaps in our knowledge can be clearly identified.

There is little doubt that the exacting research quality standards, similar to those adopted by Sherman et al. (1997; 2002), have reduced the number of studies included in the review. From a starting point of 1,499 research papers identified from a range of databases, through the various stages of screening, the number of included studies was reduced to 62. There are competing views as to whether such a rigorous exclusion process is appropriate. Some researchers will argue that rigorous research in an operational setting is impossible to achieve, and that compromises are necessary and acceptable in order to learn from the large amount of research available. Indeed, some of the authors in this book support that view. There is, however, an alternative view that only by setting exacting standards will the overall quality of research, and hence the understanding of ways to reduce crime, improve. This is the view held by the Cochrane and Campbell collaborations (www.cochrane.org/; www.campbellcollaboration.org/): international organisations that strive to disseminate research findings on health and social science interventions, based on quality research and systematic review. Their commitment to quality research and systematic review has the objective of reducing bias in reporting research outcomes— through transparency of review methods, examining all available literature published in journals and in less formal publications, ensuring that results from both positive and negative outcome studies are reviewed, and reporting only on those studies that have been rigorously conducted so that bias attributable to methodology is kept to a minimum.

THE CASE FOR QUALITY RESEARCH

The case for quality research has long been established in the field of medicine (for example, the Cochrane Collaboration). It is now no longer questioned that a treatment should be thoroughly tested before being administered to patients. Concerns over potentially harming patients through the use of untested methods are rated above the ethical arguments regarding withholding treatments that might be beneficial. The Cochrane Collaboration has been the champion of this approach in the medical field, and is now followed by the Campbell Collaboration, which supports similar standards in the field of social sciences. The Campbell Collaboration Crime and Justice Group (Farrington & Petrosino, 2001) is an international organisation that is now seeking to raise standards of research in criminal justice, and to dispute the assumption that criminal justice interventions should be implemented without adequate safeguards.

It is widely assumed that, even if an intervention is not effective in reducing crime, it is unlikely to do any harm. Since the inception of the Campbell Collaboration Crime and Justice Group and its support for systematic reviews of criminal justice interventions, this view is being challenged. For example, Petrosino, Turpin-Petrosino and Buehler (2002) gave strong evidence to the contrary in their systematic review of 'Scared Straight' programmes. 'Scared Straight' programmes were originally proposed by prison inmates and based on an assumption that delinquency could be prevented by giving youngsters at risk of offending a taste of what it would be like to be imprisoned. The project started in Rahway Prison in New Jersey, and received a great deal of international attention when televised. 'Scared Straight' projects were eventually adopted in 38 states across the US, with a number of programmes introduced in the UK without being evaluated. When a randomised controlled trial was finally conducted to assess the effectiveness of the San Quentin Squires programme (Lewis, 1983), it was found that 81 per cent of the experimental group, compared to 67 per cent of the control group, had been arrested at a 12-month follow-up.

The review by Petrosino et al. (2002) describes this and other scientifically credible evaluations that have demonstrated that attempts to scare teenagers into better behaviour is not a successful enterprise, and can even be counterproductive.

A study which similarly showed that interventions can cause harm was cited in Sherman et al. (1997). Sherman described a 30-year follow-up of a rigorous mentoring study, the Cambridge-Somerville experiment, which began in 1937:

> The results of this intensive mentoring showed no difference between treatment and control groups in criminal records, either in 1942 (Powers and Witmer, 1972) or in 1975–76 (McCord, 1978). The long-term follow-up, however, did show significantly higher levels of diagnosed alcoholism, serious mental illness, and stress-related physical health problems. A higher level of unfavourable life outcomes, although not specifically greater crime, among the treatment group seems clear. What is less clear is the meaning of the results for the value of mentoring programs today. (Sherman, et al., 1997).

This finding has not been satisfactorily explained, although possible reasons have been proposed by Sherman et al. (1997), for example: 'that mentoring is an artificial source of support which makes it harder for mentored boys to adjust as adults'; 'that the abrupt departure of these long-term counsellors from the boys' lives was as damaging emotionally to the boys as a divorce or other loss of parental involvement'; or that 'the treatment boys had no greater rate of personal problems, but when they had problems they were simply more likely to seek professional help of the kind the programme had taught them to seek'.

The conclusions drawn from the two interventions described above are that interventions that may have a superficial appeal as being likely to impact on reconvictions should be carefully evaluated before being widely implemented; there should be regular monitoring of interventions; and appropriate follow-up periods should be observed. In the *UK review*, follow-up periods ranged from 4 weeks to 10 years. Since reoffending rates vary across offences, the length of follow-up needs to take account of what is being assessed and the nature of the offending behaviour in question.

THE CASE FOR SYSTEMATIC REVIEWS

An important aspect of evaluation research is how the results are disseminated to practitioners. It is very easy in reviewing research literature to mislead as to what is effective through selectively choosing literature that supports the preferred review. It is true, however, that there is also implicit bias through negative findings being less likely to be published or cited in the literature of subsequent studies.

The Cochrane and Campbell collaborations support systematic reviews that examine all the available literature published in journals, presented at conferences, published in in-house journals, and any 'grey literature' available internationally, both positive and negative. The quality of the research is assessed, and only those studies that have been rigorously designed and conducted are included. Systematic reviews are published on the Internet and available to practitioners. This is established practice within the Cochrane Collaboration, and beginning to be implemented by the Campbell Collaboration.

THE CASE FOR RANDOMISED CONTROLLED TRIALS (RCTs)

Randomised controlled trials are generally recognised as the gold standard in evaluation design, and are widely used in medical evaluation. They minimise the methodological bias caused by selecting subjects whose selection criteria might influence results; for example, highly motivated people are more likely to do well than those less well motivated. Self-selected subjects may therefore be more likely to improve, and individual motivation rather than the type of intervention might be the most significant factor in behaviour change. Weisburd, Lum and Petrosino (2001) examined a range of studies that claimed effectiveness of interventions, and found that estimates of effect size were larger in studies where there were few precautions to minimise bias. The results were therefore not so dependable.

In the *UK review*, only two studies adopted a randomised control design: an in-prison alcohol education programme, and an experimental versus traditional probation supervision allocation. These demonstrate that it is possible to apply an RCT design in a criminal justice setting, both in prison and in the community. It is, however, recognised that it is much easier to conduct randomised controlled trials where the intervention is difficult to observe; for example, where some form of pharmaceutical medication is involved. One can quite easily randomly allocate patients to a pharmaceutical treatment or a placebo replacement without this being evident to those administering and those participating. This is more difficult where, for example, an offender is being allocated to one kind of judicial sentence rather than another. Furthermore, in this latter case, questions of just deserts, fairness of punishment, need for rehabilitation, deterrence and retribution are all introduced. Less frequently, questions of effectiveness are brought into the decision. When an offender is released from prison and reoffends, the conclusion is often not that prison didn't work, but that more prison is needed in order to be effective. Until we begin to seriously evaluate the effectiveness of interventions, this situation is unlikely to change.

Although it is recognised that it is difficult to bring about large-scale changes in sentencing and in the criminal justice system to allow for RCTs, this can be achieved. For example, the Home Office in the UK has

recently funded a substantial evaluation project of restorative justice using random allocation of offenders, and this is now under way at three sites
(Strang, 2005); and historically RCTs have been possible, exemplified by
the Borstal Typology Study (HM Prison Service, 1971), which describes a
study in which young offenders were randomly allocated to borstals with
different kinds of regimes to evaluate effectiveness. There are examples
in this book of diversions from court, and police-referred diversion to psychiatric treatment so, with determination, the wider use of randomised
controlled trials is possible within the criminal justice system.

The development of RCT methodology in the UK Criminal Justice
System (CJS) has revived interest in a growing number of researchers
who strive to achieve the highest standards of quality and certainty
on which to base their research results, and Home Office-funded RCTs
are now being encouraged (Department of Health/Home Office, 2000,
Part II, para. 6.53). Two RCT feasibility studies conducted in HMP Whitemoor in Cambridgeshire (Farrington & Jolliffe, 2002) and the Young
Offender Institute (YOI) Thorn Cross in Warrington (Farrington et al.,
2002) evaluated some of the practical issues associated with randomisation in a criminal justice setting. Threats to the feasibility of the RCT
in HMP Whitemoor were linked to the small number of prisoners receiving treatment, the heterogeneity of the population, the likely length of
the treatment, assessment case load, the occupation of treatment beds
by previously assessed prisoners and the possibility of dropouts from the
treatment (Farrington & Jolliffe, 2002).

Similar problems were encountered in the Thorn Cross study. The research aimed to identify 28 eligible participants every 5 weeks, of whom
14 were chosen at random for the intervention. Randomisation did not
occur because of case flow problems and problems with identifying sufficient numbers of eligible participants. In the main, quasi-experimental
studies or natural observational studies such as cohort studies are chosen to avoid such difficulties, and are used more commonly in the CJS
to evaluate the effectiveness of different interventions and programmes.
Despite these recognised problems, RCT methodology has been used with
more frequency and success within the US CJS and should be attempted
wherever feasible in the UK system.

COHORT STUDIES

With improvements in the quality of databases of offenders, an effective
method of assessment is the analysis of data held on large databases, such
as the Offenders Index database (Home Office, 1998) and the British Crime
Survey (Home Office, 2000). There is the potential to use such approaches
in order to examine effective interventions in offending behaviour (for

example, Lloyd, Mair & Hough, 1995; Bowles et al., 2004). Methodologies for ensuring quality of cohort studies are described in Chapter 2.

THE CASE FOR AN ECONOMIC APPROACH

A small number of studies in the *UK review* have included cost, cost-effectiveness, and costs and benefits information. Indeed, some authors have given a lead in applying cost–benefit analyses routinely to their research studies (Farrington, Hancock, Livingston, Painter & Towl, 2000; Farrington et al., 2002; Painter & Farrington, 1999; Welsh, 1999; Welsh & Farrington, 1998). Where such information has been included in studies, we have reported it, and applied an economic quality rating (Drummond, O'Brien, Stoddard & Torrance, 1997). Chapter 8, by Raymond Swaray, discusses the economic methodologies adopted and economic evaluations of interventions.

Though comparatively few in number, it is encouraging to see how many UK studies have included costs and benefits information. This compares favourably with an international systematic review of the costs and benefits of treatment interventions (Welsh & Farrington, 2000), which found only seven studies provided cost–benefit information. A systematic review of costs and benefits of sentencing (McDougall, Cohen, Swaray & Perry, 2003), in a worldwide search, found only nine studies that had properly applied costs and benefits information to this topic. It is encouraging, therefore, that 11 of the UK studies in this review presented economic information in some form.

A similar debate to that surrounding randomised controlled trials is concerned with the application of economic evaluation of criminal justice interventions. As with RCTs, this is a debate that has already been conducted in the medical field, and the value of economic evaluation accepted. It is now recognised that treatments that are highly expensive, but with little likelihood of efficacy, should not be funded, and that consideration of the balance of costs against benefits is appropriate. The National Institute for Clinical Excellence (www.nice.org.uk/), a government agency that assesses the issue of value for money, now advises the UK Government on implementation of medical treatments. Within criminal justice, however, there is still the view that the costs and benefits of a sentence or intervention should not be taken into account, and that decisions should be based on the effectiveness of the intervention, regardless of cost issues.

Cost–benefit analyses are, however, becoming increasingly important to government departments. In the UK, HM Treasury, as well as supporting a research evidence base, seeks to allocate funds to government departments on the basis of value for money. Knowledge of the benefits to be obtained from expenditure is crucial to this process, particularly as 'benefits', in criminal justice terms, incorporates savings to victims that can be achieved by number of offences reduced.

But it is argued that such a value-for-money approach raises questions of principle and ethics. This is to misunderstand what a cost–benefit analysis is trying to achieve. A good cost–benefit analysis attempts to capture the total benefits and costs to society of implementing a particular intervention or sentencing option (Cohen, 2000). This includes not only what is effective in changing offending behaviour or in reducing reconvictions, but goes further than a simple numerical count of reconvictions. A valid cost–benefit calculation will incorporate the nature of the offending and degree of seriousness, and weigh the benefits in terms of the savings in victim costs, dependent on the nature of the crime. As well as highlighting whether numbers of reconvictions have been reduced, this approach assesses whether the severity of the reoffending has also been reduced. A cost–benefit analysis therefore gives a more complete assessment of the impact of an intervention by including a victim perspective (McDougall et al., 2003).

OVERVIEW OF THE BOOK

The following chapters provide a review of the UK research evidence base at the time of writing, linked to international research and policy contexts. They describe how our knowledge and understanding has increased over recent years, building on elements that have been shown to be effective. Some of the early meta-analyses of large numbers of studies (Andrews et al., 1990; Lipsey & Wilson, 1993) identified some of the most important contributory factors to effective programmes; for example, programmes should use cognitive behavioural approaches, be structured, and address criminogenic needs and responsivity principles. Programmes are now being implemented that take account of these factors and the results of evaluations are being obtained. This allows authors to review implementation of research evidence derived from meta-analysis, as demonstrated in practice.

Chapter 2 describes the methodology used in the *UK review* of the UK literature, including the search strategy, research design quality assessment scales, and the assessment of economic methodological quality measures. The studies that were identified and rated of sufficient quality to be included in the review formed the core and basis for each of the following chapters, placed in the wider context of the research area, together with policy application and development implications.

McMurran (Chapter 3) sets the policy context and describes the increasing need for effective programmes to tackle alcohol and drug misuse. Existing research evidence is comprehensively reviewed.

Hedderman and Hough, in describing studies of diversion from prosecution at court and effective sentencing, in Chapter 4, highlight the particular difficulties of conducting rigorous research in a court environment. They make the case for a range of methodologies and outcomes in addition to reconvictions, pointing out some of the pitfalls associated with the use of reconvictions as an outcome measure.

At the time of completion of the systematic review of effectiveness (April 2003), results from studies of prison and probation interventions, particularly cognitive behavioural programmes, were very encouraging. However, in Chapter 5, Friendship and Debidin have updated the research evidence on cognitive behavioural programmes in prison and during probation, and shown that more recent studies lead to different conclusions. The authors review earlier results from the *UK review* relating these to more recent studies and the findings from international literature.

Welsh and Farrington present new evidence in Chapter 6 from two systematic reviews, incorporating meta-analytic techniques examining the effects of closed-circuit television (CCTV) and street lighting on crime. Here they contrast the different outcomes in terms of effects on crime between studies from the UK and the US for both interventions.

In Chapter 7, studies of the effectiveness of situational burglary and housing interventions are reviewed by Bennett within theoretical, research and policy contexts. Burglary-reduction studies include research on neighbourhood watch schemes, repeat-burglary prevention, property marking, multiple measures, small business initiatives, and those that attempt to reduce burglary via house redesign. Conclusions highlight lessons learned from burglary reduction initiatives for research and policy.

A number of the UK studies incorporated costs and benefits information. Swaray (Chapter 8) reviews the costs and benefits methodologies of these, and the methodologies used more generally in criminal justice settings. Findings from an international review of costs and benefits are also presented.

The final chapter (Chapter 9) summarises the findings from all the chapters on the basis of *What Works, What Doesn't, What's Promising* and *What's Unknown* (Sherman et al., 1997), highlighting UK studies and showing where there is international support for the findings. Future directions for research and policy development are proposed.

One of the main aims of this book is to provide a comprehensive summary of research evidence on crime reduction in the UK within the setting and comparison of US and international research, with a view to informing researchers, practitioners and policy makers. The following chapters seek to achieve this aim through systematic review and the appraisal and conclusions of experts in these areas of study.

REFERENCES

Andrews, D.A., Zinger, I., Hoge, R.D., Bonta, J., Gendreau, P. & Cullen, F.T. (1990). Does correctional treatment work? A clinically relevant and psychologically informed meta-analysis. *Criminology*, **28**, 369–404.

Bowles, R.B., Gordon, F., Pradiptyo, R., McDougall, C., Harris, R., Perry, A.E. & Swaray, R. (2004). *Costs and Benefits of Sentencing Options.* Unpublished Report to HM Home Office.

Cohen, M.A. (2000). To treat or not to treat?: A Financial Perspective. In C. Hollin (ed), *Handbook of Offender Assessment and Treatment* (pp. 43–9). Chichester: Wiley.

Department of Health/Home Office (2000). *Reforming the Mental Health Act (Part I: The New Legal Framework. Part II: High Risk Patients).* London: The Stationery Office.

Drummond, M.F., O'Brien, B.J., Stoddart, G.L. & Torrance, G.W. (1997). *Methods for the Economic Evaluation of Health Care Programmes* (3rd edn). Oxford: Oxford University Press.

Farrington, D.P., Ditchfield, J., Hancock, G., Howard, P., Jolliffe, D., Livingston, M.S. & Painter, K.A. (2002). Evaluation of two intensive regimes for young offenders. *Home Office Research Study 239.* London: Home Office.

Farrington, D.P., Hancock, G., Livingston, M.S., Painter, K.A. & Towl, G.J. (2000). Evaluation of intensive regimes for young offenders. *Home Office Research Findings 121.* London: Home Office.

Farrington, D.P. & Jolliffe, D. (2002). A feasibility study into using a randomised controlled trial to evaluate treatment pilots at HMP Whitemoor. *Home Office Online Report 14/02.* London: Home Office.

Farrington, D.P. & Petrosino, A. (2001). The Campbell Collaboration Crime and Justice Group. *Annals of the American Academy of Political and Social Science*, **578**, 35–49.

HM Prison Service (1971). *A Borstal Typology Study by Members of the Psychology Department.* HM Prison Wormwood Scrubs. (Unpublished).

Home Office (1998). The Offenders Index: A Users Guide. *Research Development and Statistics Directorate.* London: HMSO.

Home Office (2000). The 2000 British Crime Survey: England and Wales. *Home Office Statistical Bulletin,* 2000. London: HMSO.

Lewis, R.V. (1983). Scared straight – California style: Evaluation of the San Quentin SQUIRES program. *Criminal Justice and Behavior*, **10**, 209–26.

Lipsey, M.W. & Wilson, D.B. (1993). The efficacy of psychological, educational and behavioural treatment: confirmation from meta-analysis. *American Psychologist*, **48**, 1181–209.

Lloyd, C.G., Mair, G. & Hough, M. (1995). Explaining reconviction rates: A critical analysis. *Home Office Research Study,* 1-103. London: Home Office.

McCord, J. (1978). A thirty-year followup of treatment effects. *The American Psychologist*, **33**, 284–9.

McDougall, C., Cohen, M.A., Swaray, R. & Perry, A. (2003). The costs and benefits of sentencing: A systematic review. *The Annals of the American Academy of Political and Social Sciences*, **587**, 160–77.

Painter, K.A. & Farrington, D.P. (1999). Improved street lighting: Crime reducing effects and cost–benefit analysis. *Security Journal*, **12**, 17–32.

Petrosino, A., Turpin-Petrosino, C. & Buehler, J. (2002). Scared straight and other juvenile awareness programs for preventing juvenile delinquency: A systematic review of the randomized experimental evidence. USA: Campbell Collaboration.

Powers, E. & Witmer, H. (1972). *An Experiment in the Prevention of Delinquency: The Cambridge-Somerville Youth Study*. Montclair, NJ: Patterson Smith.

Sherman, L.W., Farrington, D.P., Welsh, B.C. & MacKenzie, D.L. (2002). *Evidence-Based Crime Prevention*. London: Routledge.

Sherman, L.W., Gottfredson, D., MacKenzie, D., Eck, J., Reuler, P. & Bushay, S. (1997). *Preventing Crime: What Works, What Doesn't, What's Promising: A Report to the United States Congress*. (www.cjcentral.com/sherman/sherman.htm).

Strang, H. (2005). *What's Happening at the Justice Research Consortium*. Retrieved 20 March 2005 from www.restorativejustice.org.uk/about-rj/Heather-Strang.htm.

Weisburd, D., Lum, C.M. & Petrosino, A. (2001). Does research design affect study outcomes in criminal justice? *Annals of the American Academy of Political and Social Science*, **578**, 50–70.

Welsh, B.C. (1999). Costs and benefits of primary prevention: A review of the literature. In D.P. Farrington and J. Coid (eds), *Early Prevention of Adult Antisocial Behaviour*. Cambridge: Cambridge University Press.

Welsh, B.C. & Farrington, D.P. (1998). Assessing the effectiveness and economic benefits of an integrated developmental and situational crime prevention programme. *Psychology, Crime and Law*, **4**, 281–308.

Welsh, B.C. & Farrington, D.P. (2000). Correctional intervention programs and cost–benefit analysis. *Criminal Justice and Behaviour*, **27**, 115–33.

CHAPTER 2

Methodology of the *UK Review* of Evidence

AMANDA E. PERRY

INTRODUCTION

This chapter discusses the methodological differences between different study designs, their associated biases and the methodology of the current *UK review*.

Study Design and Methodology

Over the last decade there has been an increasing demand in the UK Criminal Justice System (CJS) to provide an evidence base for policy and practice (for example, see McGuire's [1995] *What Works* literature), encouraging debates relating to the methodological quality of different research designs. Different study designs used to evaluate the effectiveness of interventions within the UK CJS have been conducted mainly by experts in the field and commissioned by the UK Home Office. Such research has been published on the UK Home Office website since the 1980s (see www.homeoffice.gov.uk/rds/). The use of non-randomised experimental and observational study designs is most commonly presented in the UK CJS discipline.

In the UK CJS, randomised controlled trial (RCT) methodology has been used since the 1970s, but is rarely conducted. This is due, in part, to a historical cultural resistance to the use of RCT methodology based on ethical,

Reducing Crime: The Effectiveness of Criminal Justice Interventions.
Edited by A. E. Perry, C. McDougall and D. P. Farrington. © 2006 John Wiley & Sons, Ltd.

moral and practical difficulties surrounding the random allocation of individuals to either an intervention, control or no-treatment comparison group. Reasons for not conducting RCTs tend to focus on the right of an individual to have access to treatment, and the practical difficulties in randomly assigning offenders to different types of interventions (for example, sentencing options). In the UK, experimental studies without randomisation, case-control and cohort study designs are therefore often used instead of RCTs. Sometimes a mix, or hybrid, of different study designs is used, making it difficult to assign a clear study design. Publication of more recent documentation has actively encouraged the use of RCT methodology in the UK CJS (Department of Health/Home Office, 2000, Part II, para. 6.53).

A somewhat newer and expanding area of research methodology in the UK CJS is the use of systematic review methodology through the combination of RCTs using meta-analytical techniques. Systematic review methodology traditionally stems from the healthcare discipline, and was developed in the 1970s by Professor Archibald Cochrane, a British Medical researcher who contributed greatly to the development of epidemiology as a science. A particular strength of systematic review methodology is the ability to combine the results of separate RCTs on similar outcomes to generate overall effect sizes. In addition to systematic review methodology, the Home Office is currently trialling the use of a new methodology called rapid evidence assessment (REA), which uses the principles of systematic review methodology to produce a timely response in line with policy requirements (Davies, Butler, Cassidy & Deaton, 2005).

Experimental Studies: Randomised Controlled Trials

The key premise of an RCT is the randomisation of participants to an intervention or control group; however, RCTs should only rank high in the hierarchy of study designs if they are well conducted. Often referred to as the gold standard of research design, they can be conducted using poor methodology. A well-conducted RCT should include a number of key attributes: a sample size large enough to determine the desired effect size; concealment of the allocation of randomisation; blinding of participants and investigators; reporting on the loss to follow-up and outcomes and analysis of the results by intention to treat. Intention-to-treat analysis analyses data from participants as if all have received the treatment they were assigned to at the start of the study. The analysis preserves the benefits of random assignment, yielding an unbiased estimate only with regard to the effects of being assigned to treatment, not of actually receiving the treatment.

Figure 2.1 shows an example of how incomplete follow-up data can alter the level of effectiveness using a random-effects model based on

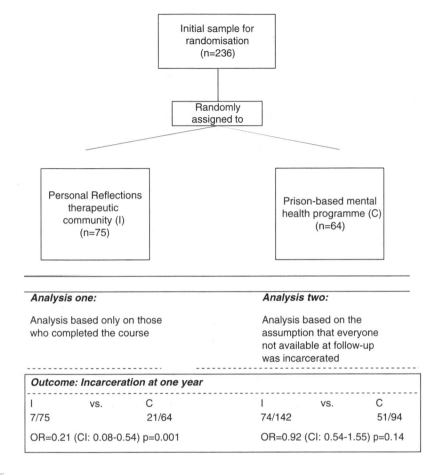

Key:

I: Intervention group
C: Comparison group
OR: Odds Ratio
CI: Confidence Interval

Figure 2.1   Example of how incomplete follow-up data can alter the level of effectiveness
Source: Based on data analysed from Sacks et al. (2004).

the assumption that all participants who were not available at follow-up were incarcerated at the one-year follow-up period. Devised to evaluate the effectiveness of a Personal Reflections therapeutic community with community-based residential aftercare in comparison to a prison-based mental health programme, the study conducted by Sacks, Sacks, McKendrick, Banks and Stommel (2004) randomly assigned offenders to an intervention or comparison group. This analysis demonstrates how the effectiveness of a study (changing from $p = 0.001$ to $p = 0.14$ after attrition) can be affected by participants who drop out of the study.

Experimental Studies Without Randomisation

Experimental studies without randomisation allocate participants to interventions using non-randomised methodology and incorporate a retrospective or prospective element. Non-randomisation is sometimes perceived as being practically easier to deal with than random assignment when managing offenders in an applied setting. The random allocation design may incorporate practical constraints for clinicians; for example, the number of offenders being referred to a particular service at any one time, and the need to provide treatment to individuals, may not allow random allocation to a treatment and waiting-list group (Farrington & Jolliffe, 2002). Where randomisation fails, it does limit the inferences that can be made about the effectiveness of an intervention due to biases associated with, for example, the selection of the sample.

A study conducted in the UK using non-random allocation of participants evaluated UK cognitive behavioural programmes conducted in prisons. The study, conducted by Friendship, Blud, Erikson and Travers (2002), used a retrospective quasi-experimental design with a matched control group to evaluate the effectiveness of two cognitive behavioural programmes: Reasoning and Rehabilitation (R&R) and Enhanced Thinking Skills (ETS). The study matched participants on current offence, sentence length, age at discharge, year of discharge, number of previous convictions and probability of reconviction. Matching participants is one way of limiting potential biases and confounding factors that may occur in the selection of the sample when not randomly allocating participants to an intervention or comparison group.

Observational Studies

In contrast to the randomised and non-randomised experimental studies described above, observational studies such as cohort, case-control or pre- and post-test studies allocate participants to groups naturally occurring; for example, everyone who was convicted of a burglary offence in 2004 and was sentenced, forms the intervention group. So, rather than the investigator manipulating or allocating the participants to an intervention or control group, the groups are naturally occurring.

Cohort Study Designs

A cohort study selects participants on the basis of exposure to a potential outcome (for example, likelihood of committing burglary). At the time the exposure status is defined, all potential participants must be free from the outcome under investigation. Eligible participants are then followed over a period of time to assess the occurrence of that outcome. Such studies can be prospective or retrospective in nature.

Prospective cohort studies offer a number of advantages for evaluating the relationship between exposure and outcome; that is, participants are free from the outcome at the time their exposure status is defined, and the sequence between exposure and outcome can be clearly established. Prospective cohort studies involving concurrent evaluations of groups receiving different interventions are generally considered more valid than studies that make comparisons with historical controls. Such methodology allows for the comparison of a full range of outcome measures with a single intervention.

Prospective cohort studies often involve following large numbers of individuals for many years, making such studies time consuming and expensive to conduct. This methodology is therefore not ideal if the research being conducted is linked to a particular policy or programme initiative with short time-scales.

Retrospective cohort studies can usually be conducted more quickly and cheaply than their prospective counterparts because all relevant events have already occurred by the time the study is initiated. This method is often used in the UK CJS because it allows researchers to investigate large datasets, using outcome measures such as reconviction or recidivism rates already available. However, retrospective cohorts rely upon the routine availability of relevant exposure data in adequate detail from pre-existing records. If this information is not available, it can result in incomplete and possibly non-comparable information for some or all study participants.

An example of a retrospective cohort study conducted in the UK and included in the current *UK review* is that by May and Wadwell (2001). Using a retrospective cohort methodology, the study assessed the impact of enforcement action on those serving a community penalty. Using three separate cohorts, determined by the level of enforcement, the Home Office's Offenders Index database was used to obtain information on reconviction rates following discharge from a community sentence.

Case-Control Studies

In contrast to a cohort study, a case-control study selects participants on the basis of presence or absence of a particular event (for example, re-arrest). The groups are then compared with respect to the proportion having a history of the event. Originally, case-control design offered a solution to the difficulties of studying diseases in healthcare settings, allowing investigators to identify affected and unaffected individuals. Researchers would then retrospectively assess their antecedent exposures. Rather than having to wait a number of years, investigators could therefore retrospectively ascertain the outcome.

Case-control studies are, however, more susceptible to bias than cohort studies. This is often attributed to the biases associated with the selection and suitability of the control or comparison group. Matching cases and controls helps to ensure that this bias is minimised, and is used to make groups comparable on confounding factors. In addition, this methodology is inefficient for the evaluation of rare risk factors (for example, reconviction of offenders aged 75 years and older) unless the attributable risk percentage is high. In contrast, case-control studies are relatively quick and inexpensive compared to other research designs such as prospective cohort studies, and are well suited to the evaluation of criminal activity where long latency periods are required.

Pre- and Post-Test Study Designs

Pre- and post-test (or before-and-after) studies evaluate the same participants before and after an intervention with no additional comparator or control group. The comparison is made within a single group of participants, rather than between participants in different groups. This makes it difficult to conclude whether any differences that might occur in the pre- to post-test evaluation are due to the intervention or some other external factor.

A review of pre- and post-test studies by Lipsey and Wilson (1993) showed that such studies produced effect sizes with an average 61 per cent greater improvement than studies that used a control group. The authors suggest that part of this exaggeration is almost certainly due to regression to the mean. Regression to the mean defines the statistical probability that, due to measurement error scores, will regress to the mean. Forming comparison groups using random allocation deals with regression to the mean as it affects both groups equally, and the effect is 'cancelled out'.

Using a pre- and post-test study design, Belton (2000) evaluated the impact of a group work programme for offenders with motoring convictions. Based on a two-year follow-up period, reconviction rates were reduced by between 22 per cent and 67 per cent. However, because of the lack of a comparison group, it is difficult to assess the direct cause-and-effect relationship between the impact of the group work programme and the reconviction rates at two years.

Systematic Review Methodology

Systematic reviews in healthcare are often referred to as secondary studies, evaluating the effectiveness of primary research (usually RCTs). They are distinct from traditional literature reviews in a number of key ways.

They seek to make transparent the process of surveying the research literature by declaring in advance all the sources of information being searched, and the criteria by which the studies will, or will not, be included. Importantly, all research studies are subject to an assessment of the quality of the research. This focuses on the study design and the authors' ability to minimise potential bias within the research. The aim of a systematic review is to present an unbiased and comprehensive review of the subject area that can be replicated. The review provides an evidence base on which practitioners can base a judgement on the applicability of the research to their own individual practice.

An example of a systematic review conducted internationally focuses on the impact of closed-circuit television (CCTV) on crime reduction. The study conducted by Welsh and Farrington (2002) produced a synthesis of 22 studies; of these 16 were conducted in the UK. The UK evidence was centred on CCTV in city centres and public housing (eight UK studies), public transport (three UK studies) and car parks (five UK studies). Overall, the review concluded that CCTV was most effective in reducing vehicle crime in car parks, but had little or no effect on public transport nor city centres. In instances, as above, where the synthesis of the research findings provides a clear result, it can have major implications for policy makers. However, in some systematic reviews in the CJS system, the results of the literature search often highlight the paucity of good-quality research in the field and lead to recommendations of further RCTs to enhance the evidence base.

Summary

Different study designs, when conducted well, each have their relative merits in understanding the effectiveness of an intervention. The weakest of the methodologies discussed in this chapter, providing the greatest limitations to ascertain cause and effect, is the pre- and post-test design. In the UK CJS the importance of understanding the cause-and-effect relationship is imperative if the quality of research is to be improved and used by policy makers and economists making informed choices about *What Works* and at *What Cost*. The next section of the chapter focuses on the methodology used in the current *UK review*.

CURRENT *UK REVIEW* METHODOLOGY

Objectives

The objective of the current systematic *UK review* was to assess all UK research evidence (between 1990 and 2002), evaluating interventions that were designed to have an impact on criminal behaviour and activity. Tables 9.1 to 9.20 (see Chapter 9) present the outcomes that relate to the criminal behaviour and activity presented in the studies.

Identification of the UK Studies

Study designs were not limited to RCT methodology, as it was thought that few, if any, would have been conducted in the UK; in addition to RCTs, experimental studies without randomisation and controlled observational studies were considered in the review if they contained a control, comparison or minimal intervention group. Because of the practical constraints associated with using comparison groups in the CJS, a number of pre- and post-test studies were identified. However, these are not presented in Tables 9.1 to 9.20 because of the limitations of the certainty of the conclusions, and problems with reliance on the data.

Types of Participants

The *UK review* contained a broad range of participants and included male and female, juvenile, young and adult offenders. In addition, it also included studies that might not have contained a participant group of offenders; for example, studies that focused on the evaluation of CCTV or neighbourhood watch schemes where housing areas were compared (as opposed to participants) with and without the intervention (Painter & Farrington, 1999).

Types of Interventions

The review included any evaluated intervention, a component of which was designed to measure the impact on criminal behaviour and/or activity. Examples of such interventions included alcohol and drug treatment, sentencing options, court diversion schemes, cognitive behavioural programmes in the prison or probation service, police targeting schemes, housing schemes, burglary reduction, street lighting and CCTV in city centres.

Types of Outcomes

Criminal behaviour and/or activity was broadly defined as the main outcome measure for the review, and was not limited to any specific offence or reporting mechanism. A range of different reporting mechanisms were recorded in the studies, including the British Crime Survey, National

Police Database, victim surveys, self-report data and court data. Criminal behaviour and/or activity encompassed:

- Predicted (from Offender Group Reconviction Score—OGRS) and actual custodial rates.
- Offences (reported by the offender), including acquisitive crime, violence, robberies, thefts, repeat burglary and victimisation, vandalism and dishonesty.
- Reconviction rates.
- Number of criminal convictions.
- Number of days engaged in illegal activity.
- Vehicle thefts.
- Shoplifting rate (per cent of items stolen).
- Number of assaults (on police officers and in accident and emergency departments).
- Number of illegal alcohol purchases.

The number of different outcomes identified from the *UK review* is an indication of the disparity with which the effectiveness of an intervention is measured in the UK CJS. Inconsistencies within the literature regarding the definition of some of these outcome measures make it difficult to combine the results of such studies.

Search Strategy for Identification of Studies

A database of published and unpublished literature was assembled from systematic searches of electronic sources and consultations with experts in the field. Searching was restricted to studies conducted in the UK between 1990 and June 2002. The following electronic databases of published literature were searched: PubMed, PsychInfo, the National Criminal Justice Reference Service (NCJRS), criminal justice abstracts, criminal justice periodicals and the Campbell Collaboration Social, Psychology and Educational Controlled Trial Register (C2-SPECTR). A further 10 databases of ongoing research, grey literature and systematic review evidence were also searched. For more details of the *UK review* see the full report (Perry et al., 2003).

In addition, websites for local government offices, the Home Office, UK universities and charities were searched for relevant material. Attempts were made to identify further studies by contacting experts and practitioners working in the field. Reference lists of all retrieved articles were examined for further potential studies.

Whilst this is not an exhaustive list, the databases covered a range of multidisciplinary resources where research on the topic and publication

1. (offender or offenders or criminal* or inmate* or probation or probationers or remand and UK) in ti, ab
2. (prisoner* or prison or prisons and UK) in ti, ab
3. "Prisoners" and UK/ all subheadings
4. (youth* or adolescent* or teen* or child* and UK) in ti, ab
5. explode "Prisons" and UK/ all subheadings
6. #1 or #2 or #3 or #4 or #5
7. crime* near (treat* or intervention* or programme*) and UK
8. early* near (treat* or intervention* or programme*) and UK
9. family* near (treat* or intervention* or programme*) and UK
10. community* near (treat* or intervention* or programme*) and UK
11. electronic monitoring* or electronic tagging* near (treat* or intervention* or programme*) and UK
12. CCTV* near (treat* or intervention* or programme*) and UK
13. drug* near (treat* or intervention* or programme*) and UK
14. alcohol* near (treat* or intervention* or programme*) and UK
15. arrest referral* near (treat* or intervention* or programme*) and UK
16. neighbourhood watch* near (treat* or intervention* or programme*) and UK
17. court* near (treat* or intervention* or programme*) and UK
18. police* near (treat* or intervention* or programme*) and UK
19. violent* or violence* near (treat* or intervention* or programme*) and UK
20. #7 or #8 or #9 or #10 or #11 or #12 or #13 or #14 or #15 or #16 or #17 or #18 or #19
21. #6 and #20

Figure 2.2 Example of search strategy

formats could be identified. The resources included unpublished and grey literature reducing the effects of publication bias. Data from the electronic databases were downloaded into an EndNote® software library system for pre-screening.

Search strategies were developed for each database separately. For full details see the full report (Perry et al., 2003). Figure 2.2 shows an example of the search strategy used for the PsychInfo database. The terms outlined were used to search the content of title and abstracts.

Selecting the Studies

Two reviewers identified potential studies by reading the titles and abstracts for relevant key words (for example, criminal justice) and key study design features such as the presence of a comparison or control group. Studies that were successful in this initial general screen were obtained in full and assessed for inclusion using the full pre-screening criteria.

The pre-screening criteria were divided into five key questions (Table 2.1). Studies were included in the review if they: (1) had been

Table 2.1 Pre-screening criteria

(1) Was the study conducted in the UK?	*Yes*	*No*
[If no to question 1, exclude]		
(2) Was the study published in or after 1990?	*Yes*	*No*
[If no to question 2, exclude]		
(3) Does the study contain at least pre- and post-test data?	*Yes*	*No*
[If no to question 3, exclude]		
(4) Does the study report on quantitative outcome measures of criminal behaviour or activity?	*Yes*	*No*
[If no to question 4, exclude]		
(5) Does the study contain enough resource information to calculate the costs?	*Yes*	*No*
[If no to question 5, but yes to questions 1–4, then include]		

conducted in the UK; (2) were published in or after 1990; (3) contained a comparison group; and (4) reported on quantitative outcome measures of crime rates, self-reported offences, recidivism or reconviction rates.

Any studies not meeting the inclusion criteria were excluded from the review. Studies that met the criteria outlined above were categorised by study design using the Maryland Scientific Methods Scale (SMS) (Sherman et al., 1997; Sherman, Farrington, Welsh & MacKenzie, 2002), methodological quality using the CRD checklists (CRD, 2001), and economic assessment using the Drummond Checklist (Drummond, O'Brien, Stoddart & Torrance, 1997).

Study Design Assessment

The main aim of the Maryland SMS (Sherman et al., 1997, 2002) is to evaluate the reliability of the effects of criminological interventions through the methodological quality of the study design. The scale, based on the work by Cook and Campbell (1979), has been used in a number of criminal justice studies to categorise study design and classify studies using the *What Works* classification system (for example, Chanhatasilpa, MacKenzie & Hickman, 2000; McDougall, Cohen, Swaray & Perry, 2003).

A particular strength of the SMS and *What Works* classification is that the framework allows different study designs to be combined together. For example, the results of non-randomised experimental studies can be combined with RCTs to assess the overall body of evidence. More traditional quantitative methods of combining studies using meta-analytic techniques do not always present such opportunities. The *What Works* method of combination is particularly relevant in the UK CJS where the majority of studies conducted are either non-randomised experimental studies or observational cohort studies.

Table 2.2 Maryland Scientific Methods Scale

Study Design	Description of Rating
Correlational study	(1) Reporting of a correlation coefficient denoting the strength of the relationship between, for example, a particular intervention and its effectiveness in preventing reoffending at a given point in time.
Pre- and post-test with no control group	(2) Reporting of a comparison group present, but this might lack comparability to the target group. Alternatively, where no comparison group is present, before-and-after measures (of offending behaviour, for example) have been obtained for the target group.
Observational cohort study with comparable group/ quasi-experimental	(3) Reporting of a controlled experimental design with comparable target and control groups present, with pre-and post comparisons being made and experimental–control comparisons on (a) specific variable/s.
Quasi-experimental/ controlled trial	(4) Reporting of a controlled experimental design, as in (3) above, but with additional controlling for other variables that might pose a threat to the interpretation of the results. Examples of controlling extraneous variables include, but are not limited to, the use of statistical procedures or matching.
Randomised controlled trial	(5) Reporting of a fully randomised experimental design in which target and control groups consist of randomly assigned individuals and appropriate measures are taken to test for the effects of the intervention.

Source: Adapted from Maryland Scientific Methods Scale (Sherman et al., 1997; 2002).

Structure and Classification Using the SMS

Using the SMS scale, studies are rated on a scale of one to five, as shown in Table 2.2.

The classification of studies using the SMS allows studies to be combined using the *What Works* system. The four *What Works* classifications are outlined below:

- *What Works*: intervention programmes which with reasonable certainty will prevent crime or reduce crime, reporting positive results from two studies (and/or schemes) scoring three or above on SMS, with supporting evidence.
- *What Doesn't*: intervention programmes which with reasonable certainty will fail to prevent crime or reduce crime, reporting negative results from two studies (and/or schemes) scoring three or above on SMS with supporting evidence.

- *What's Promising*: intervention programmes for which the level of certainty from available evidence is too low to support a generalisable conclusion, but for which there is some empirical basis for predicting that further research could support such conclusions, reporting positive results from one study (and/or scheme), scoring three or above on SMS.
- *What's Unknown:* any study (and/or scheme) not falling into any of the above categories, reporting one study with a negative or inconclusive result, scoring three or above on SMS.

Limitations of the SMS

Criticisms of the SMS documented in the literature highlight two general flaws (Sherman et al., 2002). First, the five-point scale is designed to apply equally to all experimental units, whether people, schools, prisons or communities. In some interventions, such as neighbourhood watch schemes, it is not possible to randomise individuals and such studies tend to generate intervention and control areas instead. Second, the SMS does not embrace all study designs; for example, time series designs (that is, regression discontinuity designs) are not incorporated, although they are superior to designs with only one pre-test and one post-test measure of the outcome.

The method of drawing conclusions about *What Works* can further be criticised because of its focus on statistical significance rather than on effect size. Furthermore, statistical significance does not take into account attrition within a study.

Use of the SMS in the *UK review*

Studies scoring three, four or five on the Maryland SMS were included in the main findings of the review. These studies (RCTs, experimental studies without randomisation, cohort and case-control studies with comparison groups) contain the more rigorous research designs, therefore reducing bias. Pre- and post-test studies rated as two and containing promising information cannot be relied on for policy development and are therefore not presented as part of the tables in Chapter 9. Studies rated as one on the scale (correlational studies with no before-and-after measures) were excluded from the review.

Secondary study designs such as systematic reviews, meta-analyses and reviews of the literature were included in the review. However, these were not assessed for their methodological quality. After assigning an appropriate SMS score (between three and five), general conclusions were made on *What Works*, *What Doesn't*, *What's Promising* and *What's Unknown* (Sherman et al., 1997, 2002); see Tables 9.1 to 9.20.

1. Was the assignment to treatment random?
2. Were the eligibility criteria specified?
3. Was the programme delivered blind?
4. Was the treatment allocation concealed?
5. Was there no attrition at follow-up?
6. Were the outcome assessors blinded?
7. Were the participants blinded?
8. Were the groups similar at baseline in terms of demographic details?

Figure 2.3 Quality assessment of experimental studies
Source: CRD (2001).

Methodological Quality Assessment

In addition to the SMS, the methodological quality of the studies was assessed using two quality assessment tools developed by CRD (CRD, 2001) and adapted for use in this study. Figure 2.3 was used to assess the methodological quality of randomised controlled trials, and experimental studies without randomisation. Figure 2.4 was used to assess the methodological quality of cohort study designs. The methodological quality assessment scales were scored on a scale of 0 to 8. Each question was rated as 0 or 1. A score of 0 represented that: (1) the information was either not reported; (2) the question was not applicable; or (3) the response to the question was *no*. A score of 1 represented a *yes* response to the question. The higher the score the lower the likelihood of bias.

The quality assessment of the research involved appraisal of the study's internal validity (that is, the degree to which its design, conduct and analysis minimises biases or errors). In a systematic review, the methodological quality assessment can be used to determine a minimum quality threshold for the selection of primary studies to be included in the review. In the *UK review*, the process of quality assessment was used to aid the

1. Is there a sufficient description of the groups and distribution of demographic factors?
2. Are the groups assembled at a similar point in their intervention progression?
3. Is the intervention or treatment reliably ascertained?
4. Were the groups comparable on all confounding factors?
5. Was the outcome assessment blind to exposure?
6. Was the follow-up long enough for the outcomes to occur?
7. Was the cohort followed up?
8. Were dropout rates and reasons similar across intervention and unexposed groups?

Figure 2.4 Quality assessment of cohort studies
Source: CRD (2001).

interpretation of the results and allow the generation of inferences to inform practice and research rather than threshold for inclusion.

According to the CRD guidelines, there are four sources of potential bias referred to in the literature when considering the assessment of the methodological quality of a study: selection, performance, measurement and attrition. Selection bias, often referred to as allocation bias, occurs when systematic differences between an intervention and comparison group are apparent in relation to demographic background characteristics, prognosis or responsiveness to treatment. RCTs using large numbers of participants and allocation concealment can help to protect against this bias.

Performance bias is reported when systematic differences occur within the delivery of an intervention that is being evaluated. Protection against performance bias can be generated through the use of a protocol to ensure that practitioners deliver the intervention in the same manner. Blinding of practitioners and participants can also help to reduce this bias.

Measurement bias, sometimes referred to as detection or ascertainment bias in the literature, describes systematic differences between comparison groups in how outcomes are ascertained. Blinding study participants and outcome assessors can minimise this bias.

Attrition bias is generated from a systematic difference between comparison groups in terms of withdrawals or exclusions of participants from the study sample. Attrition rates between the groups may be differential. Analysis of the results using intention to treat helps to protect against this bias, analysing participants' outcomes according to initial group allocation. In addition, data collected on why people did not complete treatment can help to ascertain whether the participants who failed to complete were any different in any way from those participants who successfully completed treatment (CRD, 1996).

In the UK CJS, attrition bias is a particular problem with studies that are conducted with participants outside a secure establishment. For example, cognitive behavioural programmes conducted in UK prisons record an average 10 per cent dropout rate. In comparison, similar programmes conducted in the community under the care of the probation service have higher dropout rates; as many as 50 per cent of individuals who begin Think First cognitive behavioural courses drop out before completing the course. Retention of such participants can be particularly difficult because of the nature of an offender's (often chaotic and socially excluded) lifestyle.

Economic Assessment

Policy makers are increasingly being made aware of not only whether an intervention is effective in reducing crime, but also whether it is cost effective. A small number of studies in the *UK review* included cost information.

---

1. Is there a well-defined question?
2. Is there a comprehensive description of alternatives?
3. Are all important relevant costs and outcomes for each alternative identified?
4. Has effectiveness been statistically established?
5. Are costs and outcomes measured accurately?
6. Are costs and outcomes valued credibly?
7. Are costs and outcomes adjusted for differential timing?
8. Is there an incremental analysis of costs and consequences?
9. Were sensitivity analyses conducted to investigate uncertainty in estimates of costs or consequences?
10. How far do study results include all issues of concern to users?
11. Are the results generalisable to the setting of interest in the review?

Figure 2.5 Economic assessment
Source: CRD (2001). Reproduced by permission of the Centre for Reviews and Dissemination.

Where this was reported, studies were rated on an 11-point checklist (Drummond et al., 1997) adapted by the CRD (CRD, 2001) (see Figure 2.5). The quality checklist ensures that all relevant methodological points are appraised in an economic evaluation, and provides insight into the occasional heterogeneity of results in economic evaluations.

Synthesis of the Results

The following section reports on the synthesis of the results through data extraction and management.

Two reviewers extracted data using a pre-determined protocol. A narrative review was performed for the nominated outcome. The data-extraction process was divided into two stages: stage one involved the data extracted for the purpose of summary tables, and stage two grouped the studies according to a number of themed areas.

The summary tables provided information on author, year, location of the study, study rating, intervention type, outcome measures, follow-up period, effectiveness, SMS score and economic score. A more detailed description of each study covering study design, objective of the study, sample description (that is, sample size, age, gender and ethnicity), methodology, results, conclusions, further comments and information on the cost of the intervention can be found in the *UK review* report (Perry et al., 2003).

Studies were grouped by intervention into a number of themed areas, as described below:

- Alcohol and drug treatment (for example, alcohol education programmes in prison and community drug treatment programmes).
- Sentencing and court diversion schemes (for example, psychiatric diversion schemes).

- Prison and probation schemes (for example, cognitive behavioural programmes).
- Crime prevention (for example, CCTV and street lighting).
- Situational crime prevention and crime reduction (for example, housing crime prevention schemes).

Table 2.3 shows the number of studies in each of the designated areas.

Due to the heterogeneous nature of the studies, it was not appropriate to perform a meta-analysis. Instead, the studies were grouped together in themed intervention areas, and are presented in Chapters 3 to 7 of this book. The *What Works* classification system used in all studies with a comparison or control group is presented in Chapter 9.

Main Findings

The search identified a total of 1,499 studies. After pre-screening this was reduced to 192. Further examination of the studies reduced the number included to 100. A total of 68 studies without a control group were excluded from the results tables. Figure 2.6 shows the process of elimination.

CONCLUSIONS

A variety of different study designs have been employed in the UK CJS, focusing mainly on non-randomisation or observational study designs. More recently, the use of RCTs has been encouraged to enable investigators to use systematic review and the new Home Office REA methodology, combining a number of similar studies to generate an effect size. In the UK, this methodology has so far been put to only limited use, and lags behind the UK health discipline and US counterparts who regularly conduct many RCTs in the CJS.

The current *UK review* displays the broad nature of both research design and outcome measures used in the UK CJS. Standardisation of these methodologies, costs and outcome measures would help to reduce this

Table 2.3 Studies identified by themed area

Themed area	Number of studies identified in each area
Alcohol and drug treatment	7
Sentencing, police and security and court diversion	20
Prison and probation	13
Crime prevention	20
Situational crime prevention	2
Crime reduction	6

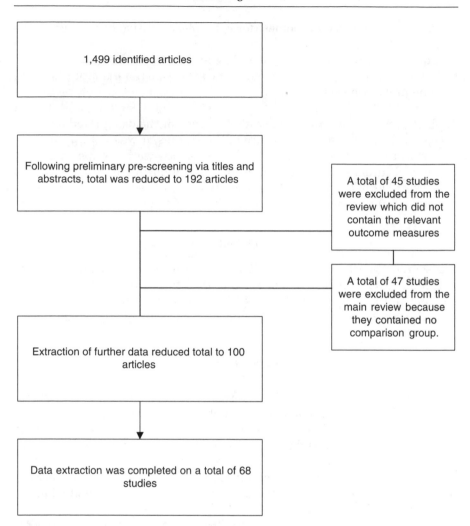

Figure 2.6 Flow chart showing the process of elimination
Source: CRD (2001). Reproduced by permission of the Centre for Reviews and
Dissemination

disparity and, in addition, would allow for comparisons to be made across
different intervention areas. The following chapters present the evidence
from the *UK review* and more recent studies in more detail.

REFERENCES

Belton, E. (2000). *Milton Keynes Group Work Programmes: A Final Evaluation.*
Milton Keynes: Oxfordshire and Buckinghamshire Probation Service.

Centre for Reviews and Dissemination (1996). *Undertaking Systematic Reviews of Research on Effectiveness*. York: University of York.

Centre for Reviews and Dissemination (2001). *Report Number 4* (2nd edn). York: University of York.

Chanhatasilpa, C., MacKenzie, D.L. & Hickman, L.J. (2000). The effectiveness of community-based programs for chemically dependent offenders: A review and assessment of the research. *Journal of Substance Abuse Treatment*, **19**, 383–93.

Cook, T.D. & Campbell, D.T. (1979). *Quasi-Experimentation: Design and Analysis Issues for Field Settings*. USA: Rand McNally.

Davies, P., Butler, G., Cassidy, D. & Deaton, S. (2005). Workshop: Rapid evidence assessment and interim evidence assessments: What they are and how to do one. '5th Annual Campbell Collaboration Colloquium: Supply and Demand for Evidence', Lisbon, 23–25 February 2005.

Department of Health/Home Office (2000). *Reforming the Mental Health Act (Part I: The New Legal Framework. Part II: High Risk Patients)*. London: The Stationery Office.

Drummond, M.F., O'Brien, B.J., Stoddart, G.L. & Torrance, G.W. (1997). *Methods for the Economic Evaluation of Health Care Programmes* (3rd edn). Oxford: Oxford University Press.

Farrington, D.P. & Jolliffe, D. (2002). A feasibility study into using a randomised controlled trial to evaluate treatment pilots at HMP Whitemoor. *Home Office Online Report 14/02*. London: Home Office.

Lipsey, M.W. & Wilson, D.B. (1993). The efficacy of psychological, educational and behavioural treatment: confirmation from meta-analysis. *American Psychologist*, **48**, 1181–209.

May, C. & Wadwell, J. (2001). Enforcing community penalties: The relationship between enforcement and reconviction. *Home Office Research Findings 155*. London: HMSO.

McDougall, C., Cohen, M.A., Swaray, R. & Perry, A. (2003). The costs and benefits of sentencing: A systematic review. *The Annals of the American Academy of Political and Social Sciences*, **587**, 160–77.

McGuire, J. (ed.) (1995). *What Works: Reducing Reoffending Guidelines From Research and Practice*. New York: Wiley.

Painter, K.A. & Farrington, D.P. (1999). Street lighting and crime: Diffusion of benefits in the Stoke-on-Trent project. In K.A. Painter and N. Tilley (eds), *Surveillance of Public Space: CCTV, Street Lighting and Crime Prevention: Crime Prevention Studies*. New York: Criminal Justice Press.

Perry, A., McDougall, C., Swaray, R., Murphy, T., Harris, R. & Bjornsson, H. (2003). *The Effectiveness of UK Criminal Justice Interventions in the Reduction of Crime: A Review of the Literature*. York: Centre for Criminal Justice Economics and Psychology, University of York.

Sacks, S., Sacks, J.Y., McKendrick, K., Banks, S. & Stommel, J. (2004). Modified TC for MICA inmates in correctional settings: crime outcomes. *Behavioural Sciences and the Law*, **22**(4), 477–501.

Sherman, L.W., Farrington, D.P., Welsh, B.C. & MacKenzie, D.L. (2002). *Evidence-Based Crime Prevention*. London: Routledge.

Sherman L.W., Gottfredson, D., MacKenzie, D., Eck, J., Reuler, P. & Bushay, S. (1997). *Preventing Crime: What Works, What Doesn't, What's Promising: A Report to the United States Congress*. (www.cjcentral.com/sherman/sherman.htm).

CHAPTER 3

Alcohol and Drug Treatments

MARY MCMURRAN

INTRODUCTION

Alcohol and drug use are both topics of great concern within criminal justice systems, but there are differences in the legislative control of each. Though legally available in the UK, alcohol is still controlled with regard to where it may be sold, by whom, and to whom, and breaking such laws is likely to result in fines and/or licensing restrictions. By contrast, the possession, sale and use of certain drugs are *de facto* against the law, with heavy sentencing for those who commit drug-specific crimes. However, despite the fact that large amounts of criminal justice expenditure and resources are directed towards managing alcohol and drug availability, problematic users abound, and there is a great need for alcohol and drug treatments in criminal justice settings.

The main concern with alcohol is that it fuels disorderly conduct and violence. In the UK, this manifests itself particularly in the form of street violence, with young, male binge-drinkers the predominant group of offenders (Richardson & Budd, 2003). Alcohol is also very often a contributory factor in incidents of domestic violence (Gilchrist et al., 2003), frequently increasing likelihood and degree of violence (Leonard, 2001). Another major issue is driving under the influence of alcohol (Ayres & Hayward, 2000). Although of lesser concern, there is some evidence that the cost of supporting a habit of heavy drinking drives some people to commit acquisitive offences (McMurran & Cusens, in press).

The drugs situation is more complex, not least because the term 'drugs' includes a wide range of substances that have many different

Reducing Crime: The Effectiveness of Criminal Justice Interventions.
Edited by A. E. Perry, C. McDougall and D. P. Farrington. © 2006 John Wiley & Sons, Ltd.

psychopharmacological effects on the individual. It seems that the main concern, however, is that drugs are substances upon which a user becomes dependent, and satisfaction of the need for drugs drives people to commit economic crimes. A recent study of offenders subjected to drug treatment and testing orders (DTTOs) reported that a drug-using offender may spend as much as £21,000 per annum on drugs, often financing this through shoplifting, burglary, drug dealing and fraud (Turnbull, McSweeney, Webster, Edmunds & Hough, 2000). Certain drugs make users more violent, with concern in this area focusing especially on crack-cocaine (Home Office, 2002a). There is also a link between drug use and prostitution, with sex workers (male and female) selling sex for drugs, and also being used as vehicles for drug distribution (May, Edmunds & Hough, 1999).

The provision of treatment within the criminal justice system is influenced by national strategies that, in turn, influence criminal justice system strategies. In the UK, Scotland, Wales, Northern Ireland and England each have their own national strategies for tackling drug- and alcohol-related concerns. The British Government's strategy on drugs, *Tackling Drugs to Build a Better Britain*, was first published in 1998, and followed by an updated version in 2002 (Home Office, 2002b). Along with greater efforts to control, prevent and treat drug misuse, it included a commitment to expand services within the criminal justice system, 'using every opportunity from arrest, to court, to sentence, to getting drug-misusing offenders into treatment' (Home Office, 2002b, p. 4). In 1999, Scotland and Northern Ireland launched their strategies, *Tackling Drugs in Scotland: Action in Partnership* (Scottish Office, 1999) and *Drug Strategy for Northern Ireland* (Northern Ireland Executive, 1999), each of which explicitly states an intention to provide treatment for drug-using offenders. Wales differed somewhat in producing a strategy for substance misuse that addressed both drugs and alcohol (National Assembly for Wales, 2000), but again included an explicit commitment to further developing treatment for substance-misusing offenders.

National alcohol strategies also commit to the treatment of alcohol-misusing offenders. Northern Ireland's *Strategy for Reducing Alcohol Related Harm* (DHSSPS, 2000), Scotland's *Plan for Action on Alcohol Problems* (Scottish Executive, 2002) and the UK Government's *Alcohol Harm Reduction Strategy for England* (Cabinet Office, 2004) all endorse the development of offender treatments.

Since 1998, Her Majesty's (HM) Prison Service for England and Wales has included a drug strategy unit devoted to the control of drugs in prisons and the promotion and co-ordination of interventions for drug users, as stated in its *Tackling Drugs in Prison* strategy. But despite the extent of alcohol-related problems among offenders, the prison service launched an alcohol strategy only as recently as December 2004 (HM Prison Service, 2004). In the accompanying *Alcohol Treatment/Interventions: Good*

Practice Guide (HM Prison Service/Department of Health, 2004) is the acknowledgement that there is no central funding for alcohol interventions and that good practice is an ideal, not a reality. There is currently no co-ordinator of alcohol interventions in the prison and probation services, even though such a role was suggested as far back as 1989 (McMurran, 1989; McMurran & Baldwin, 1989). The Northern Ireland Prison Service has operated a drug strategy since 1996, most recently revised in 2003, and this is currently being reviewed with a new combined *Drug and Alcohol Misuse Strategy*. The Scottish Prison Service is also currently working on a new addictions policy.

The probation services for England, Wales and Northern Ireland, and criminal justice social work in Scotland, have no specific drug strategies, and work with drug users is guided by sentencing, such as DTTOs, and directives on interagency working, for example membership of local drug action teams (DATs). Recently, in Scotland, special drug courts have been set up, with a range of sentencing and treatment options, dependent on what services are available locally (McIvor, Eley, Malloch & Yates, 2003). A fairly recent review of offender management in England and Wales has led to an integration of the work of prison and probation services through the creation of a National Offender Management Service (NOMS) (Carter, 2003), which may lead to changes in policy for the treatment of alcohol and drug users.

So how does the policy context affect alcohol and drug treatment in UK correctional settings? Policies are translated into the priorities that prison and probation services set, directing limited resources into what is currently seen as most pressing, either because of prevailing need or because of the political agenda. The policies that support alcohol and drug treatments in criminal justice settings must be translated into practice, which these days is guided by the process of programme accreditation. Programmes are accredited by panels of experts working to specified criteria of what makes a good programme. These criteria are based firmly on research evidence from what is known as the *What Works* movement. Driven by meta-analyses of the offender treatment literature, effective treatments and effective conditions for treatment have been identified (see review by McGuire, 2002). These conditions form the criteria by which offender treatment programmes are judged for accreditation. The 10 accreditation criteria for HM Prison Service (Correctional Services Accreditation Panel, 2002) are listed in Figure 3.1.

Essentially, evidence-based interventions targeted at crime-related issues ('criminogenic needs') are supported, and the advice is to aim these at high-risk offenders. Certain criminogenic issues are accepted within accreditation criteria as appropriate targets for treatment, and dependency on alcohol or drugs is accepted as a criminogenic need (Correctional Services Accreditation Panel, 2002).

1. There must be a clear and coherent model of change.
2. There must be a clear statement of the types of offender for whom the programme is designed.
3. A range of dynamic risk factors must be targeted.
4. Effective treatment methods must be used.
5. The programme must facilitate the offender's learning of skills.
6. The programme must be of adequate duration and intensity, and must be appropriately sequenced.
7. Attention must be paid to engaging offenders and maintaining their treatment motivation.
8. The programme must integrate with the offender's overall sentence or supervision plan.
9. The implementation of the programme must be monitored to ensure that it is run as designed (programme integrity).
10. The process and outcomes must be evaluated.

Figure 3.1 HM Prison Service's programme accreditation criteria

The result is that several accredited treatment programmes focusing on substance misuse are now used in UK criminal justice settings. These include cognitive behavioural programmes (for example, see McMurran & Priestley, 2004), 12-step programmes (Martin & Player, 2000), and therapeutic communities (Malinowski, 2003). Although these are ostensibly generic programmes that target the problematic misuse of any substance (alcohol and/or illicit drugs), it is clear that drugs are the priority, and that the range of interventions for problem drinkers is limited. While this may be understandable in the sense that drug use is a crime *per se*, there is undoubtedly still a need for specific alcohol treatments. If a treatment area is not identified as a priority, then resources to develop and maintain that treatment are scarce and interventions are not quality controlled. Without support for their development, programmes for problem drinkers in the criminal justice system may not be firmly founded on theories of problem drinking and evidence of what is effective in treatment.

ALCOHOL INTERVENTIONS

In the *UK review* evaluating criminal justice interventions that reduce crime, three methodologically acceptable studies with control group designs—all scoring four out of five on the Maryland Scale (developed by Sherman et al. in 1997 to assess the quality of study designs conducted to evaluate crime prevention in the US)—and one study with no control group were identified in relation to the effectiveness of alcohol interventions.

Only studies reporting a control group are presented in Table 9.1 (see Chapter 9) for the *What Works* classification.

The first published, a study by McMurran and Boyle (1990), classified as *Unknown* using the *What Works* classification system, investigated the effectiveness of a behavioural self-help manual with regard to young male offenders (that is, aged between 15 and 21) in England. Among offenders assessed as having a literacy level adequate for reading and understanding the manual, 45 problem drinkers were identified. Of these, 42 reported drinking 35 or more units of alcohol per week (1 unit = 8.5 grams of alcohol), which is far in excess of the current recommended safe limits of consumption (21 units or 168 grams of ethanol per week for men; Royal College of Physicians, Royal College of Psychiatrists and Royal College of General Practitioners, 1995), and well above the current average consumption for young men in this age group (21.5 units per week), which has been on the increase in recent years (Rickards, Fox, Roberts, Fletcher & Goddard, 2004). Three groups of 15 were formed, and matched for age and alcohol consumption. One group received no intervention; a second was given the self-help manual to read in their own time; and the other group was gathered together to have the manual presented to them, thus ensuring familiarisation with its contents. Reconviction data on 41 offenders were collected from the Criminal Records Office on average 15 months after release. Data were available for 13 in the no intervention group (86 per cent), of whom 8 had been reconvicted; 13 in the group given the manual to read alone (86 per cent), of whom 8 had been reconvicted; and all 15 of the group to whom the contents of the manual had been presented (100 per cent), 11 of whom had been reconvicted. There was no significant treatment effect.

Baldwin et al. (1991), classified as *What's Promising* using the *What Works* system, reported on the effectiveness of an alcohol-education course consisting of six weekly two-hour sessions, for young male offenders in Scotland. Criteria for inclusion were being aged 17 to 21 (although the control group included participants aged 22 years), having committed two or more offences, more than half of the offences being alcohol-related, and having a release date within eight weeks of the start of the course. Suitable candidates were randomly assigned to treatment or no treatment control, with 14 and 13 in each group, respectively. Comparison of the two groups indicated that, at the outset, the treatment group had significantly more property offences than the control group, and were more likely to drink in public places rather than licensed premises. Offenders were followed up on average 14 months after release, and information about drinking and offending was collected by interview from all treated and seven (60 per cent) untreated offenders. The interviewer was blind to whether the interviewee had been treated or not. In addition, information about the offender's drinking and offending was obtained by interviewing a partner, relative or close friend. Concordance of information was high. Analysis showed that those not contacted at follow-up were heavier drinkers than those contacted. Compared with the untreated group, the treated group showed significant decreases in drinking, the number of property offences, and 'offences against rules and regulations'. At follow-up, the treated group had committed significantly fewer offences against the person. Pre- to post-treatment changes on an attitudes-to-drinking questionnaire and a measure of confidence in adhering to drinking limits were significant for the treated group, but not for the untreated group.

In Singer's (1991) study, not classified under the *What Works* system due to the lack of a control group, the notion of probation as punishment was countered with the example of an alcohol-education course for young offenders in an English probation service. The course consisted of six group sessions plus two individual interviews—one pre-group interview and one at the conclusion of the group sessions. Between 1986 and 1988, 152 offenders (9 female) undertook the alcohol-education course and were assessed before and after the course on alcohol knowledge, attitudes to alcohol and drinking behaviour, and self-reported drinking, all of which showed significant positive change. At follow-up 12 months after completing the course, 63 per cent (N = 95) had not been convicted of any further crimes. Of those with five or more previous convictions—a group for whom the expected reconviction rate was 53 per cent within one year—only 42 per cent of the treated group were reconvicted.

Patterson, Macpherson and Brady's (1997) study, classified as *Unknown* using the *What Works* classification system, contained a sample of 127 white adult men (aged 16 to 70) treated in an addiction unit in Northern Ireland. The men selected for the study were diagnosed alcohol-dependent, and had spent six weeks in intensive inpatient treatment between 1986 and 1988. Seventy-three of the sample were assigned to community aftercare under the supervision of a community psychiatric nurse. This consisted of weekly home visits for the first six weeks, then monthly visits for the remainder of the year, during which they received advice, counselling and couple/family work. Community aftercare was not available to the remaining 54 patients, who were instead given hospital outpatient appointments every six weeks, when a nurse would review the patient's case. Comparison of the two groups revealed no significant differences at the outset. Five years after the date of admission, 70 (96 per cent) of the community aftercare group and 52 (96 per cent) of the hospital aftercare group were followed up by a researcher, blind to the type of aftercare the patients had received. For half the sample, a close family member was asked for information about the participant's drinking, with high concordance in 80 per cent of cases and significantly greater concordance in the community aftercare group. Where concordance was poor, the participant appeared to be under-reporting his alcohol consumption. Significantly, more of the community aftercare group were abstinent at follow-up, and this group suffered significantly fewer blackouts. Overall, 14 per cent of the sample had committed criminal offences, and 4 per cent had been in prison, but there were no differences between treatment conditions.

The research on the effectiveness of alcohol treatments is slight, and leaves us in no position to draw conclusions. But methodological questions can be raised in relation to these studies, consideration of which may be useful in future research.

A major research issue is a combined one of who to select for treatment and what outcomes to measure. If offending is to be used as an outcome measure, then attention needs to be paid to selecting offenders for whom this is a logical outcome of treatment. In McMurran and Boyle's (1990) study, offenders selected were heavy or problematic drinkers, but the connection between drinking and offending was not established, and so there may not have been a logical connection between reducing drinking and reducing offending. In the study by Patterson et al. (1997), offending was again used as an outcome measure with no pre-intervention assessment of offending and no identification of any relationship between drinking and offending. Related to this selection criterion is the question of what crime outcome measures to use. Alcohol is more commonly related to violent offending, although there is evidence of a relationship with acquisitive offending, particularly among those with alcohol-misuse disorders (McMurran & Cusens, in press). In what types of crime might one logically expect to see a reduction after treatment? Both selection criteria and outcome measures need to be carefully thought through in relation to each other.

If the logic is that offending is reduced by tackling the mediator of drinking, then it is useful to measure the impact of any treatment on this mediator. In McMurran and Boyle's (1990) study, the failure to reduce reoffending may have been because the intervention did not reduce drinking or because reducing drinking had no impact on offending. In order to tease out these issues, it is important to measure changes in both drinking and offending, as in the Baldwin et al. (1991) study.

Another major issue of concern in the studies reviewed is that of sample sizes. McMurran and Boyle (1990) and Baldwin et al. (1991) examined small numbers of offenders, but the numbers in Patterson et al.'s (1997) study are lowest of all, despite the greater total number of participants. Patterson et al.'s sample was not an offender sample, and of the 122 people followed up, only 14 per cent were identified as offenders. The authors do not make it clear that 14 per cent equals a mere 17 individuals spread over two conditions, yet they compare offending across the two treatment groups and comment on the absence of any significant difference.

Apart from nine female offenders in Singer's (1991) sample, the studies here focus on men. The extent of the need for alcohol interventions in female offender populations remains largely ignored and, consequently, services specific to their needs remain underdeveloped. While it is true that men are responsible for more alcohol-related aggression than women, there is growing concern about women and violence (Muncer, Campbell, Jervis & Lewis, 2001). There may also be different criminal consequences of women's drinking with, perhaps, acquisitive offending or sex work figuring more prominently.

The intensity of the intervention is another area of concern. Meta-analyses show that higher 'dosage' treatments (that is, longer and more frequent sessions) for high-risk offenders are most effective in reducing recidivism (Lipsey, 1992, 1995). 'Intensive' treatment, as defined by Lipsey (1995) in his meta-analysis, lasted 26 weeks or more, with two or more contacts per week, and more than 100 hours of treatment. In practice, around 50 hours of intervention is taken as a rough minimum for a programme to be considered for accreditation in the UK. Baldwin et al.'s (1991) and Singer's (1991) interventions were around 12 hours' duration, and McMurran and Boyle's (1990) considerably shorter. These programmes would not stand up to scrutiny by an accreditation panel today. Indeed, Singer's (1991) comment about 'the demanding and disciplined nature of the course' (p. 614) shows just how views have changed. These days, a demanding course is unlikely to be less than 20 two-hour sessions and is usually considerably longer.

However, there is tension here between the offender treatment literature and the alcohol treatment literature. In alcohol treatments, brief interventions, including advice, self-help manuals and brief motivational enhancement therapy, have a good record of effectiveness, particularly with people with less severe drinking problems who request help (see review by Heather, 2004). Many offenders, particularly younger ones, are not dependent on alcohol, but rather have problems associated with binge drinking (Richardson & Budd, 2003), although whether they volunteer for treatment or not is a moot point. The drive towards accreditation of intensive programmes for high-risk offenders means that there is little interest in supporting the design and evaluation of briefer programmes. This differs from the approach in clinical settings, where cognisance of limited resources and the need for cost-effectiveness has led to a stepped care model of treatment, in which a minimal intervention is given first and, if this does not work, successively more intensive interventions are given until the client shows signs of benefit. Economising in this way means that scarce resources can be shared among more people.

DRUG INTERVENTIONS

In the *UK review*, four methodologically acceptable studies with control group designs—three scoring three, and one scoring four out of five on the Maryland Scale—and three studies with no control group were identified in relation to the effectiveness of drug interventions. (See Table 9.2 for further details.)

In Merseyside, Parker and Kirby (1996), classified as *What's Promising* using the *What Works* classification system, examined the effect of methadone treatment on acquisitive crime. By examining trends in drug use and various types of crime in Merseyside boroughs over 16 years, they found evidence in support of a relationship between heroin use and acquisitive crime, particularly burglary and theft. The researchers compared a sample of 209 heroin users (40 per cent female) registered at a drug treatment clinic with 103 unmatched drug users (30 per cent female) recruited via needle exchange schemes in the community. The mean age of the clinic sample was 31, and that of the community sample 27, while across both groups men were significantly older than women (32 and 29 years respectively). The investigators relied on self-reported drug use and crime, but ran a validity check on the clinic sample's reports against urine tests and police reports. Although there was some under-reporting of drug use and crime, the authors considered self-report to be of adequate validity. Compared with the treatment group, the community sample had used more drugs, specifically heroin, cocaine, crack and non-prescribed methadone, in the month prior to interview. Most participants in the treatment group claimed to have reduced their drug taking as a result of treatment (71 per cent), with about a fifth claiming to have stopped (22 per cent). More women than men in the treatment group reduced their drug use. The community sample spent more on drugs—an average of £375 per week compared with £75 per week for the treatment group. At the time of interview, 75 per cent of those studied had at least one criminal conviction, with a mean of 16 cautions and convictions per person. Convictions for theft, fraud and offences of violence were significantly more likely in the community sample, and members of this group were significantly more likely to get their income from acquisitive crime, prostitution and drug dealing. On admission, 90 of the treatment group reported funding their drug use through theft and fraud. At follow-up interview, this was significantly decreased by 50 per cent to 46 individuals. There was no pre- to post-treatment difference in drug dealing. Significantly more of the treatment group was in paid employment at interview, compared with at admission.

McCusker and Davies (1996), classified as *What's Promising* according to the *What Works* system, compared heroin users treated in three drug clinics within one region of the UK, using a case-control matching design. A registered practitioner at one of the three clinics prescribed pharmaceutical heroin (diamorphine), whereas practitioners at the other two clinics prescribed methadone. Other than that, services were highly similar in counselling and healthcare. The heroin-prescribed group numbered 27, of whom 88 per cent were male. These were matched for age, sex, drug use and treatment history with a methadone-prescribed group, numbering 39, of whom 85 per cent were male. A range of assessments was conducted at referral and then again after six months. At follow-up, 1 (4 per cent) of the heroin-prescribed group and 14 (36 per cent) of the methadone-prescribed group had dropped out of treatment, and the heroin-prescribed group had maintained significantly more regular contact with services. Differences at baseline between the two groups were identified, with fewer of the heroin-prescribed group reporting having recently used heroin, and the reported mean monthly expenditure being less for this group, at £17 compared with £67 for the methadone group. At follow-up, the heroin-prescribed group had had their medication increased, compared with a decrease in the methadone-prescribed group, and both groups were using illicit drugs, including non-prescribed heroin. Judging from the mean amount spent monthly at follow-up, the methadone group had reduced their drug intake (£43) while the heroin prescribed group remained the same (£17). A considerable percentage of each group admitted to *not* aiming for abstinence—63 per cent of the heroin-prescribed and 26 per cent of the methadone-prescribed group—which actually rose to 80 per cent and 40 per cent, respectively, at follow-up. Employment status did not differ between the two groups at the outset, and did not change over time, with about three-quarters being unemployed. At referral, 37 per cent of the heroin-prescribed group were on probation or awaiting trial, which remained virtually the same at follow-up (38 per cent), compared with 21 per cent of the methadone group at referral, rising to 32 per cent at follow-up. When participants were asked to report the number of days in the past month that they had engaged in any illegal activity—drug possession excepted—the methadone-prescribed group reported more at first assessment and a greater reduction at follow-up (a mean of 5.9 days dropping to 4.2 for the methadone group, compared with 1.9 dropping to 1.7 for the heroin prescribed group).

In Inner London, the Haynes (1998) study was not classified using the *What Works* classification system due to the lack of a comparison group. The study surveyed 112 probation referrals to a drug treatment service. Their mean age was 27 years, 17 per cent were female, 21 per cent were black, and 38 per cent had a problem with opiates or cocaine at referral. Data were collected from probation service records and drug service case notes. Of the 112 referrals, 83 (74 per cent) were available at follow-up on average 15 months after referral. Of the 83 people followed up, 52 (63 per cent) had reoffended, with acquisitive offending most common

(64 per cent of reoffenders), followed by drug offences (12 per cent) and offences of violence (12 per cent). Comparing participants' offending before and after intervention, the numbers committing the more serious offences of violence and burglary had dropped (from 17 per cent to 12 per cent for violence; 22 per cent to 10 per cent for burglary), whereas the numbers committing less serious property offences increased (from 45 per cent to 54 per cent). The number of contacts with the drug and probation services predicted reoffending, with fewer contacts associated with a higher likelihood of reoffending.

Martin and Player (2000), classified as *What's Promising* by the *What Works* classification system, evaluated a 12-step therapeutic community for drug and alcohol misusers in prison. They studied 200 men who had been referred to the treatment programme in prisons in London and the southeast of England. The men were mostly in their twenties, and three-quarters were white British. All 200 participants were interviewed, and information regarding offending was verified from prison records. The 200 formed three groups: (1) programme graduates (N = 95, 47.5 per cent); (2) programme drop-outs (N = 35, 17.5 per cent); and (3) non-starters, who had been referred but never started treatment (N = 70, 35 per cent). The men in the overall sample were recidivist offenders, with programme graduates being more serious offenders than non-graduates and serving longer sentences. When asked to identify their main drug of choice, 29 per cent cited heroin, 20 per cent alcohol and 19 per cent cocaine, with more graduates using heroin and cocaine. Almost all the men agreed that drug use had led to their offending, particularly acquisitive offending to support their habit, and about a quarter said that drug-induced behaviour had led to the offence. Follow-up information on reconviction was collected from the Home Office's Offenders Index database. A subset of 75 men was interviewed at follow-up: 42 graduates, 13 dropouts and 20 non-starters. At follow-up, breath, hair or urine samples were taken for testing for the person's drug of choice only. Reconviction data on all but one member of the sample at a mean post-release period of 13 months showed that significantly fewer graduates (N = 19; 20 per cent) than non-graduates (N = 41; 39 per cent) had been reconvicted. From interviews, it was evident that significantly fewer of those who were totally abstinent, or abstinent from their drug of choice (N = 47; 21 per cent) had been reconvicted compared with those who had continued to use their drug of choice (N = 23; 56 per cent).

Coid, Carvell, Kittler, Healey and Henderson (2000; undated), in a study not classified by the *What Works* system due to the lack of a comparison group, interviewed 221 opiate addicts (70 per cent male; 69 per cent white British) at a community clinic in East London. Three-quarters were self-referred, the others being referred by GPs, drug counsellors and probation officers. Most had used a range of illicit drugs, although heroin was the primary drug of addiction. The majority (84 per cent) had a criminal history and many had financed their drug use by drug dealing (65 per cent) and theft (62 per cent). Prior to treatment, only 15 per cent had funded their drug use through legal means. Most (67 per cent) believed that their drug use and offending were linked. A subgroup of 116 (52 per cent) of the initial sample was identified for follow-up six months after starting methadone-reduction treatment. Of these, 81 (70 per cent) were still in treatment and therefore available for interview. The interviewees had used heroin on only 11 days in the previous month, compared with 25 days in the month before treatment began, and had spent £19 per day compared with £42 per day prior to treatment. Use of drugs other than heroin remained the same, except for illicit methadone, usage of which was reduced. Comparing self-reported criminal activity for six months before treatment and six months since treatment began, the mean number of days involved in crime was significantly less for drug dealing and theft, and illegal earnings from drug dealing, theft and burglary were also reduced significantly.

Keen, Rowse, Mathers, Campbell and Seivewright (2000), again not classified by the *What Works* system due to the lack of a comparison group, conducted a retrospective study of 57 patients on methadone maintenance prescription in two GP practices in Sheffield. Of the 135 methadone maintenance patients registered at the practices, 69 (51 per cent) attended for consultations during the month of the study, of whom 57 were interviewed. Thirty-seven were male and 20 female, with an average age of 34. They had been addicted but untreated for an average of eight years, and in treatment for an average of four-and-a-half years. Crime data were accessed from police records, with 52 participants identified as having a criminal record. Comparisons were made between pre-treatment and in-treatment periods. The total number of convictions and cautions reduced by 39 per cent; convictions for theft and fraud and cautions reduced by 52 per cent; and time spent in prison reduced by 82 per cent—all of which decreases were significant. Men showed a significantly greater decrease in criminality than women.

Metrebian et al. (2001), classified as *What's Unknown* by the *What Works* system, studied long-term opiate-dependent individuals in a West London clinic specialising in offering injectable opiates. Over a one-and-a-half-year period, 58 injecting opiate users who could or would not give up injecting were identified and offered injectable pharmaceutical heroin or methadone. Behaviour change was assessed at 3-, 6- and 12-month intervals using a validated interview procedure—the Opiate Treatment Index. Of the 58 participants, 37 (64 per cent) chose injectable heroin and 21 per cent) injectable methadone. The two groups were mainly males (70 per cent and 76 per cent respectively), white (92 per cent and 75 per cent), with an approximate age of 37. At baseline, the heroin-prescribed group was significantly more likely to have used illicit heroin and in greater amounts, and to have used crack-cocaine, than the methadone-prescribed group. At 12 months, more of the heroin-prescribed group were still in treatment (59 per cent) compared with the methadone-prescribed group (48 per cent). Treatment dropouts were more likely to be male, but there were also group differences, with dropouts in the heroin-prescribed group being older and having longer injecting careers. Of those still in treatment at 12 months, the heroin-prescribed group (N = 22) had significantly reduced their illicit heroin use, whereas the methadone-prescribed group (N = 10) had not. Criminal activity, scored from the Opiate Treatment Index but not specified in this paper, was significantly reduced in the heroin-prescribed group but not the methadone-prescribed group.

Research on the effectiveness of drug treatments on crime is somewhat better than that for alcohol treatments and, in general, the outcomes are positive. However, attention to the detail of these research studies indicates that some caution needs to be exercised when drawing conclusions.

The most obvious limitations in these studies relate to sampling. In studies where two groups have been compared, the groups differ at the outset on key variables. Parker and Kirby's (1996) treatment group contained more women, were older and used fewer drugs than the no-treatment group. Despite being matched on age, sex, drug use and treatment history, McCusker and Davies' (1996) groups differed at baseline in that the heroin-prescribed group was using less heroin than the methadone-prescribed group just before treatment, and more were on probation or awaiting trial. Metrebian et al.'s (2001) heroin-prescribed group was using more heroin and crack-cocaine than the methadone-prescribed group just before treatment. These differences mean that any observed treatment effects are confounded by the different initial status of the control or comparison groups.

Samples also suffered attrition, meaning that the data on those still in treatment did not necessarily reflect the data on the sample as a whole, with differential attrition across groups exacerbating this problem. Comparing treatment completers with treatment non-completers, as in the Martin and Player (2000) study, is not comparing like with like. Treatment non-completers have been shown to display a high risk of reoffending as measured by statistical risk calculation scales (Wormith & Olver, 2002). Care must be taken, therefore, to minimise missing cases and assiduously to follow up those who are identified as study participants. Missing data should not simply be ignored, but rather dealt with in a statistically appropriate manner (Hollis & Campbell, 1999).

The majority of the studies focus on heroin users and acquisitive offending. There is an underpinning rationale, articulated and evidenced by Parker and Kirby (1996), that heroin use is costly and so users are driven by economic necessity to commit acquisitive crimes. Logically, therefore, reducing heroin use will lead to a reduction in acquisitive offending. The only study that compared treated with untreated heroin users showed lower prevalences of theft, burglary, fraud, drug dealing and prostitution in the treated sample (Parker & Kirby, 1996). Two studies compared treatment type—pharmaceutical heroin compared to methadone—with one finding that self-reported crime reduced more with methadone (McCusker & Davies, 1996) and the other finding that crime reduced more with heroin (Metrebian et al., 2001). Studies comparing a single sample of heroin users before and after treatment found significant reductions in drug dealing, theft and fraud (Coid et al., 2000; Keen et al., 2000).

Focusing on heroin use and acquisitive crime is understandable and, perhaps, sensible; however, it is worth noting that most heroin users use other drugs as well. These other drugs may also lead to acquisitive offending to support the habit; even if drugs are cheap, many users have low incomes and are unable to finance drug use legitimately. Additionally, attenuation of heroin use may lead to an increase in the use of other drugs associated with problems other than acquisitive crime; for example, an increase in alcohol use and violence. Furthermore, drug possession and drug use are in themselves crimes, and so are legitimate crime targets. It may therefore be worth taking a broader perspective on drug use and crime rather than focusing mainly heroin and acquisitive crime.

It is interesting to note that all but one of the drug-treatment studies was conducted within health or specialist drug services, whose priorities are not crime reduction. Where the service's priority is health, and where professionals see the drug user as their client, ethical dilemmas are raised when crime becomes a primary focus. One consequence of this is the use of inadequate measures of crime. For example, asking about the number of days when the participant engaged in the all-inclusive 'any illegal activity' leaves one wondering what sort of offences had been committed and whether or not they were related to drug use. Self-reported crime can be acceptable for research purposes (Thornberry & Krohn, 2000), but criminal record checks are preferable as corroboration, if not as the gold standard.

One advantage of work in health and drug services is that it arguably leads to a greater likelihood that changes in drug use and associated variables are measured. Where people remain in treatment, their drug use and often their spending on drugs is assessed. In offender samples, the effectiveness of drug treatment is often evaluated with crime alone as the outcome measure, and no information about changes in drug use (Hollin et al., 2004). By contrast, Shewan, Macpherson, Reid and Davies (1996) reported the effectiveness of a drug-treatment programme in a prison in Edinburgh, comparing 30 prisoners prescribed methadone as well as receiving counselling, with prisoners referred to the programme but who did not start or did not complete it. Although the two groups were not strictly comparable, the treatment group significantly reduced drug use in prison compared with controls, but in this case there was no post-release follow-up. The study by Martin and Player (2000) is the best example of the measurement of both substance use and crime, producing evidence that abstinence is associated with a lower likelihood of recidivism. Self-reported alcohol use and drug use are acceptable for research purposes (Del Boca & Darkes, 2003; McMurran, Hollin, & Bowen, 1990; O'Farrell, Fals-Stewart & Murphy, 2003), but, again, corroboration by drug testing is desirable.

Multi-agency drug treatments are now common. Probation services link with other agencies to provide treatment under DTTOs (Turnbull et al., 2000). More recently, drug courts refer to such local treatment services as are available (Eley, Malloch, McIvor, Yates & Brown, 2002). Information from these comprehensive services suggests that attention needs to be paid to keeping people in services. In a recent study, Hough, Clancy, McSweeney and Turnbull (2003) collected Offenders Index information on 174 DTTO referrals and found a high incidence of reconviction at 2 years (80 per cent). Reconviction was significantly less likely amongst those who completed their order (53 per cent) than those whose order was revoked (91 per cent). Looking at the number of convictions per person per year, an upward trend was observed, peaking the year before the DTTO and dropping thereafter. When completers and non-completers were compared, this trend was evident only for completers. In this study, 67 per cent of the sample (N = 108) had their orders revoked, and the authors commented that 'the key to success in DTTOs lies in retaining people on their orders' (p. 5). See Table 9.3 (Chapter 9) for more details on the *What Works* classification system.

CONCLUSIONS

The alcohol and drug research studies identified in the *UK review* evaluating criminal justice interventions that reduce crime are few in number and suffer serious methodological problems. Although methodological flaws may preclude any definitive conclusion that alcohol and drug treatments work in reducing reoffending, they likewise preclude any definitive conclusion that they do *not* work. More research into the effectiveness of alcohol and drug treatments would be informative, but only if studies are well designed and well executed. Attention needs to be paid to the issues identified above, which are summarised in Figure 3.2.

In policy terms, it is clear that alcohol policies need to be translated into treatments and targets. In the UK, only one accredited treatment programme specifically for alcohol-related offenders exists, targeting drink driving (see Hollin et al., 2002). Although other programmes for substance

1. *Selection* – For each individual, assess the relationship between alcohol or drug use and crime. Evaluate the effectiveness of the intervention on crime logically. That is, use specific crimes as outcome measures only where there is a connection between substance use and that type of crime.

2. *Controls* – Ensure that control or comparison groups are matched on relevant measures (for example, age, sex, criminality, substance use), or that there is randomisation to control groups.

3. *Sample sizes* – Use as large a sample size as possible.

4. *Crime outcome measures* – Specify the type, frequency and severity of crime that is connected with the substance use and that is expected to decrease. In clinical samples, measure this before the intervention as well as after.

5. *Substance use outcome measures* – Measure the effect of the intervention on substance use, otherwise it is impossible to say if the intervention has been successful or unsuccessful by its effect on this key mediator. Focusing only on one drug of choice may miss problems related to other drugs, particularly if a different substance becomes the drug of choice after treatment.

6. *Official records versus self-report* – Self-reported substance use and crime are commonly used in research. Validation self-report, through official record checks, urinalysis, hair analysis or corroboration by others, in at least a subsample of the participants, is desirable.

7. *Blind follow-up* – At follow-up, researchers should be blind to the condition to which the participant was allocated.

8. *Missing data* – Minimise missing data by taking care to follow up the sample. Where there are missing data, do not simply ignore this in data analysis, but rather use techniques that take any potential bias into account.

Figure 3.2 Key methodological recommendations

use may include problem drinkers, it seems that, in reality, services may not be extended to problem drinkers. Certainly, evaluations in this area are few, and it may be that the focus should be directed to alcohol use and crime specifically (for example, see McMurran & Cusens, 2003).

The question of how intensive a substance use treatment programme needs to be requires further examination. Undoubtedly, high-risk offenders and serious long-term drug users are unlikely to benefit from minimal interventions, yet there are offenders passing through the criminal justice system for whom early-stage interventions may have a beneficial effect. It seems unlikely that stepped care could be effective and efficient with substance users in the community, but would not translate in some way to criminal justice settings.

Retaining offenders in treatment programmes is a topic of current concern in UK criminal justice settings, given the high dropout rates in community samples (Hollin et al., 2002, 2004; Hough et al., 2003) and the knowledge that that non-completers are not only more likely to reoffend than completers, but may possibly be more likely to offend than untreated offenders (Cann, Falshaw, Nugent & Friendship, 2003). Attention to methods of retaining offenders in treatment is required. However, programme non-completers may be higher-risk offenders than completers and the same factors may predict non-completion, therefore it is not logical to assume that retention in treatment will necessarily lead to success with this group. Attention to methods of selection is also required to minimise the dropout problem.

One other aspect revealed in Hough et al.'s (2003) DTTO study is that of regional variations in treatment outcome. There are regional variations in drug use (Turnbull et al., 2000), and there are also regional variations in services. This suggests that there is value in regional research across the UK, comparing client groups, service provision and ways of working to identify what works with whom and where.

Like probation service DTTOs, prisons also have multi-agency interventions, with counselling, assessment, referral, advice and throughcare services (CARATs) in all prisons providing support and advice for drug misusers during their time in prison, and directing prisoners into drug rehabilitation and detoxification programmes. Studies of the effectiveness of these services would be useful.

Finally, one aspect that is under-investigated is what works for specific groups, for example, women offenders, black and minority ethnic groups, and offenders with mental health problems.

REFERENCES

Ayres, M. & Hayward, P. (2000). Motoring offences and breath test statistics. *Home Office Statistical Bulletin 24/01*. London: Home Office.

Baldwin, S., Heather, N., Lawson, A., Ward, M., Robb, E., Williams, A., Greer, C., Gamba, S. & Robertson, I. (1991). Effectiveness of pre-release alcohol education courses for young offenders in a penal institution. *Behavioural Psychotherapy*, **19**, 321–31.

Cabinet Office (2004). *Alcohol Harm Reduction Strategy for England*. London: Cabinet Office Strategy Unit.

Cann, J., Falshaw, L., Nugent, F. & Friendship, C. (2003). Understanding what works: Accredited cognitive skills programmes for adult men and young offenders. *Home Office Research Findings 226*. London: Home Office.

Carter, P. (2003). *Managing Offenders, Reducing Crime: A New Approach*. London: Cabinet Office Strategy Unit.

Coid, J., Carvell, A., Kittler, Z., Healey, A. & Henderson, J. (2000). The impact of methadone treatment on drug misuse and crime. *Home Office Research Findings 120*. London: Home Office.

Coid, J., Carvell, A., Kittler, Z., Healey, A. & Henderson, J. (Undated). Opiates, criminal behaviour and methadone treatment. Accessed 21 September 2004. www.homeoffice.gov.uk/rds/pdfs/crimbehav.pdf.

Correctional Services Accreditation Panel (2002). *Programme Accreditation Criteria*. London: Home Office.

Del Boca, F.K. & Darkes, J. (2003). The validity of self-reports of alcohol consumption: State of science and challenges for research. *Addiction*, **98** (Supplement 2), 1–12.

DHSSPS (2000). *Strategy For Reducing Alcohol Related Harm*. Belfast: Northern Ireland Executive, Department of Health, Social Services, and Public Safety.

Eley, S., Malloch, M., McIvor, G., Yates, R. & Brown, A. (2002). *The Glasgow Drug Court in Action: The First Six Months*. Edinburgh: Scottish Executive Social Research.

Gilchrist, E., Johnson, R., Takriti, R., Weston, S., Beech, A. & Kebbell, M. (2003). Domestic violence offenders: Characteristics and offending related needs. *Home Office Research Findings 217*. London: Home Office.

Haynes, P. (1998). Drug using offenders in south London: Trends and outcomes. *Journal of Substance Abuse Treatment*, **15**, 449–56.

Heather, N. (2004). Brief interventions. In N. Heather & T. Stockwell (eds), *The Essential Handbook of Treatment and Prevention of Alcohol Problems* (pp 117–38). Chichester: Wiley.

HM Prison Service. (2004). *Addressing Alcohol Misuse: A Prison Service Alcohol Strategy for Prisoners*. London: HM Prison Service.

HM Prison Service/Department of Health. (2004). *Alcohol Treatment/ Interventions: Good Practice Guide*. London: HM Prison Service Drug Strategy Unit.

Hollin, C.R., McGuire, J., Palmer, E., Bilby, C., Hatcher, R. & Holmes, A. (2002). Introducing Pathfinder programmes into the Probation Service: An interim report. *Home Office Research Study 247*. London: Home Office.

Hollin, C., Palmer, E., McGuire, J., Hounsome, J., Hatcher, R., Bilby, C. & Clark, C. (2004). Pathfinder programmes in the probation service: a retrospective analysis. *Home Office Research, Development and Statistics Directorate Online Report No 66/04*. London: Home Office.

Hollis, S. & Campbell, F. (1999). What is meant by intention to treat analysis? Survey of published randomised controlled trials. *British Medical Journal*, **319**, 670–74.

Home Office (2002a). *Tackling Crack: A National Plan*. London: Home Office.

Home Office (2002b). *Tackling Drugs to Build a Better Britain*. London: Home Office.

Hough, M., Clancy, A., McSweeney, T. & Turnbull, P.J. (2003). The impact of drug treatment and testing orders on offending: Two-year reconviction results. *Home Office Research Findings 184*. London: Home Office.

Keen, J., Rowse, G., Mathers, N., Campbell, M. & Seivewright, N. (2000). Can methadone maintenance for heroin-dependent patients retained in general practice reduce criminal conviction rates and time spent in prison? *British Journal of General Practice*, **50**, 48–9.

Leonard, K.E. (2001). Domestic violence and alcohol: What is known and what do we need to know to encourage environmental interventions? *Journal of Substance Use*, **6**, 235–47.

Lipsey, M.W. (1992). Juvenile delinquency treatment: A meta-analytic inquiry into the variability of effects. In L.T.D Cook, H. Cooper, D.S Cordray, H. Hartman, L.V. Hedges, R.J. Light, T.A Louis & F. Mosteller (eds), *Meta-Analysis for Explanation: A Casebook* (pp 83–127). New York: Russell Sage Foundation.

Lipsey, M.W. (1995). What do we learn from 400 research studies on the effectiveness of treatments with juvenile delinquents? In J. McGuire (ed.), *What Works: Reducing Reoffending Guidelines From Research and Practice* (pp 63–78). New York: Wiley.

Malinowski, A. (2003). 'What works' with substance users in prison? *Journal of Substance Use*, **8**, 223–33.

Martin, C. & Player, E. (2000). *Drug Treatment in Prison: An Evaluation of the RAPt treatment programme*. Winchester: Waterside Press.

May, Y., Edmunds, M. & Hough, M. (1999). Street business: The links between sex and drug markets. *Police Research Series, Paper 118*. London: Home Office.

McCusker, C. & Davies, M. (1996). Prescribing drug of choice to illicit heroin users: The experience of a UK community drug team. *Journal of Substance Abuse Treatment*, **13**, 521–31.

McGuire, J. (2002). Integrating findings from research reviews. In J. McGuire (ed.), *Offender Rehabilitation and Treatment: Effective Programmes and Policies to Reduce Reoffending* (pp 3–38). Chichester: Wiley.

McIvor, G., Eley, S., Malloch, M. & Yates, R. (2003). Establishing drug courts in Scotland: Early experiences of the pilot drug courts in Glasgow and Fife. *Crime and Criminal Justice Research Programme, Research Findings 71*. Edinburgh: Scottish Executive.

McMurran, M. (1989). Services for prisoners who drink. *Prison Service Journal*, **75**, 5–6.

McMurran, M. & Baldwin, S. (1989). Services for prisoners with alcohol-related problems: A survey of UK prisons. *Addiction*, **84**, 1053–58.

McMurran, M. & Boyle, M. (1990). Evaluation of a self-help manual for young offenders who drink. *British Journal of Clinical Psychology*, **29**, 117–19.

McMurran, M. & Cusens, B. (2003). Controlling alcohol-related violence: A treatment programme. *Criminal Behaviour and Mental Health*, **13**, 59–76.

McMurran, M. & Cusens, B. (in press). Alcohol and acquisitive offending. *Addiction Research and Theory*.

McMurran, M., Hollin, C.R. & Bowen, A. (1990). The consistency of alcohol self-report measures in a male young offender population. *British Journal of Addiction*, **85**, 205–8.

McMurran, M. & Priestley, P. (2004). Addressing substance-related offending (ASRO): A structured cognitive-behavioural programme for drug users in probation and prison services. In B. Reading & M. Weegman (eds), *Group Psychotherapy and Addiction*. London: Whurr.

Metrebian, N., Shanahan, W., Stimson, G.V., Small, C., Lee, M., Mtutu, V. & Wells, B. (2001). Prescribing drug of choice to opiate dependent drug users: A comparison of clients receiving heroin with those receiving injectable methadone at a West London drug clinic. *Drug and Alcohol Review*, **20**, 267–76.

Muncer, S., Campbell, A., Jervis, V. & Lewis, R. (2001). 'Ladettes', social representations, and aggression. *Sex Roles*, **44**, 33–44.

National Assembly for Wales (2000). *Tackling Substance Misuse in Wales*. Cardiff: National Assembly for Wales.

Northern Ireland Executive (1999). *Drug Strategy for Northern Ireland*. Belfast: Northern Ireland Executive.

O'Farrell, T.J., Fals-Stewart, W. & Murphy, M. (2003). Concurrent validity of a brief self-report drug use frequency measure. *Addictive Behaviors*, **28**, 327–37.

Parker, H. & Kirby, P. (1996). Methadone maintenance and crime reduction on Merseyside. *Police Research Group, Crime Detection and Prevention Series, Paper 72*. London: Home Office.

Patterson, D.G., Macpherson, J. & Brady, N.M. (1997). Community psychiatric nurse aftercare for alcoholics: A five-year follow-up study. *Addiction*, **92**, 459–68.

Richardson, A. & Budd, T. (2003). Young adults, alcohol, crime, and disorder. *Criminal Behaviour and Mental Health*, **13**, 5–17.

Rickards, L., Fox, K., Roberts, C., Fletcher, L. & Goddard, E. (2004). *Living in Britain: General Household Survey 2002*. London: HMSO.

Royal College of Physicians, Royal College of Psychiatrists, Royal College of General Practitioners (1995). *Alcohol and the Heart in Perspective: Sensible Limits Reaffirmed*. London: RCP, RCPsych, RCGP.

Scottish Executive (2002). *Plan for Action on Alcohol Problems*. Edinburgh: Scottish Executive.

Scottish Office (1999). *Tackling Drugs in Scotland: Action in Partnership*. Edinburgh: The Scottish Office.

Sherman, L.W., Gottfredson, D., Mackenzie, D., Eck, J., Reuler, P. & Bushay, S. (1997). Presenting Crime: What Works, What Doesn't, What's Promising: A report to the United Nations Congress. (http://www.cjcentral.com/sherman/sherman.htm).

Shewan, D., Macpherson, A., Reid, M.M. & Davies, J.B. (1996). The impact of the Edinburgh Prison (Scotland) drug reduction programme. *Legal and Criminological Psychology*, 1, 83–94.

Singer, L.R. (1991). A non-punitive paradigm of probation practice: Some sobering thoughts. *British Journal of Social Work*, 21, 611–26.

Thornberry, T.P. & Krohn, M.D. (2000). The self-report method for measuring delinquency and crime. In D. Duffee, R.D. Crutchfield, S. Mastrofski, L. Mazerolle & D. McDowall (eds), *Criminal Justice 2000 (v. 4): Innovations in Measurement and Analysis* (pp 33–83). Washington DC: US Department of Justice.

Turnbull, P.J., McSweeney, T., Webster, R., Edmunds, M. & Hough, M. (2000). Drug treatment and testing orders: Final evaluation report. *Home Office Research Study 212*. London: Home Office.

Wormith, J.S. & Olver, M.E. (2002). Offender treatment attrition and its relationship with risk, responsivity, and recidivism. *Criminal Justice and Behavior*, 29, 447–71.

CHAPTER 4

Diversion from Prosecution at Court and Effective Sentencing

CAROL HEDDERMAN AND MIKE HOUGH

INTRODUCTION

Decisions made in the courtroom are amongst the most important in the criminal process. Judgements about guilt or innocence are made, and the guilty may be deprived of their liberty. However, evidence to help sentencers and others reach difficult decisions remains scant. Whilst justice is intimately concerned with the weighing of evidence in individual cases, there are, as we shall discuss below, some systematic tensions between doing justice and carrying out the sort of rigorous research that permits generalisations about effective sentencing.

The cases that reach the court stage of the criminal justice process have made it through a series of decision-making filters. First, the offender decides to commit an offence, and the victim—or a witness—decides to report it to the police. Then the police decide whether to record the offence, and if the identity of the offender is unclear, they decide whether to investigate and, if so, to what depth. If the police are able to identify the offender and the evidence is sufficient, the police then have to consider whether it is in the public interest to caution the offender or refer the case to the Crown Prosecution Service (CPS). The CPS must decide whether the evidence is enough to sustain a prosecution and whether a prosecution would be in the public interest. Figure 4.1 shows the impact of these decisions on the number of cases coming

Reducing Crime: The Effectiveness of Criminal Justice Interventions.
Edited by A. E. Perry, C. McDougall and D. P. Farrington. © 2006 John Wiley & Sons, Ltd.

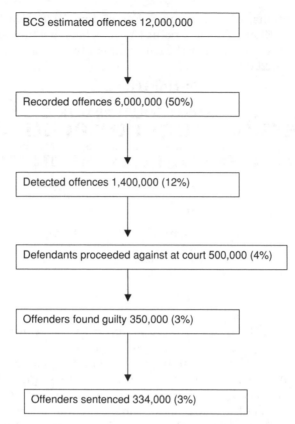

Figure 4.1 Relationship between level of victimisation reported in British Crime Survey and the criminal justice system processing of indictable offences, 2003 (Home Office, 2004a)

to court.[1] It shows cases rather than individuals and tells us little about the true extent of offending amongst those who pass through the system. Nevertheless, this pattern does suggest that the role of courts in reducing crime through the way that they deal with offenders is likely to be less influential than changes in the police's ability to catch offenders. In other words, the probability of arrest and sanction—of any sort—appears to be a greater determinant of crime rates than the choice of sanction made by

---

[1] This flow chart is derived from the figures presented in Figure 1.1 of 'Criminal Statistics, England and Wales, 2003' (Home Office, 2004a). It should be noted that the British Crime Survey (BCS) records crimes against household and individuals whereas the recorded crime figures cover indictable and 'tried either way' offences and some serious summary offences and includes offences (for example, shoplifting) against organisations. Also, court figures are based on the number of *court appearances*, whereas the BCS and police figures are based on number of *offences*.

the courts (Bottoms, 2004; Langan & Farrington, 1998; Von Hirsch, Bottoms & Burney, 1999). This is a point that has been acknowledged by the Carter report commissioned by the Government to review the 'correctional services' (Carter, 2003).

EVALUATING COURT PRACTICE

The *UK review* yielded very few evaluations of sentencing options that reached high standards of methodological quality. The reasons for this are not accidental. Sentencers who see their jobs as tailoring sentences to the precise circumstances of an offence and an offender are unlikely to agree to the principle of randomised controlled trials (RCTs), though some have been mounted in North America. Quasi-experimental designs are not exposed to this problem, but the difficulties in assembling genuinely comparable control groups are intense. Age, gender, number of previous convictions and experience of drug dependence are all important predictors of the risk of reconviction, and control groups need to be matched as closely as possible on all these factors. As will be discussed below, there are serious limitations on the validity and reliability of key outcome measures, including reconviction rates (for example, Lloyd, Mair & Hough, 1994; Mair, Lloyd & Hough, 1997). Finally, there is a tendency to abstract the findings of high-quality evaluative research from their specific context, and to over-generalise about the effectiveness of 'proven' interventions.

Researchers are well aware of the need to 'raise their game'. Often, the obstacles to doing so lie with funders rather than evaluators. The major sentencing initiatives in England and Wales are usually evaluated by researchers working on contract to central government. Research designs are usually specified in the invitation to tender, RCTs are very rarely proposed, and quasi-experimental designs are rarely required and rarely affordable. Drug treatment and testing orders (DTTOs) are a good example. The first full evaluation report relied simply on 'pre-post' measures of self-reported offending and drug use, with no control groups (Turnbull, McSweeney, Webster, Edmunds & Hough, 2000). The conclusions were inevitably heavily qualified. The subsequent reconviction study relied on internal comparisons between 'completers' and 'dropouts', and on opportunistically assembled control groups of (fairly) similar offenders who had been given other sentences (see Hough, Clancy, Turnbull & McSweeney, 2003).

Researchers in this predicament face a dilemma. Do they relay to their policy colleagues only those 'copper-bottomed' findings whose replicability is guaranteed? Or do they accept the here-and-now realities of political life, in which real decisions have to be made against short time-frames with less than perfect evidence? The route taken in the DTTO evaluation was to 'lower the bar' so that *something* of value could be said, albeit with a degree of uncertainty, rather than saying *very little* of value, but with complete confidence. Given the paucity of information about court-related outcomes, this chapter follows a similar strategy.

COURT DIVERSION

Even after the CPS has made the decision to prosecute and brought the case to court, a minority of offenders will be diverted at pre-conviction or pre-sentence because the standard range of responses is considered either inadequate or inappropriate. Examples include restorative justice schemes, schemes where an offender is treated for a mental health or substance misuse problem, or schemes in which an ongoing relationship exists between the offender and victim in domestic violence cases.

Diversion is often contingent on the offender agreeing to undergo treatment or to carry out or refrain from certain activities. Non-compliance usually results in the offender re-entering the formal sentencing process. A general toughening of attitudes towards offending has led to little patience with non-compliance (Hedderman & Hough, 2004), with the result that most of the schemes that were formerly offered as an alternative to formal processing are now accessed as a condition of a court order, an obvious example being the DTTO (Turnbull et al., 2000).

The provision of 'treatment' in a criminal justice context is predicated on the implicit or explicit assumption that if an underlying problem is addressed, reoffending (generally measured through reconviction) will also fall. Yet research into the factors related to onset, persistence and desistance suggests that offending is the result of the interaction of a number of factors (Farrington, 1997). Thus, tackling only one element of the problem is not likely to be the most successful approach, as numerous reviews of *What Works* have made clear (for example, Gaes, Flanagan, Motiuk & Stewart, 1999; Vennard & Hedderman, 1998; Webster, Hedderman, Turnbull & May, 2001).

Moreover, while it is thought reasonable to consider the impact of such schemes on reconviction rates, it is also legitimate to assess them on other criteria. This includes not only looking at other reconviction benefits (for example, a diminution in seriousness), but also whether, for example, reducing substance misuse yields other social benefits such as offenders being able to sustain employment or care for their children for longer periods with less state assistance and while experiencing fewer health problems.

Psychiatric Diversion Schemes

Work from the *UK review* identified three studies from four publications (Baldwin et al., 1991; Cooke, 1991a, 1991b; James et al., 2002). Two of the three studies are discussed in more detail below. Evidence from the *UK review* using the *What Works* classification system identified one study with *What's Promising* results (Cooke, 1991a, 1991b), and the other two studies as *What's Unknown* results (Baldwin et al., 1991; James et al., 2002). The Baldwin study is not discussed further here as it is not a psychiatric deversion sheme. See Table 9.4 (Chapter 9) for further details.

Two different interview-based studies of the male remand population during the 1990s found that nearly 10 per cent were in need of some form of immediate psychiatric help, and other studies have shown that this was true of at least 5 per cent of the sentenced prison population (James et al., 2002). The rates in the female remand and sentenced population were twice as high. Court-based psychiatric assessment and referral schemes are intended to increase the speed and frequency with which mentally ill defendants or convicted offenders are identified so that they can be diverted into treatment. They involve locating psychiatric professionals (usually community psychiatric nurses) at a magistrates' court who can advise the court on the need for treatment and either arrange a formal hospital admission in severe cases or arrange a referral to appropriate community-based services.

The first court-based psychiatric diversion schemes in England and Wales were established in the late 1980s at a small number of courts. By 2002 there were around 150 such schemes in operation (James et al., 2002). One study (Hudson, James & Harlow, 1995, cited in James et al., 2002) found strong evidence of their value in increasing identification rates as nearly two out of five of those subjected to compulsory admission after a period on remand had not been diagnosed as mentally ill while on remand. James et al.'s (2002) review of the literature on such schemes concluded that they could also dramatically cut the time from arrest to admission and reduce the call on prison remand places. However, whether schemes actually achieved this varied considerably because of differences in the way they operated.

James et al.'s (2002) own study of outcomes followed up subjects identified by court psychiatric teams between 1992 and 1996 who were admitted to hospital. A comparison group was selected from the same hospitals. Of the original 537 court admissions, only 214 were finally matched with comparable community admissions and included in the study. As the cases excluded from the study were similar to the included cases on a range of important factors (for example, age, gender, ethnicity, presence of mental illness, substance misuse), the loss of cases is unlikely to have biased the results.

The results showed that 41 per cent of those admitted to hospital through a court scheme were readmitted within two years, but only 12 per cent were readmitted through the courts. For those admitted through a court scheme, and a community admissions comparison group, readmission was associated with clinical rather than criminological factors.

It is sometimes suggested that court-based schemes give priority to patients on the grounds of their offending rather than clinical need. Certainly, James et al. (2002) study found that community-based admissions required more intensive nursing and were responsible for more incidents of violence. On the other hand, it was found that 75 per cent of the court-admission group had been in a psychiatric hospital within the previous two years; and over 40 per cent of the community admissions had a criminal record. This supports the claims by charities such as Revolving Doors (www.revolving-doors.co.uk) that many of those who are referred to treatment through court-based schemes are not new patients.

The two-year rate of reconviction for community cases in James et al.'s (2002) study was 5 per cent, whereas 28 per cent of court-admission cases were reconvicted. However, this can also be compared with the 56 per cent rate for those given non-medical disposals at court. The authors also draw attention to the fact that the court admission group had a lower number of people convicted, fewer offences and fewer instances of sentencing in the two years following their court appearance, as opposed to the two years preceding it. However, the community group showed the same improvements. Under these circumstances, it seems likely that the reduction in offending is as likely to be explained as much by selection effects, maturation, spontaneous remission or regression to the mean[2] as treatment.

The only other rigorous study of a court-based diversion scheme for offenders with mental health problems identified in the *UK* review which showed some evidence of impact for the first such scheme in Scotland (Cooke, 1991a, b). The *UK review* also identified a study (Baldwin et al., 1991) which showed some evidence of the impact of a court-referred behavioural/alcohol education course.

The Scottish court diversion scheme began in 1984, and involved the procurators fiscal (the Scottish equivalents of Crown prosecutors in England and Wales) referring offenders who were suspected of having psychological difficulties for psychological and psychiatric treatment before or (generally) instead of prosecution. The scheme was employed only where the defendant faced minor charges. Initial research results indicated that most of those diverted were first offenders, that their offences were generally not planned, and that the risk of detection was low. Reconviction analysis based on the records of 120 of those referred to the scheme over 12 months from 1985 to 1986 found that 25 were reconvicted, and that drink driving and breach of the peace were the most common offences at a further conviction. Cooke reports that 15 per cent of those who received

---

[2] Regression to the mean describes the situation where extreme scores in the first observation tend to shift towards the mean on subsequent observations. See: Cook, T.D. & Campbell, D.T. (1979). *Quasi-experimentation design and analysis issues for field settings*. Chicago: Rand McNally.

treatment were reconvicted compared with 41 per cent of those who did not, but the actual figures on which these percentages are based are not reported and reconviction periods ranged from 23 to 34 months. Also, Cooke acknowledges, the difference may simply indicate selection effects, with those least likely to reoffend being most likely to accept treatment.

EFFECTIVE SENTENCING

A total of eight studies were identified by the *UK review,* five of which are discussed below (Deering, Thurstone & Vanstone, 1996; Home Office, 1993; May, 1999a, 1999b; May & Wadwell, 2001; Oldfield, 1997). The three studies not discussed in detail in this chapter (Dobash, Cavanagh & Lewis, 1996 and Dobash and Dobash, 1996; Dobash, Dobash, Cavanagh & Lewis, 1999; Dodgson, et al., 2001) are presented with all 10 studies in Table 9.15 (see Chapter 9). Chapter 5 includes further discussion regarding sentencing options specifically relating to probation orders and probation interventions covered by four of the eight studies (Deering et al., 1996; Home Office, 1993; May, 1999a, 1999b; Oldfield, 1997), which are also presented in Table 9.15.

Assuming that the offender is convicted, he or she will usually be sentenced to custody or some form of community penalty. For adults, the main forms of community sentences are discharges, fines, community rehabilitation orders (formerly probation orders), community punishment orders (formerly community service orders) and community punishment and rehabilitation orders (formerly combination orders). Following the introduction of the Powers of Criminal Courts (Sentencing) Act 2000, the courts in England and Wales now also have the power to impose curfew orders, which require offenders to remain indoors for certain parts of the day with compliance monitored by means of an electronic tag. The Crime and Disorder Act of 1998 empowered the courts to impose DTTOs on offenders with severe drug habits who are at risk of imprisonment. Regular testing is used to check compliance with the order.

In considering the effectiveness of sentencing, one must decide what criterion of effectiveness is to be applied (Moxon, 1998). Arguably, effectiveness in sentencing embraces issues of equity. The sentence awarded in a particular case may be judged effective because it is proportionate (commensurate with seriousness of offence and the offender's culpability) or consistent (treating like cases alike).

Usually, however, effectiveness is distinguished from equity. The latter is generally reckoned to include concepts such as proportionality and appropriateness, and the former relates to the instrumental aims pursued by the sentencer. Issues about effectiveness are not straightforward even when they are limited in this way to the question 'did the sentence in this case do what it was intended to do by the sentencer?'

Traditionally, the aims of sentencing have been characterised as punishment, general or individual deterrence, incapacitation and rehabilitation (Thomas, 1979). These aims have recently been recast and put into statute in the Criminal Justice Act 2003 as punishment, deterrence, incapacitation, rehabilitation, protection of the public and reparation. While there are circumstances where sentencers treat one aim or another as paramount, more often they seek to address more than one aim on a single sentencing occasion. Thus it is sometimes difficult to say which aim's effectiveness should be measured even in a single case. It is therefore of questionable legitimacy to assess a sentence's crime-reductive impact using reconviction rates when it was not imposed with the intention of reducing reoffending (Mair et al., 1997). In fact, changes in reconviction rates are the most commonly used measure of sentencing impact only partly because reoffending is such a salient issue. The very absence of standardised units with which to measure the effectiveness of aims such as punishment, protecting the public and general deterrence is also an important factor in narrowing our field of vision (Moxon, 1998).

This chapter does not examine the 'incapacitative' effects of imprisonment and other sentences that significantly curtail the liberty of offenders. Imprisonment clearly has some preventative effect, simply by keeping offenders out of circulation, but the size of this effect is very difficult to quantify, and certainly falls beyond the reach of conventional evaluation methods. For a recent review, we refer the reader to Bottoms (2004), which concludes that there are clearly some incapacitation effects, though these are smaller than is often assumed, for a variety of reasons related to the identification of the 'best bets' for incapacitation and the natural pattern of offending careers. The Bottoms (2004) review suggests that the key policy issue is whether incapacitation strategies are a cost-effective way of preventing crime.

Reconviction rates serve as outcome measures for both rehabilitative and special deterrent sentencing strategies. Accepting that reconviction rates do measure some aspect of sentencing impact, and that they also enable both types of sentences and the content of similar sentences to be compared, reconviction rates must still be viewed with caution, as numerous authors have explained (see, for example, Lloyd et al., 1994; Moxon, 1998). Difficulties include:

• Reconviction is not a direct measure of offending. Varying clear-up rates and subsequent decisions about processing by individual criminal justice personnel can affect whether an offence results in a conviction, whether a string of offences becomes one reconviction or many, and the type of conviction an event is recognised as (for example, an attempt to break into a domestic dwelling may end up as a conviction for criminal damage or attempted burglary).

- Different studies count recidivism differently. Some North American studies include re-arrest and re-imprisonment alongside reconviction. In the UK, each sentencing occasion, rather than every offence, is usually counted as a conviction, so a spate of offending over a short period may actually be counted as just one reconviction.
- Generally, even the best statistical modelling can only control for static criminal history variables as, until recently, this was the only information easily available. Dynamic factors such as a current drug problem may affect both the likelihood that a particular sentence is imposed, and the chances that a sentence will be effective.
- Corrections made for pseudo-reconvictions[3] will be rather crude until more studies are routinely based on analyses of the Police National Computer (PNC) data, which includes date of offence, rather than Offenders Index data, which does not.
- Differences in the reconviction rates of particular sentences or programmes may indicate that they work (assuming other explanations can be discounted/controlled for), but they do not provide insight into why an intervention works or which parts of it work.

Despite these limitations, as a recent review has concluded, reconviction rates remain the most commonly used empirical measure of reoffending and programme evaluation because they are the most readily accessible (Friendship, Street, Cann & Harper, 2004).

Reconviction studies of sentencing effectiveness take one of two broad forms:

- Those that compare different sentences (discharges, fines, community punishment, electronic monitoring, probation and custody).
- Those that assess the value of a particular component of a given sentence (for example, an alcohol treatment programme delivered as a condition of a community rehabilitation order).

Comparing Different Types of Sentences

Of almost 1.5 million offenders dealt with for indictable and summary offences in 2003, 69 per cent were fined, 13 per cent received a community sentence that involved some form of supervision in the community, and about 7 per cent were sentenced to custody. The remainder received other sentences, including discharges. Limiting this breakdown to the 334,000 offenders dealt with for indictable offences (as shown in Figure 4.1),

---

[3] Pseudo-reconvictions are convictions that are recorded after the start of a sentence, but which relate to offences committed before it began. Thus, they are not a measure of the impact of the current sentence.

23 per cent were fined, 33 per cent were given a community sentence, 24 per cent were sentenced to custody, and 20 per cent received other sentences (Home office, 2004a).

It is inappropriate to compare the raw reconviction rates for different sentences. The courts use different sentences for different sorts of offenders, with different risks of reconviction and, as noted above, to achieve a range of different objectives. The sorts of offenders who are typically fined are inherently less likely to reoffend than those given forms of intensive probation supervision. In isolation, their lower reconviction rates tell us nothing about the effectiveness of the two disposals in preventing crime.

An examination of trends over time in 'raw' reconviction rates can tell us something about impact. Between 1993 and 2001, when the number of sentenced prisoners in England and Wales rose from 28,000 to 46,000 and the prison population as a whole rose from 44,000 to 74,000, the raw two-year reconviction rate rose from 57 per cent to 61 per cent (Home Office, 2004b). Part of this rise in reconviction rates is explained by the inclusion of additional offences into the 'Standard List' used to calculate reconviction rates (Home Office, 2003). However, this is not a complete explanation. The increase in reconvictions over time suggests either that the nature of the offenders received into prison had changed significantly, or that prison is becoming less effective even as its use increases. Between 1993 and 1999, reconviction rates for community penalties remained relatively stable at between 56 per cent and 57 per cent (Home Office, 2004c) However, the latest figures (Home Office, 2004b) show a raw reconviction rate of 61 per cent for 2001. The probation service's court order caseload rose over this period from 97,000 to 120,000, and its entire criminal supervision caseload (that is, including the supervision of offenders on release from prison) rose from 145,000 to 207,000 (Home Office, 2004c).

Occasionally, special analyses are conducted that allow both for differences in the types of offenders receiving different sentences, and for pseudo-reconvictions. However, there are clear limits on the range of information that can practically be collated on offenders centrally. This means that even when such modelling is carried out, it is not clear whether the emergent differences in reconviction rates reflect differences in efficacy or result from some other unknown differences between offenders (for example, the within-type seriousness of offences all classified as grievous bodily harm). This is most obviously true when studies compare probation orders with and without conditions (Home Office, 1993; Oldfield, 1997). Clearly, for all such cases the courts concluded that probation was a more suitable sentence than any other. This suggests that the offenders are broadly comparable, though statisticians in the Home Office (1993) have acknowledged that those on orders with conditions tend to be higher risk when criminal history variables are allowed for, and are likely to have more personal problems; after all, they will have been given conditions such as attending a drug rehabilitation centre or a psychiatric clinic for a reason.

A study published in 1997, conducted by researchers at the Home Office, showed that the two-year reconviction rates were 60 per cent for probation, 52 per cent for community service and 61 per cent for orders that combined probation and community service. The average reconviction rate for these orders was 57 per cent. However, controlling for pseudo-reconvictions brought this down to 53 per cent, which is identical to the rate for those discharged from prison in the same year (Kershaw & Renshaw, 1997).

Another study used the same dataset to examine the effectiveness of non-custodial sentences by comparing actual reconviction rates with those expected on the basis of age, sex and criminal history for those given such disposals (Moxon, 1998). The actual reconviction rates of those given conditional discharges (39 per cent) or fined (43 per cent) were one percentage point better than expected. The reconviction rates for those given community service (48 per cent) and probation (55 per cent) were, respectively, two and three percentage points lower than expected. However, these results were not corrected for pseudo-reconvictions.

A recent statistical bulletin since the *UK review* has provided more up-to-date information on reconviction rates by sentence for adults released from prison or commencing a community sentence in 2001 (Spicer & Glicksman, 2004). This also modelled actual reconviction rates against a predicted rate, though the way in which this was calculated differed from the approach adopted by Moxon in that it controlled for a change in the case mix over time. However, once again, pseudo-reconvictions were not allowed for because the study was based on Offenders Index cases, so the date of offence was not available. This is an important limitation, in that community penalties are systematically more prone to finding pseudo-reconvictions in the reconviction follow-up period than custodial ones.

With this proviso in mind, the analysis showed an *actual* reconviction rate for those released from custody of 58.2 per cent compared to a *predicted* rate of 60.1 per cent. The difference was statistically significant at $p \leq 0.05$. For those commencing community penalties, the *actual* reconviction rate was 51.2 per cent compared with a *predicted* rate of 51.7 per cent. This difference was not statistically significant. The cautious conclusion to draw from this—bearing in mind the point about pseudo-reconvictions—is that there is currently little to choose between imprisonment and community penalties in terms of the prevention of reoffending.

As noted at the start of the chapter, randomised controlled trials of sentencing are very rarely conducted in England and Wales for ethical and practical reasons, practitioner resistance being the most difficult obstacle to overcome. The Deering et al. (1996) study identified in the *UK review* circumvented these difficulties by allocating offenders sentenced to probation to normal supervision or supervision with additional cognitive behavioural elements. There were only 60 offenders in the original pool, and a third of the 30 given additional 'treatment' had to be excluded from the final analysis because they failed to complete.[4] However, this is an approach that might be adapted to test between community interventions of comparable severity, assuming the non-completion issue could be resolved.

One of the few studies identified in the *UK review* that included information on some social factors as well as criminal history, age and sex, is that conducted by May (1999a, 1999b). Based on a sample of more than 7,000 cases from 6 probation areas sentenced in 1993, this showed that sentencers' choices between community penalties (community service, probation and combination orders) were shaped more by social factors than criminal history. For example, males who had no social problems recorded were more likely to be sentenced to community service than other offenders. However, this did not entirely explain the reconviction rates for this sentence. As the author concluded, this indicates that the sentence itself may have had a positive effect on reconviction. Possible reasons for this are suggested by McIvor's (1992) earlier work in Scotland that involved interviewing offenders, supervisors, judges and recipients of the offender's labours. McIvor found that a high proportion of offenders felt that they acquired new skills and/or a sense of satisfaction and increased self-confidence from the work they had completed. Those who felt most positively about the work were the least likely to be reconvicted.

Overall, research studies and statistical analyses that have looked at differences in the effectiveness of broad sentence types have usually taken differences in criminal history into account. But, as mentioned above, corrections for pseudo-reconvictions have not always been made. Studies that allow for social factors such as homelessness, poor education and substance misuse, which influence both the choice of sentence and risk of reconviction, are rare. Currently, it would be unsafe to argue that one sentence is inevitably or, even usually, more effective than another, especially as the content and delivery of community penalties, and the sorts of offenders made subject to them, have been shown to vary so much between one site and another. Their content has also changed, especially over the last five years, as the government has sought to reinvent community penalties in the light of the *What Works* literature (Raynor, 2004), which stresses the importance of, among other things, tailoring sentences for individuals and bringing together different types of interventions to maximise effects (see, for example, the review by Vennard & Hedderman, 1998). This question is of even less relevance following the implementation

---

[4]Of course, the handling of dropouts in an analysis of this sort is of critical importance to the outcome.

of the Criminal Justice Act (CJA) 2003 as sentencers are now empowered to impose a much wider mix of community conditions in a single 'generic' community sentence, using 'custody plus' and 'custody minus' to mix those elements with short spells in custody.

The Effectiveness of 'New' Sentences

The impact of curfew orders using electronic monitoring was examined by Sugg, Moore & Howard (2001). The original sample consisted of all 375 of those given such an order in 12 months spanning 1996 to 1997 in three pilot areas. However, only 269 offenders' records could be traced, although this was not thought to have resulted in bias. Eight offenders were excluded because their convictions had been overturned; 61 per cent (N = 160) of those on curfew orders were also made subject to other community sentences.

The expected two-year reconviction rate for those on curfew orders (based on actuarial modelling) was 67 per cent. The actual figure was 73 per cent. However, this was similar to the reconviction rate for a comparison group of offenders who received other community penalties over the same time period. These offenders also had reconviction rates that were higher than predicted. The authors argued that the most likely explanation for this is that the algorithm used to calculate an expected rate is based on national data and does not take into account local factors such as the police clear-up rate. The comparison group in this analysis had been sentenced to straight probation orders.

When the two-year reconviction results for 160 offenders on joint orders were compared with the 101 offenders on standalone curfew orders, the former were at a higher risk of being reconvicted (70 per cent versus 62 per cent), and more of them were convicted (exact figures not reported).

DTTOs represent a viable and important new order, designed to tackle dependent drug users with extensive criminal records. As discussed above, the evaluation would, in an ideal world, have had a much more powerful experimental design. Nevertheless, some firm conclusions can be drawn, especially when the results are set beside other studies (see Hough et al., 2003; Turnbull et al., 2000).

The two-year reconviction rates for the DTTO offenders were high. Overall, 80 per cent of the 174 offenders on whom data are available had been reconvicted within two years. This figure was eight percentage points higher than the rate of reconviction for all offenders with demographic and criminal profiles comparable to the DTTO group. This partly reflects limitations in the methods of calculating expected rates, which cannot take into account key predictive factors such as dependent drug use. But equally important, the divergence could be largely attributed to the very large gap of 15 percentage points between observed and expected rates in one of the three pilot sites. The conclusion to be drawn is that the way in which a programme is implemented can critically determine outcome.

The study also showed low completion rates: only 30 per cent of the sample finished their order successfully. There were also very marked differences in reconviction rates between completers (only 53 per cent of whom were reconvicted) and revokes, of whom 91 per cent were reconvicted. By comparison, the evaluation of the Scottish DTTO pilot (McIvor, 2004), with a similar methodology, showed much higher completion rates (of 48 per cent), and much lower overall reconviction rates (66 per cent). Meanwhile, a further—and larger—reconviction study of DTTOs in England and Wales shows that at a time when probation areas were under pressure to meet DTTO commencement targets, reconviction rates south of the border rose to 90 per cent (Home Office, 2004b). Taking these findings together, one can say with a degree of confidence that schemes should aim to maximise retention if they are to minimise reconviction rates, and that incentives to maximise the number of commencements will probably drive up reconviction rates. The overall conclusion that the way in which DTTOs are actually implemented determines the level of success, is a robust one.

One further finding from the DTTO evaluation in England and Wales deserves mention here. It was possible to compare conviction rates over a number of years for the DTTO sample, and for '1A6 orders', the predecessors of DTTOs that lacked mandatory testing powers and were less demanding of offenders. The results showed that annual conviction rates in the five years before the orders were made were lower for the 1A6 group; however, reconviction rates were remarkably similar. This could indicate that DTTOs were relatively more effective, achieving the same results with a higher-risk group. Alternatively, the DTTO group, who were slightly older on average, may have simply been closer to the end of their natural drug-using 'careers'.

MAKING SENTENCES MORE EFFECTIVE

The evidence on diversion schemes is thin, and in any case there are compelling reasons beyond crime-preventive ones for diverting people with mental health problems, for example, or problems of drug dependence, from the criminal process. In the absence of overwhelming evidence that they actually promote reoffending, the presumption must be in their favour—providing that diversion does not offend against principles of equity.

The evidence is also lamentably sketchy about the effectiveness of sentences in rehabilitating or deterring offenders. We can say with some confidence that different sentences do not have grossly different reconviction outcomes. The differences between sentence types, after taking account of demographics and criminal histories, are marginal. Nevertheless, an improvement in reconviction rates is worth striving for, even if only a percentage point shift in low single figures.

The current quasi-experimental methods used to examine sentencing outcomes are obviously unsatisfactory. Where formal control groups are selected and compared, there are always going to be questions about how comparable the groups actually are. In an ideal world, for researchers the solution is to 'sell' the RCT approach to sentencers, but in our view this remains a remote prospect. There may be a few exceptions, such as comparing broadly similar sentences of comparable penal weight. However, securing widespread practitioner support for RCTs is a risky and long-term project. Given that sentencers are instructed to limit the use of custody to cases where the offence is 'so serious', only custody will do, the chances of a custody/non-custodial RCT are minimal. It is likely that there has been increased scope for some forms of non-custodial sentencing RCTs, as the new provisions introduced by the CJA 2003 allow sentencers greater freedom in building their own 'bespoke' community orders.

In the middle term, the most cost-effective research strategy for assessing sentencing impact is probably to be found in the construction of 'virtual control groups', whereby statistical modelling techniques are used to calculate expected reconviction rates for offender groups of any given demographic and criminal profile. Early work with the Home Office's Offender Group Reconviction Scale seemed promising, but the technical—yet largely soluble—problems with this approach have become clearer over time. The Home Office plans to merge its own reconviction database with that of the Police National Computer, which will solve the problem of pseudo-reconvictions.

In the meantime, while evaluations and research may not be able to say much about the choice between sentence types for different offenders, we can say quite a lot about how to make the sentences that are imposed more effective, especially those involving community supervision.

In the late 1990s, the government in England and Wales embarked on the transformation of probation and prison interventions under the banner of an Effective Practice Initiative by revising them, or devising new ones, in the light of *What Works* principles. The first step was to develop and roll-out cognitive behavioural programmes; other interventions were to follow. The value of these programmes is reviewed in Chapter 5.

Beginning with cognitive behavioural programmes is understandable, as the literature shows these to be the most effective (for reviews see McGuire, 1995; Vennard & Hedderman, 1998). However, some of the other equally important messages contained in the literature were given less attention (Hedderman, 2004). This includes recognising that, as offenders commonly have more than one problem, they need more than one form of assistance; that follow-up work after attending a programme is an essential element; that no intervention works for everyone and that selection criteria should therefore be adhered to closely; that there is a balance to be struck between programme integrity and matching delivery to offenders' learning styles (responsivity); and that programmes should be delivered by well-trained and well-resourced staff. Early reconviction results from evaluations of cognitive behavioural programmes in prison and in the community suggest that cognitive behavioural programmes have had limited impact in the UK, and that this is at least partly because these other *What Works* principles have not been given enough attention (Clarke, Simmons & Wydall, 2004; Falshaw, Friendship, Travers & Nugent, 2003; Hollin et al., 2004).

It is self-evident that for a sentence to stand a chance of being effective, an offender must actually undergo it. This is not usually a problem in relation to prison, as escape levels are low. Although they have improved in recent years, attendance rates for community sentences are still poor. For example, only around half of those on probation and community service orders in three studies conducted in 1999 and 2000 attended all appointments without any unacceptable absences (Hedderman & Hearnden, 2001). For some of the new interventions that have been trialled under the Effective Practice Initiative, attendance rates of 50 per cent would be a significant improvement. For example, Haslewood-Pocsik, Merone and Roberts's (2004) study evaluated a scheme designed to help offenders into employment, and McMahon, Hall, Haywood, Hudson & Roberts's (2004) evaluation of basic skills training for offenders found that so few offenders completed the programmes that their impact could not be assessed quantitatively.[5]

In Hollin et al.'s (2004) recent examination of the impact of five different forms of cognitive behavioural programmes delivered in a probation setting, the results were analysed in two ways. First, the two-year reconviction rates of those allocated to the programme and a matched comparison group were examined. This indicated that the programme was ineffective. However, an analysis in which programme completers, non-completers and the comparison group were compared showed that completers had lower reconviction rates than the other two groups. The question that cannot be answered from this analysis is how the results would have looked if more of the offenders who were allocated to the programme had attended it.

---

[5] The exact attrition rates cannot be calculated readily from these reports, but in McMahon et al.'s (2004) study 1,003 offenders were assessed as probably having basic skills deficits, 155 were subject to an in-depth assessment, and 20 were available for interview having completed relevant training. Twenty-two offenders completed the two employment programmes evaluated by Haslewood-Pocsik et al.'s (2004) study, compared with an original target of 400.

Although their analysis is based on only 275 cases being supervised in a single probation area in 1996, May and Wadwell (2001), identified in the *UK review*, found that offenders who had at least one unacceptable absence had a lower than predicted reconviction rate where appropriate enforcement action was taken. Offenders had a higher than predicted reconviction rate when enforcement action was not in line with the requirements of the National Standards (Home Office, 1995) current at that time.

While it is rather depressing to conclude that the evidence on sentencing effectiveness is rather poor quality and limited, we have at least been able to identify some of the reasons for this. RCTs are desirable in the abstract, and it would be helpful if researchers could develop more meaningful ways of assessing effectiveness to provide faster feedback than reconviction. However, the primary obstacles to overcome involve ensuring that the reasons particular sentences are used are clear and compatible in individual cases; that more offenders undergo the sentences courts impose on them; and that interventions delivered pre-court and post-sentence reflect all, rather than a few, *What Works* principles. Perhaps most important in properly understanding sentencing effectiveness, sentencers must accept that the relative effectiveness of different sentences should be scrutinised scientifically rather than assumed on the basis of historic and common practice.

REFERENCES

Baldwin, S., Heather, N., Lawson, A., Robertson, I., Mooney, J. & Braggins, F. (1991). Comparisons of effectiveness: Behavioural and talk-based alcohol education courses for court referred young offenders. *Behavioural Psychotherapy*, **19**, 157–72.

Bottoms, A. (2004). Empirical research relevant to sentencing frameworks. In A. Bottoms, S. Rex & G. Robinson (eds), *Alternatives to Prison: Options for an Insecure Society*. Cullompton: Willan Publishing.

Carter, P. (2003). *Managing Offenders, Reducing Crime: A New Approach*. London: Cabinet Office Strategy Unit.

Clarke, A., Simmonds, R. & Wydall, S. (2004). Delivering cognitive skills programmes in prison: A qualitative study. *Home Office Online Report 27/04*. London: Home Office.

Cooke, D.J. (1991a). Psychological treatment as an alternative to prosecution: A form of primary diversion. *The Howard Journal*, **30**, 53–65.

Cooke, D.J. (1991b). Treatment as an alternative to prosecution: Offenders diverted for treatment. *British Journal of Psychiatry*, **158**, 785–91.

Deering, J. Thurstone, R. & Vanstone, M. (1996). Individual supervision: An experimental programme in Pontypridd. *Probation Journal*, **43**(2), 70–76.

Dobash, R., Cavanagh, K. & Lewis, R. (1996). Changing violent men. *Probation Journal*, **43**(4), 217–18.

Dobash, R. & Dobash, E.R. (1996). *Re-education Programmes for Violent Men: An Evaluation*. London: HMSO.

Dobash, R., Dobash, E.R., Cavanagh, K. & Lewis, R. (1999). A research evaluation of British programmes for violent men. *Journal of Social Policy, 28*(2), 205–33.

Dodgson, K., Goodwin, P., Howard, P., Llewellyn-Thomas, S., Mortimer, E., Russell, N. & Weiner, M. (2001). Electronic monitoring of released prisoners: An evaluation of the Home Detention Curfew Scheme. *Home Office Research Study 222*. Home Office Research, Development & Statistics Directorate. London: HMSO.

Falshaw, L., Friendship, C., Travers, R. & Nugent, F. (2003). Searching for 'What Works': An evaluation of cognitive skills programmes. *Home Office Research Findings 206*. London: Home Office.

Farrington, D.P. (1997). Human development and criminal careers. In M. Maguire, R. Morgan & R. Reiner (eds), *Oxford Handbook of Criminology* (2nd edn). Oxford: Clarendon Press.

Friendship, C., Street, R., Cann, J. & Harper, G. (2004). Introduction: The policy context and assessing the evidence. In G. Harper & C. Chitty (eds), The impact of corrections on re-offending: A review of 'what works'. *Home Office Research Study 291*. London: Home Office.

Gaes, G.G., Flanagan, T.J., Motiuk, L. & Stewart, L. (1999). Adult correctional treatment. In M. Tonry & J. Petersilia (eds), *Crime and Justice: A Review of Research* (Vol. 26) (pp 361–426). Chicago: University of Chicago Press.

Haslewood-Pocsik, I., Merone, L. & Roberts, C. (2004). The evaluation of the employment pathfinder: Lessons from Phase I and a survey from Phase 2. *Home Office Online Report 22/04*. London: Home Office.

Hedderman, C. (2004). Testing times: How the policy and practice environment shaped the creation of the What Works evidence-base. *VISTA, 8*, 182–8.

Hedderman, C. & Hearnden, I. (2001). To discipline or punish? Enforcement under National Standards 2000. *VISTA, 6*(3), 215–24.

Hedderman, C. & Hough, M. (2004). Getting tough or being effective: What matters? In G. Mair (ed.), *What Matters in Probation*. Cullompton: Willan Publishing.

Hollin, C., Palmer, E., McGuire, J., Hounsome, J., Hatcher, R., Bilby, C. & Clark, C. (2004). Pathfinder Programmes in the probation service: A retrospective analysis. *Home Office Online Report 66/04*. London: Home Office.

Home Office (1993). Reconvictions of those given probation and community service orders in 1987. *Home Office Statistical Bulletin 18/93*. London: Home Office.

Home Office (1995). *National Standards for the Supervision of Offender in the Community 2000*. London: Home Office.

Home Office (2003). Prison statistics, England and Wales, 2001. *Command Paper 5743*. London: HMSO.

Home Office (2004a). Criminal Statistics, England and Wales, 2003. *Command Paper 6361*. London: HMSO.

Home Office (2004b). Offender management caseload statistics 2003, England and Wales. *Home Office Statistical Bulletin 15/04*. London: Home Office.

Home Office (2004c). *Probation Statistics, England and Wales, 2001*. London: Home Office.

Hough, M., Clancy, A., Turnbull, P.J. & McSweeney, T. (2003). The impact of drug treatment and testing orders on offending: Two-year reconviction results. *Home Office Research Findings 184*. London: Home Office.

Hudson, D. James, D. & Harlow, P. (1995). *Psychiatric Court Liaison to Central London*. London: Riverside Mental Health.

James, D., Farnham, F., Moorey, H., Lloyd, H., Hill, K., Blizard, R. & Barnes, T.R.E. (2002). Outcome of psychiatric admission through the courts. *RDS Occasional Paper 79*. London: Home Office.

Kershaw, C. & Renshaw, G. (1997). Reconvictions of prisoners discharged from prison in 1993, England and Wales. *Home Office Statistical Bulletin 5/97*. London: Home Office.

Langan, P. & Farrington, D.P. (1998). *Crime and Justice in the United States and in England and Wales 1981–1996*. US: Bureau of Justice Statistics.

Lloyd, C., Mair, G. & Hough, M. (1994). Explaining reconviction rates: A critical analysis. *Home Office Research Study 136*. London: Home Office.

Mair, G., Lloyd, C. & Hough, M. (1997). The limitations of reconviction rates. In G. Mair (ed.), *Evaluating the Effectiveness of Community Penalties*. Aldershot: Avebury.

May, C. (1999a). Explaining reconviction following a community sentence: The role of social factors. *Home Office Study 192*. London: Home Office.

May, C. (1999b). The role of social factors in predicting reconviction for offenders on community penalties. *Home Office Research Findings 97*. London: Home Office.

May, C. & Wadwell, J. (2001). Evaluating community penalties: The relationship between enforcement and reconviction. *Home Office Research Findings 155*, 1–4. London: HMSO.

McGuire, J. (1995). *What Works: Reducing Reoffending*. Chichester: Wiley.

McIvor, G. (1992). *Sentenced to Serve: The Operation and Impact of Community Service by Offenders*. Aldershot: Avebury.

McIvor, G. (2004). *Reconviction Following Drug Treatment and Testing Orders*. Edinburgh: Scottish Executive.

McMahon, G., Hall, A., Hayward, G., Hudson, C & Roberts, C. (2004). Basic skills programmes in the probation service: an evaluation of the basic skills pathfinder. *Home Office Research Findings 203*. London: Home Office.

Moxon, D. (1998). The role of sentencing policy. In P. Goldblatt & C. Lewis (eds), Reducing reoffending: An assessment of research evidence on ways of dealing with offending behaviour. *Home Office Research Study 187*. London: Home Office.

Oldfield, M. (1997). What worked? A five-year study of probation reconvictions. *Probation Journal*, **44**(1), 2–10.

Raynor, P. (2004). The Probation Service 'Pathfinders': Finding the path and losing the way? *Criminal Justice*, **4**(3), 309–25.

Spicer, K. & Glicksman, A. (2004). Adult reconviction: Results from the 2001 cohort. *Home Office Online Report 59/04*. London: Home Office.

Sugg, D., Moore, L. & Howard, P. (2001). Electronic monitoring and offending behaviour—reconviction results for the second year of trials of curfew orders. *Home Office Research Findings 141*. London: Home Office.

Thomas, D.A. (1979). *Principles of Sentencing*. London: Heinemann.

Turnbull, P.J., McSweeney, T., Webster, R., Edmunds, M. & Hough, M. (2000). Drug treatment and testing orders: Final evaluation report. *Home Office Research Study 212*. London: HMSO.

Vennard, J. & Hedderman, C. (1998). Effective interventions with offenders. In Reducing offending: An assessment of research evidence on ways of dealing with offending behaviour. *Home Office Research Study 187*. London: Home Office.

Von Hirsch, A., Bottoms, A. & Burney, E. (1999). *Criminal Deterrence and Sentence Severity: An Analysis of Recent Research*. Oxford: Hart Publishing.

Webster, R., Hedderman, C., Turnbull, P.J. & May, T. (2001). Building bridges to employment for prisoners. *Home Office Research Study 226*. London: Home Office.

CHAPTER 5

Probation and Prison Interventions

CAROLINE FRIENDSHIP AND MIA DEBIDIN[1]

INTRODUCTION

The report *Preventing Crime: What Works, What Doesn't, What's Promising* (Sherman et al., 1997), produced for the US Department of Justice, re-examined the evidence on what interventions are effective in reducing offender reconviction rates, and found that those based on cognitive behavioural theory and practice have the most impact in this area. In the UK, reviews of the literature by McGuire and Sherman, with other colleagues, were summarised in Goldblatt and Lewis (1998), and were influential in the creation of the £250 million, three-year Crime Reduction Programme (CRP) in 1999 (see Welsh, Farrington, Sherman & MacKenzie, 2002). The main purpose of the CRP was to obtain evidence of the most effective methods for reducing crime, and it included a wide range of initiatives used by police and crime and disorder partners, including the prison and probation services. In addition, the impetus for offending behaviour programmes was supported by the publication in 1998 of Her Majesty's Inspectorate of Probation (HMIP) reports *Strategies for Effective Offender Supervision* and *Evidence-Based Practice: A Guide to Effective Practice* (HMIP, 1998a, 1998b), which set out the principles and foundation of what has since become the *What Works* movement within the prison and probation services.

---

[1] All opinions expressed by the authors within this chapter are independent of the views of the Home Office.

Reducing Crime: The Effectiveness of Criminal Justice Interventions.
Edited by A. E. Perry, C. McDougall and D. P. Farrington. © 2006 John Wiley & Sons, Ltd.

As part of a commitment to *What Works* principles and evidence-based practice, in 1998/9 the *Guide to Effective Practice* announced that a number of Pathfinder programmes would be developed for use with offenders under community supervision, and a system of accrediting the design and delivery of such programmes would be established. The result was the Joint Prisons/Probation Accreditation Panel, set up to build on existing arrangements in the prison service, which is currently known as the Correctional Services Accreditation Panel (CSAP, 2004). Thus, from the mid-1990s, a range of pre-accredited and accredited offending behaviour programmes were set up and implemented in the prison and probation services in England and Wales. The first few cognitive skills programmes accredited by the panel were rapidly rolled out across both services, while many new programmes were adapted and developed for accreditation.

Currently, the prison service lists 19 fully or provisionally accredited programmes (including 7 drug treatment programmes) and 6 programmes not yet accredited or under development. The probation service lists 16 fully or provisionally accredited programmes (including two drug treatment programmes) with a further 2 under development.

International Literature on Offending Behaviour Programmes

There is considerable evidence from meta-analytic studies and systematic reviews, originating mainly from North America, to support the effectiveness of offending behaviour programmes. These findings are sufficiently consistent and robust to draw some conclusions about *What Works*. McGuire (2002) summarised the findings from 30 meta-analytical reviews of evaluations in the international literature published between 1985 and 2001. These studies indicate reductions in reconviction rates ranging from 6 to 15 percentage points for some types of intervention (Losel, 1995) and report reductions as high as 20 per cent for interventions adhering to *What Works* principles of risk, need, responsivity and programme integrity (Vennard & Hedderman, 1998; Vennard, Sugg & Hedderman, 1997). The literature also indicates that behavioural, or cognitive behavioural, treatment methods, including social skills and cognitive skills training programmes, reinforcement and incentive programmes, have proven effectiveness in reducing recidivism (Pearson, Lipton, Cleland & Yee, 2002). Cognitive behavioural programmes also have the highest mean effect size for drug-use relapse of the various treatment modalities (Lipton, Pearson, Cleland & Yee, 1998).

Reviews of international literature have also found that conclusions about treatment programmes that focus on anger management, victim awareness, living skills and different types of sex offenders await sufficient robust evidence and rigorous evaluation of their effectiveness. At the same time, there have been no offending behaviour treatment programmes that have been sufficiently evidenced as interventions that 'do not work' to reduce reoffending.

Programme Outcomes in England and Wales

The evidence-base for offending behaviour programmes in England and Wales is still in the early stages of development, due mainly to insufficient time having elapsed for reconviction outcome studies to be completed. However, the results of outcome studies are beginning to emerge. The findings from a limited number of reconviction outcome studies of cognitive behavioural programmes (including sex offender treatment programmes—SOTPs) in the UK prison service and National Probation Service (NPS) have shown some effectiveness with some offenders, but not all. Several studies that evaluated programmes prior to and after accreditation have been completed in both prisons and the community, producing mixed outcomes. In addition to outcomes on effectiveness, this research also covers programme implementation and delivery, with a common finding of problems and shortfalls.

Implementing Interventions Effectively

The evidence suggests that implementation problems are likely to have affected the success of offending behaviour programmes in reducing reoffending. For example, a recent qualitative study of prison-based enhanced thinking skills (ETS) and reasoning and rehabilitation (R&R) programmes found that issues of implementation, timing of participation in sentence, motivation and resettlement arrangements were all important considerations in programme outcomes (Clarke, Simmonds & Wydall, 2004). Programme participants and staff suggested that long waiting lists affected offenders' motivation, that there was a need for post-programme booster work prior to release, and that institutional support for the programmes was important in enhancing the impact of programmes and could be strengthened by staff awareness training and role-model training for non-programme staff.

Research on offending behaviour programmes has highlighted three main problems in delivering these interventions effectively, including:

- the rapid expansion of programmes
- targeting programmes ineffectively
- higher than expected attrition rates (that is, offenders not starting or not completing programmes).

Although there is little published evidence on the effect of large-scale expansion on the effectiveness of programmes, speculation among experts suggests that treatment quality might be compromised (Gendreau,

Goggin & Smith, 1999). The monitoring of programme quality is thought to be particularly important at a local level because of the many different features of implementation that can influence overall programme effects, such as the characteristics of the implementer, environment and the target population (Elliott, Hatot & Sirovatka, 2001).

Rapid expansion of offending behaviour programmes in the prison and probation services may have affected the quality of implementation and programme delivery. For example, in the prison service, expansion of ETS and R&R went from 30 sites and 746 completions in 1995/96 to 130 sites and 6,383 completions in 2002/03. The equivalent targets for probation tripled in three years, from 10,000 to 30,000 completions between 2001/02 and 2003/04 (although these targets were subsequently reduced to 12,000 in 2002/03 and 15,000 in 2003/04).

Cognitive skills programmes are expected to produce the greatest impact for medium-risk offenders (Andrews, Bonta & Hoge, 1990). Since the *UK review*, there has been some evidence that programmes may not be targeting offenders as intended. For example, the proportion of high-risk offenders decreased over the three prison-based ETS and R&R studies, and the proportion of medium-risk offenders increased (Cann, Falshaw, Nugent & Friendship, 2003; Falshaw, Friendship, Travers & Nugent, 2003; Friendship, Blud, Erikson & Travers, 2002). The proportion within the low-risk group also increased, peaking in the second evaluation. This suggests a shift in programme targeting, initially to lower-risk offenders and more recently to medium-risk offenders. Similarly, the evaluation of the Think First programme in the community found that only 37 per cent of offenders targeted for the programme fell within the recommended range of Offender Group Reconviction Scale (OGRS) risk scores (Ong, Harsent, Roberts, Burnett & Al-Attar, 2004). The national evaluation of ETS, R&R and Think First found that only 54 per cent of offenders with a programme order fell into the appropriate medium-risk range (Hollin et al., 2004).

Many prison and probation service interventions have suffered higher than expected attrition rates. For example, approximately 10 per cent of offenders failed to complete prison-based ETS and R&R (Cann et al., 2003); 41 per cent of these left through their own choice. Completion rates for community-based offending behaviour programmes have been even lower. For example, Stewart-Ong, Harsent, Roberts, Burnett and Al-Attar (2003) found that 28 per cent of offenders completed Think First, and that attrition tended to occur early in the programme. On average, non-completers attended less than a quarter of the core programme and half completed fewer than 4 of the 22 sessions. Just over a third of non-starters and non-completers were reallocated to new programmes following non-attendance. Other community-based research has reported completion rates of 73 per cent (Sugg, 2000), 45 per cent (Belton, 2002), 39 per cent (Steele & Van Arendsen, 2001) and 35 per cent (Hollin et al., 2004).

THE RESEARCH EVIDENCE

Therapeutic Communities (Prison)

The aim of a therapeutic community (TC) is to examine an individual's behaviour at a community level in order for problem behaviour to be explored and appropriate behaviour to be developed. The community challenges an individual's behaviour, but also provides a support network to facilitate change. Therapeutic communities are typically found in mental health settings and in the independent or voluntary sector with exceptions such as HMP Grendon, which has run a modified therapeutic community for imprisoned offenders since 1962 (see Genders & Player, 1995). Lees, Manning and Rawlings (1999) have undertaken a systematic review on the wider TC literature. The studies that met the criteria for the *UK review* are all prison based. Two studies relate to HMP Grendon's TC and, in addition, recent research has reported on a Christian-centred TC based in four other prisons. (See Table 9.6 in Chapter 9 for more details on the *What Works* classification system.)

The HMP Grendon TC has been the subject of a number of research studies (for example, Robertson & Gunn, 1987; Cullen, 1994, 1997). In the *UK review*, two reconviction studies were identified, both of which had produced *What's Promising* results according to the *What Works* classification (Marshall, 1997; Taylor, 2000). The studies compared offenders admitted to the TC at Grendon with a waiting list comparison, using a quasi-experimental design. Marshall (1997) examined reconviction rates within four years and found lower rates for the admitted group than the waiting list. These results, however, were not statistically significant at an acceptable level; that is, a 95 per cent confidence level. The study reported statistical significance at the level of 1 in 10 probability that the finding occurred by chance (that is, 90 per cent confidence level). The study also found that longer residency at HMP Grendon TC led to greater reduction in reconviction. This study was replicated by Taylor (2000) using a seven-year follow-up and found similar results, although prisoners who stayed in the TC for at least 18 months had a significantly lower reconviction rate ($p < 0.05$). Both studies were able to control for differences in criminal histories between the admitted and waiting list groups.

Burnside, Adler, Loucks and Rose (2001) produced results classified as *What's Unknown* using the *What Works* classification system. The study examined a Christian-centred therapeutic programme (Kainos) operating on the wings of four prisons in England and Wales (the Verne, Highpoint North, Highpoint South, and Swaleside). It used a cohort design where one-year reconviction rates for offenders in the therapeutic community were compared to one-year rates for offenders retrospectively identified from a national sample. The comparison group sample had similar sentence lengths and came from similar prisons, but no account was taken of criminal history or personal characteristics. One-year reconviction rates were 23 per cent for the intervention group and 26 per cent for the comparison group. There were no statistically significant differences between these two rates even when the analysis controlled for differences in criminal history and personal characteristics between the two groups. These findings, however, were based on sample of only 84 TC residents, and thus may have had insufficient power to detect any small but significant programme effects on reconviction. This study showed modest improvements in prisoners' attitudes and behaviour; for example, anti-offending attitudes and attitudes towards Christianity.

Intensive Regimes (Prison)

High intensity training (HIT) interventions were designed by the prison service and modelled on aspects of American boot camps to reduce offending behaviour in young offenders (YOs) through the use of 'discipline', 'hard work' and 'earned privileges' (Farrington, Hancock, Livingston, Painter & Towl, 2000). Two different HIT regimes were evaluated using control groups to compare the actual and predicted reconviction outcomes at one-year and two-year follow-up periods, as well as outcomes of psychological tests given before and after the intervention, and identified as part of the *UK review*. Table 9.7 in (see Chapter 9) provides more detail using the *What Works* classification system.

The HIT regime implemented in 1996 at Thorn Cross Young Offenders Institute was a 25-week programme that emphasised physically challenging activities with throughcare and aftercare, including programmes to address offending behaviour and arrangement of work and training places on release. At the follow-up period one year after discharge, the actual reconviction rate for 177 young offenders from Thorn Cross was significantly less than their predicted rate (35 per cent compared to 47 per cent), while the actual reconviction rate for the 127 comparison group YOs showed no significant change from their predicted rate (55 per cent compared to 56 per cent). At the two-year follow-up period, the percentage of offenders actually convicted was similar to the predicted percentage for both the Thorn Cross YOs (66 per cent compared to 65 per cent, respectively) and their comparisons (75 per cent compared to 75 per cent, respectively), although the Thorn Cross group took significantly longer to reoffend (about two months) and committed significantly fewer offences than the comparison group (3.5 versus 5.1) (Farrington et al., 2000, 2002). Direct comparison of the actual reconviction rates between the Thorn Cross group and the comparison group would not be meaningful because there were significant differences between the groups in their predicted rates of reoffending.

The HIT regime at Colchester, implemented in 1997, was a 12-week programme that involved progression from austere to more privileged conditions and emphasised physically challenging activity alongside educational opportunities. At the one-year follow-up period, the reconviction rate for the 61 Colchester YOs (30 per cent) was not significantly different from that of the 97 comparison YOs (31 per cent). The same was found at the two-year follow-up, although the percentage actually reconvicted was about 6 per cent less than predicted for both groups (Colchester 44 per cent compared to 51 per cent; control group 53 per cent compared to 58 per cent). The groups were also similar in their average time to reconviction; however, the Colchester YOs committed slightly fewer offences on average than their comparison group (1.5 compared to 2) (Farrington et al., 2002). The small number of offenders used in the analyses suggests that the findings should be treated with caution.

While there were no significant differences between the Thorn Cross, Colchester and control group offenders in their performance on psychological tests, the Colchester group had significantly more positive attitudes than the control group at the end of their sentence. It was not possible to attribute the successful outcomes to any particular component of the HIT regimes; however, the comparison of findings for Thorn Cross and Colchester led to the conclusion that physical training aspects had not made a difference to reconviction outcomes (Farrington et al., 2000, 2002). The inconclusive results from this single study of high-intensity training regimes thus led to their categorisation as *What's Unknown* in the *UK review*.

Cognitive Behavioural Programmes (Prison)

Cognitive behavioural programmes (CBPs) were designed to reduce reoffending by improving offenders' skills of effective problem-solving, creative and critical thinking, social perspective taking, moral reasoning, management of emotions and use of social skills. Currently, there are more than 35 CBPs in use in both custodial and community settings in England and Wales, designed as offending behaviour programmes and divided into general offending behaviour programmes and specialised programmes for particular types of offenders, for example, sex offenders and violent offenders.

The R&R and ETS programmes are two general offending behaviour programmes that were implemented in prisons in England and Wales in 1992. A previous review of the international literature (MacKenzie, 2002) and a meta-analytic study (Tong & Farrington, in press) both concluded that the R&R programme was effective in reducing reoffending. ETS was modelled on the R&R programme (developed in Canada), but it is a shorter programme (21 sessions compared to 38) and was developed by psychologists in HM Prison Service.

Since the *UK review*, the two programmes have been evaluated together in three separate studies of their use with imprisoned offenders, spanning 10 years of their delivery in the UK. All three studies used the same method of comparing reconviction outcomes for a group of offenders who had been selected for the programmes with a group of offenders who had not been selected for programmes that were individually and retrospectively matched on several static risk factors, such as risk of reoffending, sentence length, current offence and year of discharge.

The first study consisted of 670 adult male offenders who had participated in one of the two programmes between 1992 and 1996, and a comparison group of 1,801 adult male offenders who had not participated in a programme. It found a significant difference in the reconviction rates for medium- to low-risk offenders (a reduction of 14 percentage points), and for medium- to high-risk offenders (a reduction of 11 percentage points) after two years. The low- and high-risk offenders in the programme group also had reconviction rates lower than their comparison groups, but these were not statistically significant (Friendship et al., 2002; Friendship, Blud, Erikson, Travers & Thornton, 2003).

The second study conducted since the *UK review* consisted of 649 adult male offenders who had participated in one of the two programmes between 1996 and 1998, and a comparison group of 1,947 adult male offenders who had not taken part in the programmes. This study found no differences between the two-year reconviction rates of the two groups that were compared. Further analysis of programme dropouts, of the time between treatment completion and release or the time to first reconviction, of each programme separately, and of the quality of delivery, did not produce any significant results in this study (Falshaw et al., 2003, 2004).

The third study consisted of a sample of 2,195 adult male offenders who had participated in one of the two programmes between 1998 and 2000, and another sample of 1,534 young offenders who had taken part in one of the programmes between 1995 and 2000. Their comparison groups consisted of 2,195 adult males and 1,534 young offenders respectively, individually matched as described above for the previous two studies. This study found no differences between the one- and two-year reconviction rates for adult men or young offenders and their comparison groups. Further analysis found that offenders who completed the programmes had a significantly lower reconviction rate after one year than their matched comparisons. This amounted to a reconviction rate 2.5 percentage points lower for adult men who completed their programme, and a rate 4.1 percentage points lower for young offenders who completed their programme. These differences for completers were not seen at the two-year follow-up (Cann et al., 2003). Although the research design allowed for statistical control of important differences in risk factors between the programme group offenders and their comparisons, it did not control for dynamic factors such as offence-related needs and motivation to change, which therefore cannot be ruled out as alternative explanations for the outcomes seen for programme completers.

The negative results from the three most recent studies since the *UK review* of the ETS and R&R programmes, two of which were in prison (Cann et al., 2003; Falshaw et al., 2003) and one of which was in the community (Hollin et al., 2004) suggest that these two CBPs would be categorised from *What's Promising* to *What's Unknown* in UK interventions. However, the positive results of the first study make this categorisation less fitting, and they might be better classed as 'what has worked or what sometimes works' until experimental research design can be used to test their effectiveness. Tables 9.8 and 9.9 in Chapter 9 present the classification from the *UK review*.

The sex offender treatment programme (SOTP) is another CBP that was nationally established in HM Prison Service in 1992. This programme aimed to reduce offending behaviour by changing offenders' attitudes towards their offence(s), enhancing their victim empathy and developing their skills in management of risk factors to prevent relapse. The first version of the programme consisted of 80 hours of treatment, and the second version extended this time to 170 hours. Since the *UK review*, one further study has been conducted in this area. The study evaluated the reconviction outcomes of 647 adult male offenders who had participated in these two versions of the SOTP prior to 1996, compared to a matched control group of 1,910 adult male offenders who had not taken part in the programmes. It found that offenders who participated in the SOTP had a lower rate of reconviction for sexual offences than the comparison group, but that this difference was not statistically significant. However, a statistically significant lower reconviction rate for the SOTP group was found when sexual and violent offences were combined. While a lower rate of reconviction was found for all SOTP offenders, the differences were statistically significant for offenders with a medium- to low risk and medium- to high risk of reconviction ($p < 0.01$ and < 0.05 respectively). The very low rate of reconviction for sex offenders (that is, less than 5 per cent within two years of release), and the differences between the SOTP and comparison group on factors that were not controlled (such as motivation), were referred to by the researchers as difficulties in attributing the outcomes to a treatment effect, but as the difference in outcomes was maintained when various risk factors were controlled (for example, sexual convictions, violent convictions and risk of sexual reconviction), the researchers concluded that the SOTP had produced a positive impact on reoffending (Friendship, Mann & Beech, 2003a, 2003b). The positive results from this single study of prison-based Sex Offender Treatment Programmes suggest that these programmes are *What's Promising* interventions for reducing further offending.

A number of pre- to post-treatment test studies (for example, Beech, Fisher, Beckett & Scott-Fordham, 1998; Beech, Erikson, Friendship & Ditchfield, 2001) have also reported findings favourable to the prison-based SOTP, but these did not fulfill the criteria of the *UK review* and have therefore not been discussed in any further detail.

Cognitive Behavioural Programmes (Probation)

A summary of programme evaluation findings published by the Home Office NPS in July 2002 described findings from several evaluation studies of offending behaviour programmes in England and Wales. In addition to the reconviction outcomes summarised from primary studies of offending behaviour programmes in prisons that have been included in the *UK review* (Friendship et al., 2002) and subsequent studies (Friendship et al., 2003), and excluded from the *UK review* (for example, Beech et al., 1998), it describes reconviction outcomes from primary studies of various programmes delivered in the community, including the West Midlands SOTP, R&R and aggression replacement training (ART), and South Yorkshire drink impaired drivers course (DIDC). The summary reported reduced reconviction outcomes for participants in all of these programmes; however, the research was not described in enough detail to determine how well the primary studies fit the criteria of this review, and there was some indication that a few studies may not have been sufficiently robust to have been included.

The findings reported for the ART and DIDC programmes are based on very small samples, and outcomes for the programme completers were compared with poorly matched comparison groups. A reconviction rate of 32 per cent was found for 153 offenders sentenced to ART, in contrast to a rate of 41 per cent for the matched comparison group. A reconviction rate of 14 per cent was reported for the 86 offenders who completed DIDC, in contrast to a rate of 21 per cent found for the comparison group of 56 offenders who received a custodial sentence. These summarised findings suggest that these two programmes are *What's Promising* interventions for the NPS, although the primary research might indicate that they would be more accurately classified as *Unknown* until they have been rigorously evaluated.

For the R&R programme, a drop of 16 per cent in the reconviction rate for offenders within the Mid Glamorgan probation area is reported for the one-year follow-up period. After two years, the reconviction rate had begun to rise. These outcomes were based on a sample of 107 offenders in the treatment group and 82 offenders in the comparison group (Raynor & Vanstone, 2001).

Finally, the West Midlands SOTP is described as having cut reconviction for sexual offences by 7.4 per cent, for violence by 11.4 per cent, and for other offences such as theft by 22 per cent. The primary study was included in the *UK review*. The study evaluated the SOTP in the community between January 1995 and June 1996, with a three-year follow-up period. The sample consisted of 155 adult male offenders in the treatment group and 74 in the untreated comparison group who had been recommended for treatment but given alternative sentences instead. It found significant reductions in reconviction rates for the treated child sex abusers and non-significant reductions in reconviction for treated rapists and exhibitionists. The sample sizes for two of the treated groups were too small for tests of statistical significance to be meaningful. The research concluded that sex offenders who participated in community-based sex offender treatment were less likely to be convicted of sexual, violent or other offences than untreated sex offenders. The results were also described as being consistent with earlier research from a sex offender treatment evaluation project (STEP) (Allam, 1998). The findings of this single study suggest that the West Midlands SOTP is a *Promising* cognitive behavioural programme for the probation service.

Another study evaluated a different cognitive behavioural programme designed to reduce further sexual offending. The Cherwell Group programme was implemented in Oxfordshire probation service around 1990. An evaluation of the programme compared reconviction outcomes for 63 men who completed the programme to a matched control group of untreated sexual offenders under supervision in the three years prior to the programme. One member of the treatment group was reconvicted in the average follow-up period of 30 months, in contrast to 9 who were reconvicted in the comparison group. This research was based on a small number of offenders and the criteria used for matching is not clear, thus the conclusions should be treated with some caution. See Table 9.10 in Chapter 9 for more details on the *What Works* classification system.

A third study of community-based sex offender treatment evaluated seven different programmes under the STEP. The project consisted of four short-term programmes, two longer rolling programmes, and one year-long residential programme. Reconviction outcomes for 133 offenders who were referred to 1 of the 7 programmes were compared with those for 191 sex offenders who were given probation orders in 1990; 8 per cent of the programme group were reconvicted of an offence within 2 years, in contrast to 29 per cent of the comparison group. Calculation of the risk of reconviction scores for the two groups compared showed that the control group had a predicted reconviction rate of 23 per cent, in contrast to the predicted rate of 13 per cent for the treatment group (Hedderman & Sugg, 1996).

Since the *UK review*, the NPS has recently published a summary of findings from an evaluation of the Think First programme, one of its general offending behaviour programmes based on cognitive behavioural theory (Stewart-Ong et al., 2004). The summary describes lower reconviction rates at follow-up periods of 6, 9 and 12 months for offenders who completed the programme, compared with offenders who never started a programme or who dropped out before completion. It also refers to an earlier evaluation that found that a group of offenders who had participated in the programme in the community had a significantly higher rate of reconviction than the comparison group made up of offenders who had received a custodial sentence (Stewart-Ong et al., 2004). Both sets of findings should be viewed with caution, as the method used in the first-mentioned study could not rule out other plausible explanations for the results, such as selection effects, and the method used in the second study did not appear to be comparing like with like. At best, the findings from these two studies are inconclusive and suggest that the community-based Think First programme should be categorised as *Unknown*.

Since the *UK review*, a large-scale evaluation has been completed for community-based cognitive behavioural programmes, including ETS, R&R, Think First and a similar programme designed for use with individuals instead of groups (Priestley One-to-One), as well as a programme designed for drug-misusing offenders (Hollin et al., 2004). This research examined programmes delivered nationally across the probation service between 2000 and 2001, with a sample of 2,230 offenders given a community order to attend a programme, and a comparison group of 2,645 offenders who had not been given a programme order.

The evaluation reported reconviction rates of 55 per cent for offenders who completed treatment, 77 per cent for offenders who had not completed treatment (made up of non-starters and dropouts), and 58 per cent for the comparison-group offenders. It also reported a reconviction rate of 70 per cent for all offenders given a programme order, and that these patterns were maintained after statistically controlling for differences between the groups on important risk factors. Additionally, it analysed reconviction outcomes for offenders by level of risk and reported no difference between low-risk completers and the low-risk comparison group, and a significantly higher reconviction for low-risk non-completers. High-risk completers were reconvicted significantly less than the high-risk comparison group, while high-risk non-completers were similar to the comparison group. Offenders in the medium-risk band, who were 'appropriately targeted' for treatment, showed lower reconviction rates for completers and higher rates for non-completers compared to the rates for medium-risk comparison offenders. The results were similar across all five programmes evaluated (Hollin et al., 2004). The authors argued that the reconviction findings for completers and non-completers provided evidence supportive of a treatment effect; however, the research design did not control for the effects of other factors that might explain the results, such as differences in motivation or levels of offence-related needs between the different groups of offenders used in the analysis. At best, the results from this study suggest that these programmes are *Promising* community interventions, although they might be equally categorised as *Unknown* until they are more rigorously evaluated with experimental design. See Table 9.11 (Chapter 9) for more details on the *What Works* classification system.

Employment Projects (Probation) in the *UK Review*

Employment has a strong link to reconviction in the offender rehabilitation literature; for example, Motiuk (1998) found that, for male offenders, the strongest predictors of reoffending after release were, in order of importance, employment, substance abuse, associates, marital/family status and personal/emotional problems. Policy initiatives relating to employment have been evident in England and Wales, such as prison initiatives that include Welfare to Work and Inmate Development and Preparation for Release (IDPR) (see Webster, Hedderman, Turnbull & May, 2001).

In the *UK review*, only one study was identified as providing reconviction evidence for England and Wales regarding employment initiatives, and this was the ASSET probation employment scheme (Sarno, et al., 2000; Sarno, Hearnden & Hedderman, 2001). Reconviction data was not available for another scheme, called Springboard, which was also examined within this study. Both schemes provided help for offenders from guidance workers and included a six-week part-time job related programme that incorporated job search skills and aimed to develop the offenders' confidence and motivation in relation to employment. The target age group was 16- to 25-year-olds. One-year reconviction rates showed that 43 per cent of those on ASSET (n = 219) were reconvicted, compared to 56 per cent in a comparison group (n = 90) who were referred to ASSET, but did not attend. These differences were statistically significant. The study acknowledged the limitation of the comparison group; in particular, it is likely that there were systematic differences in attender and non-attender characteristics. See Table 9.12 in Chapter 9 for more details on the *What Works* classification system.

Motoring Offending Projects (Probation) in the *UK Review*

Only one intervention was identified in the *UK review* that specifically targeted car crime and, as the author (Wilkinson, 1997) notes, crime-prevention schemes have been the main focus in this area and not interventions to reduce reoffending. The study evaluated the effectiveness of the long-standing Ilderton motor project based in South London (see Martin & Webster, 1994). The programme provided an opportunity for offenders involved in car crime to pursue an interest in cars in a pro-social manner. Ilderton is a large garage where young offenders can learn how cars function and are maintained and, in doing so, their offending can be challenged in a disciplined environment. The study (a quasi-experimental design) had a small sample of 35 offenders in the intervention group and 40 in the comparison group. It matched the comparison group on relevant criminal history, such as conviction for a similar motoring offence at a similar point in time; however, some systematic differences did arise between the two groups, particularly the offenders' previous number of offences for car crime. General reconviction within one, two and three years was reported, all of which were statistically significantly lower for the intervention group. There were also significant differences in the average number of motoring offences per year during the follow-up. See Table 9.13 in Chapter 9 for more details on the *What Works* classification system.

Restorative Justice in the *UK Review*

Restorative justice (RJ) programmes give victims of crime the opportunity to explain to the offender the impact of his or her offence(s). Generally, such initiatives aim to reduce reoffending, restore the relationship between victim and offender, and to improve the victim's experience of the criminal justice system (see Marshall, 1999, for a comprehensive review). One research study was identified in the *UK review* as having adequate methodology to be included (Miers, Maguire, Goldie, Sharpe & Hale, 2001). In terms of reconviction outcomes the study examined five RJ schemes across England and Wales: two relating to adult offenders and three for juveniles. Reconviction rates for offenders who experienced a scheme were compared to similar offenders who had not.

For the adult schemes, West Yorkshire showed a significant reduction in reconviction, with RJ scheme offenders reconvicted at a rate of 44 per cent (n = 153) within two years, compared to 56 per cent (n = 79). There was also evidence that RJ offenders were convicted for less serious offences. In contrast, the West Midlands scheme showed no significant reduction in reconviction within two years, although RJ offenders had lower reconviction rates of 44 per cent (n = 147), compared to 54 per cent (n = 83) for similar offenders. For juvenile offenders, there were no significant differences in reconviction rates between offenders who experienced one of the three schemes and comparison offenders who did not. Currently, a Home Office-funded RCT is being conducted in the UK that will build and improve on the evidence provided in the above study. The evidence from the two adult schemes shows *What's Promising* results, while the findings from the juvenile scheme remain as *What's Unknown*. See Table 9.14 in Chapter 9 for more details on the *What Works* classification system.

Probation Orders in Probation Interventions in the *UK Review*

There has been a comprehensive body of evaluative research that relates to *What Works* with offenders on probation. The research has examined both differential probation sentences and also specific probation interventions. The review identified six studies that fulfilled the methodological criteria. Deering, Thurston & Vanstone (1996) examined the efficacy of the supervision of offenders on standard probation orders. The study randomly allocated the first 60 offenders given a probation order without additional requirements to one of two groups from 1 September 1993. The experimental group (n = 29) received experimental supervision in the form of a new assessment approach and cognitive behavioural skills training, and the controls received traditional supervision (n = 30). One-year reconviction rates were 37 per cent for the experimental group and 50 per cent for controls, suggesting that experimental supervision was more effective in reducing reconviction than traditional supervision. It needs to be noted, however, that this study was a small-scale research project with a very small sample, and these low numbers resulted in the observed difference in reconviction rates between the experimental and control group not being statistically significant. The evidence was classified as *What's Promising* using the *What Works* classification system. See Table 9.15 in Chapter 9 for further details on the *What Works* classification system.

A Home Office (1993) report, covering a similar period as the study above, compared probation orders with requirements, with no additional requirements, and with community service. Two-year reconviction rates were examined for the three samples of offenders resulting in a 65 per cent rate for probation orders with a day centre or 4A requirement (4A and 4B probation orders are no longer used), 50 per cent for other probation orders, and 54 per cent for community service orders. It was not possible, however, to make judgements about the relative effectiveness of the disposals due to the different characteristics of the offenders receiving each disposal. Statistical adjustment was made to control for differences such as age, number of previous convictions and most serious previous conviction, which reduced the reconviction rate for the probation order with requirement group.

In a similar vein, May (1999a, 1999b) examined two-year reconviction rates for probation only, probation orders with a treatment requirement, community service and combination orders using a 1993 sample. Reconviction rates were 53 per cent probation only, 58 per cent probation with requirements, 43 per cent community service and 53 per cent combination orders. This may suggest community service orders were most effective in reducing reconviction, but probably reflects that less serious offenders would be given such a disposal. This study is classified as *What's Promising* using the *What Works* classification system—see Table 9.15 in Chapter 9 for further details.

Research following this theme is also found in Oldfield (1997), who examined probation only, probation orders with requirements 4A and 4B, and prison. In the five years following the commencement of these orders, the probation-only group had a 47 per cent reconviction rate, the probation group 4A a 41 per cent rate, probation 4B a 63 per cent rate and, finally, prison also a 63 per cent rate. As above, the caveat of the research is that more serious offenders are likely to be sentenced to custody, and so it is not a valid measure of effectiveness to simply compare these rates. This study is classified as *What's Promising* using the *What Works* classification system. See Table 9.15 in Chapter 9 for further details.

An evaluation of intensive community supervision for young offenders (Bottoms, 1995) compared the effect of heavy-end intermediate treatment (HEIT), other intermediate treatment (OIT), custody (CUS) and straight supervision orders (SUPs) in terms of reconviction outcomes. Fourteen months after the end of treatment, reconviction rates were HEIT (74 per cent), OIT (65 per cent), CUS (81 per cent) and SUP (61 per cent), and there were no significant differences between these rates. This study is classified as *What's Unknown* using the *What Works* classification system. See Table 9.15 in Chapter 9 for further details.

Finally, Williams and Creamer (1997) compared four different experimental probation orders with differing requirements in Scotland run in different areas. The outcome under observation was custodial disposals. The study compared predicted custodial rates using a specifically developed risk predictor with actual custodial rates. The study found that all experimental probation orders yielded actual custodial rates that were lower than the predicted rate; however, an important consideration here is that the reduction in custodial rates may be an artifact of the predictor rather than a result of the experimental probation supervision. For example, if a risk predictor over-predicts, actual rates of custody will appear lower in the absence of any intervention. This study is classified as *What's Promising* using the *What Works* classification system. See Table 9.15 for further details.

CONCLUSIONS

Making definitive conclusions regarding effectiveness of probation and prison offender interventions based on the research evidence from England and Wales is limited by the following factors:

- Few reconviction studies have fulfilled the standard of research specified for the *UK review* and this is highlighted by a more inclusive Home Office review of *What Works* with offenders (Harper & Chitty, 2004).
- Very few studies in this review have achieved an RCT methodology.

- Quasi-experimental design studies reported here have used different techniques to construct or match a comparison group.
- The comparability between the intervention group and comparison group on theoretically relevant variables (for example, criminal history) has not been adequate in many quasi-experimental reconviction studies reported here.
- There are differences in the length of follow-up reported in reconviction studies.
- The type of interventions attended are fundamentally different in many respects, such as theoretical ethos, factors targeted, methods used and duration.
- Small sample sizes are included in the intervention evaluations.
- There are differences in the assessment measures used by individual interventions (for example, risk-assessment protocols).

In addition to using primary outcome studies, and in order to extend our understanding of *What Works* in the field of offender rehabilitation, it is important to consider the role of combined outcome studies. The Campbell Collaboration is following the lead of the Cochrane Collaboration in aiming to develop and maintain standards for systematic reviews in the fields of education, social and criminological research (Davies, Nutley & Smith, 2000). There is a need in England and Wales to develop meta-analytical studies and systematic reviews; for example, a meta-analysis of R&R was recently conducted (Tong & Farrington, in press). However, because of the problems outlined above, these methods can be compromised by the lack of comparability between studies. It is recommended that a more strategic approach is adopted in England and Wales to document primary outcome studies and to make this data available for combination in both meta-analytical studies and systematic reviews.

In summary, based on the evidence from evaluation studies of the interventions and programmes included in the initial *UK review*, there were no studies that were identified as *What Works* or *What Doesn't Work*. Studies falling into *What's Promising* or *What's Unknown* are shown below:

- *What's Promising*: Prison-based therapeutic communities (HMP Grendon), a probation employment project, a motoring offending project, adult restorative justice. In relation to sentencing: court-mandated programmes for violent men, an experimental probation scheme, community service orders, probation orders with requirements, probation orders with no requirements, and enforcement action.
- *What's Unknown*: Prison-based ETS and R&R, and SOTP in the community (originally *What's Promising*), intensive regimes for young offenders and Christian-centred therapeutic programmes, juvenile restorative

justice. In relation to sentencing: electronic monitoring, final warnings and intensive treatment and supervision orders.

Since the *UK review*, the additional two studies focusing on the evaluation of ETS and R&R courses change the original classification in the review from *What Works* to *What's Unknown*, with three more recent studies showing negative results (Cann et al., 2003; Hollin et al., 2004; Falshaw et al., 2003) and one study showing a positive result (Friendship et al., 2002, 2003). One further study focusing on SOTP treatment for offenders shows promising results, supporting the rest of the literature in this area, which suggests that SOTP reduces reoffending behaviour (Friendship et al., 2003a, 2003b).

REFERENCES

Allam, J. (1998). *Effective Practice in Work With Sex Offenders. A Reconviction Study Comparing Treated and Untreated Offenders*. West Midlands: Probation Service Sex Offender Unit.

Andrews, D.A., Bonta, J. & Hoge, R.D. (1990). Classification for effective rehabilitation: Rediscovering psychology. *Criminal Justice and Behavior*, **17**, 19–52.

Beech, A., Erikson, M., Friendship, C. & Ditchfield, J. (2001). A six-year follow-up of men going through probation-based sex offender treatment programmes. *Home Office Research Findings 144*. London: Home Office.

Beech, A., Fisher, D., Beckett, R. & Scott-Fordham, A. (1998). An evaluation of the prison sex offender treatment programme. *Home Office Research Findings 79*. London: Home Office.

Belton, E. (2002). *Think and Change Programme: Reconviction Study April 1999–April 2000*. Unpublished report for National Probation Service, Thames Valley.

Bottoms, A.E. (1995). *Intensive Community Supervision for Young Offenders: Outcomes, Process and Cost*. Cambridge: Institute of Criminology.

Burnside, J., Adler, J., Loucks, N. & Rose, G. (2001). Kainos programme evaluation. *Executive Summary 17*. London: Home Office.

Cann, J., Falshaw, L., Nugent, F. & Friendship, C. (2003). Understanding What Works: Accredited cognitive skills programmes for adult men and young offenders. *Home Office Research Findings 226*. London: Home Office.

Clarke, A., Simmonds, R. & Wydall, S. (2004). Delivering cognitive skills programmes in prison: A qualitative study. *Home Office Research Findings 242*. London: Home Office.

Correctional Services Accreditation Panel (2004). *Correctional Services Accreditation Panel Annual Report 2003–2004*. London: National Probation Directorate.

Cullen, E. (1994). Grendon: The therapeutic prison that works. *Therapeutic Communities: International Journal for Therapeutic and Supportive Organizations*, **15**(4), 301–11.

Cullen, E. (1997). Can a prison be a therapeutic community: The Grendon template. In E. Cullen, L. Jones and R. Woodward (eds), *Therapeutic Communities for Offenders*. Chichester: Wiley.

Davies, H.T.O., Nutley, S.M. & Smith, P.C. (2000). *What Works? Evidence-Based Policy and Practice in Public Services*. Bristol: The Policy Press.

Deering, J., Thurston, R. & Vanstone, M. (1996). Individual supervision: An experimental programme in Pontypridd. *Probation Journal*, **43**(2), 70–76.

Elliott, D., Hatot, N.J. & Sirovatka, P. (2001). *Youth Violence: A Report of the Surgeon General*. US: National Library of Medicine. www.ncbi.nlm.nih.gov/books.

Falshaw, L., Friendship, C., Travers, R. & Nugent, F. (2003). Searching for 'What Works': An evaluation of cognitive skills programmes. *Home Office Research Findings 206*. London: Home Office.

Falshaw, L., Friendship, C., Travers, R. & Nugent, F. (2004). Searching for 'What Works': HM Prison Service Accredited Cognitive Skills Programmes. *British Journal of Forensic Practice*, **6**, 3–13.

Farrington, D.P., Ditchfield, J., Hancock, G., Howard, P., Jolliffe, D., Livingston, M.S. & Painter, K.A. (2002). Evaluation of two intensive regimes for young offenders. *Home Office Research Findings 239*. London: Home Office.

Farrington, D.P., Hancock, G., Livingston, M.S., Painter, K.A. & Towl, G. (2000). Evaluation of intensive regimes for young offenders. *Home Office Research Findings 121*. London: Home Office.

Friendship, C., Blud, L. Erikson, M. & Travers, R. (2002). An evaluation of cognitive behavioural treatment for prisoners. *Home Office Research Findings 161*. London: Home Office.

Friendship, C., Blud, L., Erikson, M., Travers, R. & Thornton, D. (2003). Cognitive-behavioural treatment for imprisoned offenders: An evaluation of HM Prison Service's Cognitive Skills Programme. *Legal and Criminological Psychology*, **8**, 103–14.

Friendship, C., Mann, R. & Beech, A. (2003a). The prison-based Sex Offender Treatment Programme: An evaluation. *Home Office Research Findings 205*. London: Home Office.

Friendship, C., Mann, R.E. & Beech, A.R. (2003b). An evaluation of a national prison-based treatment program for sexual offenders in England and Wales. *Journal of Interpersonal Violence*, **18**, 744–59.

Genders, E. & Player, E. (1995). *Grendon: A Study of a Therapeutic Prison*. Oxford: Clarendon Press.

Gendreau, P., Goggin, C. & Smith, P. (1999). The forgotten issue in effective correctional treatment: program implementation. *International Journal of Offender Therapy and Comparative Criminology*, **43**, 180–87.

Goldblatt, P. & Lewis, C. (1998). Reducing offending: An assessment of research evidence on ways of dealing with offending behaviour. *Home Office Research Study 187*. London: Home Office.

Harper, G. & Chitty, C. (eds) (2004). The impact of corrections on re-offending: A review of what works. *Home Office Research Study 291*. London: Home Office.

Hedderman, C. & Sugg, D. (1996). Does treating sex offenders reduce reoffending? *Home Office Research Findings 45*. London: Home Office.

Her Majesty's Inspectorate of Probation (1998a). *Strategies for Effective Offender Supervision*. London: Home Office.

Her Majesty's Inspectorate of Probation (1998b). *Evidence-Based Practice: A Guide to Effective Practice*. London: Home Office.

Hollin, C., Palmer, E., McGuire, J., Hounsome, J., Hatcher, R., Bilby, C. & Clark, C. (2004). Pathfinder programmes in the probation service: A retrospective analysis. *Home Office Online Report 66/04*. London: Home Office.

Home Office (1993). Reconvictions of those given probation and community service orders in 1987. *Home Office Statistical Bulletin 18/93*. London: Home Office.

Lees, J., Manning, N., & Rawlings, B. (1999). Therapeutic community effectiveness. *NHS CRD Report Number 17*. York: University of York.

Lipton, D.S., Pearson, F.S., Cleland, C. & Yee, D. (1998). How Do Cognitive-Behavioural Programmes for Offenders Compare with Other Modalities: A Meta-Analytic Perspective. (Preliminary Findings from CDATE). Presented at the Stop and Think Conference, 9–11 March 1988. York: UK.

Losel, F. (1995). The efficacy of correctional treatment: A review and synthesis of meta-evaluations. In J. McGuire (ed.), *What Works: Reducing Reoffending— Guidelines From Research and Practice*. Wiley: Chichester.

MacKenzie, D.L. (2002). Reducing the criminal activities of known offenders and delinquents. Crime prevention in the courts and corrections. In L.W. Sherman, D.P Farrington, B.C. Welsh & D.L. MacKenzie (eds), *Evidence-Based Crime Prevention* (pp 330–404). London: Routledge.

Marshall, P. (1997). A reconviction study of HMP Grendon therapeutic community. *Home Office Research Findings 53*, 1–4. London: Home Office.

Marshall, T. (1999). *Restorative Justice: An Overview*. London: Home Office.

Martin, J. & Webster, D. (1994). *Review of Motor Projects*. London: Home Office.

May, C. (1999a). Explaining reconviction following a community sentence: The role of social factors. *Home Office Research Study 192*. London: Home Office.

May, C. (1999b). The role of social factors in predicting reconviction for offenders on community penalties. *Home Office Research Findings 97*. London: Home Office.

McGuire, J. (2002). Criminal sanctions versus psychologically-based interventions with offenders: A comparative empirical analysis. *Psychology, Crime and Law*, **8**, 183–208.

Miers, D., Maguire, M., Goldie, S., Sharpe, K. & Hale, C. (2001). Exploratory evaluation of restorative justice schemes. *Crime Reduction Research Paper 9*, 113. London: Home Office.

Motiuk, L. (1998). Using dynamic factors to better predict post-release outcome. *Forum on Corrections Research*, **10**(3), 14–20.

National Probation Service (2002). Reducing reconviction rates. *Service Briefing. National Probation Service Issue 4*. London: National Probation Service.

Oldfield, M. (1997). What worked? A five year study of probation reconvictions. *Probation Journal*, **44**(1), 2–10.

Ong, G., Harsent, L., Roberts, C., Burnett, R. & Al-Attar, Z. (2004). Think First Prospective Research Study: Effectiveness and Reducing Attrition. What Works Programme Evaluation Findings June 2004. (National Probation Service). London: Home Office.

Pearson, F.S., Lipton, D.S., Cleland, C.M. & Yee, D.S. (2002). The effects of behavioural/cognitive-behavioural programs on recidivism. *Crime & Delinquency*, **4**(3), 476–96.

Raynor, P. & Vanstone, M. (2001). Straight thinking on probation: Evidence-based practice and the culture of curiosity. In G.A. Bernfeld, D.P. Farrington & A.W. Leschied (eds), *Offender Rehabilitation in Practice: Implementing and Evaluating Effective Programs* (pp 189–203). Chichester: Wiley.

Robertson, G. & Gunn, J. (1987). A ten-year follow-up of men discharged from Grendon prison. *British Journal of Psychiatry*, **151**, 674–78.

Sarno, C., Hearnden, I., Hedderman, C., Hough, M., Nee, C. & Herrington, V. (2000). Working their way out of offending: An evaluation of two probation employment schemes. *Home Office Research Study 218*. London: Home Office.

Sarno, C., Hearnden, I. & Hedderman, C. (2001). From offending to employment: A study of two probation schemes in inner London. *Home Office Research Findings 135*, 1–4. London: Home Office.

Sherman, L.W., Gottfredson, D.C., MacKenzie, D.L., Eck, J., Reuter, P. & Bushway, S.D. (1997). *Preventing Crime: What Works, What Doesn't, and What's Promising.* Washington DC: National Institute of Justice, US Department of Justice.

Steele, R. & Van Arendsen, J. (2001). *Reconviction of Offenders on Think First: A Twelve Month Follow Up of Offenders Expected to Complete Think First Between September 2000 and September 2001.* Unpublished report from Merseyside Probation Area Research and Information Services, National Probation Service.

Stewart-Ong, G., Harsent, L., Roberts, C., Burnett, R. & Al-Attar, Z. (2003). Evaluation of the Pre-Accreditation Version of Think First: A Community-Based Cognitive-Behavioural Programme for Persistent Offenders. (Unpublished). Cited in G. Stewart-Ong, L. Harsent, C. Roberts, R. Burnett & Z. Al-Attar (2004). Think First Prospective Research Study: Effectiveness and Reducing Attrition. What Works NPD Programme Evaluation Findings June 2004. (National Probation Service). London: Home Office.

Stewart-Ong, G., Harsent, L., Roberts, C., Burnett, R., & Al-Attar, Z. (2004). *Think first prospective research study: effectiveness and reducing attrition.* What Works NPD Programme Evaluation Findings June 2004. (National Probation Service). London: Home Office.

Sugg, D. (2000). South Yorkshire Drink Impaired Drivers Scheme. *Service Briefing. National Probation Service Issue 4.* London: National Probation Service.

Taylor, R. (2000). Seven-year reconviction study of HMP Grendon therapeutic community. *Home Office Research Findings 115,* 1–4. London: Home Office.

Tong, L.S.J. & Farrington, D.P. (in press). How effective is the Reasoning and Rehabilitation Programme in reducing reoffending? A meta-analysis of evaluations in three countries. *Psychology, Crime and Law.*

Vennard, J. & Hedderman, C. (1998). Effective interventions with offenders. In P. Goldblatt & C. Lewis (eds), Reducing offending: An assessment of research evidence on ways of dealing with offending behaviour. *Home Office Research Study 187.* London: Home Office.

Vennard, J., Sugg, D. & Hedderman, C., (1997). The use of cognitive-behavioural approaches with offenders: Messages from the research. Part I. *Home Office Research Study 171.* London: Home Office.

Webster, R., Hedderman, C., Turnbull, P.J. & May, T. (2001). Building bridges to employment for prisoners. *Home Office Research Study 226.* London: Home Office.

Welsh, B.C., Farrington, D.P., Sherman, L.W. & MacKenzie, D.L. (2002). What do we know about crime prevention? *International Annals of Criminology, 40,* 10–31.

Wilkinson, J.M. (1997). The impact of Ilderton motor project on motor vehicle crime and offending. *British Journal of Criminology, 37*(4), 568–851.

Williams, B. & Creamer, A. (1997). Evaluating Scottish special probation schemes: In G. Mair (ed), *Evaluating the Effectiveness of Community Penalties.* Aldershot: Avery.

CHAPTER 6

CCTV and Street Lighting: Comparative Effects on Crime

Brandon C. Welsh and David P. Farrington

INTRODUCTION

The main aim of this chapter is to report on the results of two systematic reviews, incorporating meta-analytical techniques, which examined the effects of closed-circuit television (CCTV) surveillance cameras and improved street lighting on reducing crime (see also Farrington & Welsh, 2002a, 2002b; Welsh & Farrington, 2002, 2003). Within these two systematic reviews, the studies identified from the *UK review* are presented in Tables 9.16 and 9.17 in Chapter 9.

The chapter also compares the relative effectiveness of these two interventions in preventing crime. In addition to CCTV and street lighting as situational crime-prevention measures (Clarke & Homel, 1997), two key interests underlie this comparative perspective: one of a historical, and the other of a contemporary nature. The more historical interest pertains to the widespread use of improved street lighting in the US in the 1970s, and its subsequent abandonment as a policy option. Following the dramatic increase in crime in the 1960s, many American towns and cities embarked upon major street-lighting programmes as a means of reducing crime, and this led to a detailed review of the effectiveness of street lighting in preventing crime by Tien, O'Donnell, Barnett and Mirchandani (1979) as part of the National Evaluation Program of Law Enforcement Assistance Administration funding. On the basis of the 15 most methodologically

Reducing Crime: The Effectiveness of Criminal Justice Interventions.
Edited by A. E. Perry, C. McDougall and D. P. Farrington. © 2006 John Wiley & Sons, Ltd.

rigorous evaluations, Tien et al. (1979) concluded that their results were mixed and generally inconclusive.

The review was interpreted as showing that street lighting had no effect on crime. However, it relied on what is now called a 'vote-counting' method, focusing on how many evaluations produced statistically significant results. Unfortunately, statistical significance depends partly on the effect size and partly on the sample size. Many criminological evaluations are based on relatively small numbers, which means that a practically important effect size may not be statistically significant. Vote-counting methods were supplanted in the 1980s by meta-analysis, which focuses on the effect size and estimates of weighted mean effect sizes of interventions (Lipsey & Wilson, 2001). If Tien et al. (1979) had carried out a meta-analysis, it is likely that different conclusions would have been reached.

Tien et al.'s (1979) review effectively ended research on street lighting and its effects on crime in the US. Because it found the evidence to be mixed and generally inconclusive (many of the programmes were, in fact, effective), it should have led instead to attempts to evaluate the effects of street lighting using more adequate designs, and should have stimulated efforts to determine in what circumstances improved street lighting might or might not lead to reductions in crime.

The contemporary interest in comparing these two situational crime-prevention measures arises largely from the current UK experience of the widespread use of one of these measures (CCTV) as a government-funded method of reducing crime, and the complete dismissal by the government of the other (improved street lighting). In the UK, CCTV has been, and continues to be, the single most heavily funded non-criminal justice crime-prevention measure. Over the three-year period from 1999 to 2001, the British Government made available £170 million for 'CCTV schemes in town and city centres, car parks, crime hot-spots and residential areas' (Home Office Policing and Reducing Crime Unit, 2001, p. 8). In previous years (1996 to 1998), CCTV accounted for more than three-quarters of total Home Office spending on crime prevention (Koch, 1998, p. 49).

There is concern that this funding may have been based partly on political considerations (for example, the popularity of CCTV with the public), and partly on a handful of apparently successful schemes that were more often than not evaluated using simple one-group (no control group) before-and-after designs. Such evaluations were conducted with varying degrees of competence (Armitage, Smyth, & Pease, 1999, p. 226), and were often lacking in professional independence from government (Ditton & Short, 1999, p. 202). In addition to this was a complete dismissal at the time by the Home Office of a number of high-quality UK studies showing that improved street lighting had a desirable effect on crime. In a recent review of these studies, Pease (1999) stated that 'the capacity of street lighting to influence crime has now been satisfactorily settled' (p. 68). That substantial funding was poured into CCTV schemes on the basis of questionable research, while the effectiveness of improvements to street lighting was supported by high-quality research, raises serious questions about the use of public resources to prevent crime in the UK.

This chapter now turns to a description of the methods used in the two systematic reviews of the effects of CCTV and street lighting on reducing crime, followed by a presentation of the results and, finally, conclusions and directions for policy and future research.

METHODS

Criteria for Inclusion of Evaluation Studies

In selecting evaluations for inclusion in the reviews, the following criteria were used:

1. Either CCTV or improved street lighting was the focus of the intervention. For evaluations involving one or more other interventions, only those evaluations in which CCTV or improved street lighting was the main intervention were included.
2. The principal aim of the schemes was the reduction of crime, and that there was an outcome measure of crime. The most relevant crime outcomes were violent and property crimes.
3. The evaluation design was of high methodological quality, with the minimum design involving before-and-after measures of crime in experimental and comparable control areas. Control areas are needed in order to counter threats to internal validity. According to Cook and Campbell (1979) and Shadish, Cook, and Campbell (2002), this is the minimum design that is interpretable, corresponding to level 3 on the Scientific Methods Scale (Farrington, Gottfredson, Sherman, & Welsh, 2002; Sherman et al., 1997).
4. The total number of crimes in each area before the intervention was at least 20. The main measure of effect size was based on changes in crime rates between the before-and-after time periods. It was considered that a measure of change based on an N below 20 was potentially misleading. Also, any study with less than 20 crimes before would have insufficient statistical power to detect changes in crime. The criterion of 20 is probably too low, but we were reluctant to exclude studies unless their numbers were clearly inadequate.

Search Strategies

The following four search strategies were carried out to identify CCTV or improved street lighting evaluations meeting the criteria for inclusion in the two systematic reviews:

1. Searches of online data bases. The following data bases were searched: SPECTR, Criminal Justice Abstracts, National Criminal Justice Reference Service (NCJRS) Abstracts, Sociological Abstracts, Social Science Abstracts (SocialSciAbs), Educational Resources Information Clearing-house (ERIC), Government Publications Office Monthly Catalog (GPO Monthly), Psychology Information (PsychInfo), and Public Affairs Information Service (PAIS) International. These databases were selected because they had the most comprehensive coverage of criminological, criminal justice and social science literature. They are also among the top databases recommended by the Campbell Crime and Justice Coordinating Group, and other systematic reviews of interventions in the field of crime and justice have used them (for example, Braga, 2001).

   For the CCTV systematic review, the following terms were used to search these databases: 'closed circuit television', 'CCTV', 'cameras', 'social control', 'surveillance' and 'formal surveillance'. When applicable, 'crime' was then added to each of these terms (for example, 'CCTV and crime') to narrow the search parameters. For the street lighting systematic review, the following terms were used: 'street lighting', 'lighting', 'illumination' and 'natural surveillance'. Again, when applicable, 'crime' was then added to narrow the search parameters.

2. Searches of literature reviews on the effectiveness of the interventions in preventing crime (Eck, 2002; Fleming & Burrows, 1986; Nieto, 1997; Painter, 1996; Pease, 1999; Phillips, 1999; Poyner, 1993; Ramsay & Newton, 1991; Tien et al., 1979).[1]

3. Searches of bibliographies of CCTV and street lighting reports.

4. Contacts with leading researchers.

Both published and unpublished reports were included in the searches. Furthermore, the searches were international in scope and not limited to the English language (one non-English language evaluation report is included in the CCTV review).

The search strategies resulted in the identification of 83 evaluations (49 for CCTV and 34 for street lighting). Of these, 76 were obtained and analysed; the other seven, which may or may not have met the criteria for inclusion, could not be obtained. Of these 76 evaluations, 32 met the

---

[1]The review by Tien et al. (1979) identified 103 street-lighting projects carried out in the US in the 1970s, but considered that only 15 (listed on pp. 51–54) met their minimum methodological standards. We attempted to obtain 11 of these 15 evaluation reports. For the other four studies (conducted in Baltimore, Chicago, Richmond (Virginia), and Washington DC) Tien et al. (1979) could not determine from the reports that there was any kind of experimental-control comparison. Hence, we did not attempt to obtain and screen every possible study on street lighting and crime conducted prior to Tien et al. (1979), but only those studies that conceivably might meet our criteria for inclusion. We did, however, attempt to obtain and screen every possible study conducted after Tien et al.'s (1979) review.

criteria for inclusion (19 for CCTV and 13 for street lighting), and 41 did not (25 for CCTV and 16 for street lighting) and were thus excluded from the systematic reviews. The three remaining studies (all CCTV) met the criteria for inclusion, but did not provide the data required in order to be included in the meta-analysis (see below).[2]

RESULTS

This chapter attempts to estimate the comparative effectiveness of the two interventions in preventing crime, based on the highest-quality research evidence available. (Table 6.1 presents summary information on each of the 32 included studies.) To address this and other questions of interest, results obtained in the included evaluations on the effects of CCTV and improved street lighting on crime are analysed using the statistical technique of meta-analysis.

A meta-analysis is essentially a statistical summary of comparable effect sizes reported in each evaluation. In order to carry out a meta-analysis, a comparable measure of effect size and an estimate of its variance is needed for each programme evaluation (Lipsey & Wilson, 2001; Wilson, 2001). In the case of CCTV and street-lighting evaluations, the measure of effect size had to be based on the number of crimes in the experimental and control areas before and after the intervention, as this was the only information that was regularly provided during the evaluations. Here, the odds ratio (OR) is used as the measure of effect size. For example, in the Doncaster CCTV evaluation (Skinns, 1998), the odds of a crime after, given a crime before, in the control area were 2,002/1,780, or 1.12. The odds of a crime after, given a crime before, in the experimental area were 4,591/5,832, or 0.79. The OR was therefore 1.12/0.79, or 1.42, which was statistically highly significant (p < 0.0001).

The OR is calculated from the following table:

	Before	After
Experimental	a	b
Control	c	d

Where a, b, c, d are numbers of crimes

$$OR = ad/bc$$

---

[2]Information on the unobtainable and excluded evaluations is available from the first author, Brandon C. Welsh, in the Department of Criminal Justice, University of Massachusetts, Lowell, US.

Table 6.1 Summary of CCTV and improved street-lighting evaluations

Author and Publication Date	Place	Period (months)		Other Interventions	Outcome Measure
		Pre	Post		
CCTV in City Centres					
Brown (1995)	Newcastle UK	26	15	No	Survey
Brown (1995)	Birmingham UK	12	12	No	Records
Short & Ditton (1996)	Airdrie UK	24	24	No	Records
Skinns (1998)	Doncaster UK	24	24	Yes	Records
Armitage et al. (1999)	Burnley UK	12	12	No	Records
Farrington et al. (2005)	Cambridge UK	11	11	No	Survey/Records
Mazerolle et al. (2002)	Cincinnati N	23	6	No	Records
Mazerolle et al. (2002)	Cincinnati H	23	4	No	Records
Mazerolle et al. (2002)	Cincinnati F	24.5	3.5	No	Records
Street Lighting in City Centres					
Poyner & Webb (1997)	Birmingham UK	12	12	No	Records
Atlanta RC (1974)	Atlanta	12	12	No	Records
DIFL (1974)	Milwaukee	12	12	No	Records
Wright et al. (1974)	Kansas City MO	12	12	No	Records
Sternhell (1977)	New Orleans	51	29	No	Records
CCTV in Residential/Public Housing					
Musheno et al. (1978)	New York	3	3	No	Survey
Street Lighting in Residential/Public Housing					
Shaftoe (1994)	Bristol UK	12	12	No	Records
Painter & Farrington (1997)	Dudley UK	12	12	No	Survey/SR

Study	Location				
Painter & Farrington (1999)	Stoke UK	12	12	No	Survey
Inskeep & Goff (1974)	Portland OR	6 or 11	6 or 11	No	Records
Harrisburg PD (1976)	Harrisburg	12	12	No	Records
Lewis & Sullivan (1979)	Fort Worth	12	12	No	Records
Quinet & Nunn (1998)	Indianapolis	6–9	6–9	Yes	Records
CCTV in Car Parks					
Poyner (1991)	Guildford UK	24	9	Yes	Records
Tilley (1993)	Hartlepool UK	15	30	Yes	Records
Tilley (1993)	Bradford UK	12	12	Yes	Records
Tilley (1993)	Coventry UK	8/16	8/16	Yes	Records
Sarno (1996)	Sutton UK	12	12	Yes	Records
Street Lighting in Car Parks					
Poyner (1991)	Dover UK	24	24	Yes	Records
CCTV in Public Transportation					
Burrows (1980)	Underground S	12	12	Yes	Records
Webb & Laycock (1992)	Underground N	46	26	Yes	Records
Webb & Laycock (1992)	Underground C	28	32	Yes	Records
Grandmaison & Tremblay (1997)	Montreal	18	18	No	Records

Notes
Cincinnati: N = Northside, H = Hopkins Park, F = Findlay Market; RC = Regional Commission; DIFL = Department of Intergovernmental Fiscal Liaison; SR = self-reports; PD = police department; 8/16 = 8 for experimental, 16 for control (in both pre and post); Underground: S = Southern sector; N = Northern line, C = Central.

The variance of OR is calculated from the variance of LOR (the natural logarithm of OR):

$$V(LOR) = 1/a + 1/b + 1/c + 1/d$$

The OR has a very simple and meaningful interpretation. It indicates the proportional change in crime in the control area compared with the experimental area. An OR greater than 1.0 indicates a desirable effect of the intervention, while an OR less than 1.0 indicates an undesirable effect. In this example, the OR of 1.42 indicates that crime increased by 42 per cent in the control area compared with the experimental area. However, an OR of 1.42 could also indicate that crime decreased by more than 30 per cent in the experimental area compared with the control area, since the change in the experimental area compared with the control area is the inverse of the OR, or 1/1.42 here.

In order to produce a summary effect size in a meta-analysis, each effect size is weighted according to the inverse of the variance. This was another reason for choosing the OR, which has a known variance (Fleiss, 1981, pp. 61–7).[3]

We also investigated the important issues of displacement of crime and diffusion of crime-prevention benefits. Displacement is often defined as the unintended increase in targeted crimes in other locations following from the introduction of a crime-reduction scheme. Five different forms of displacement have been identified by Reppetto (1976): temporal (change in time), tactical (change in method), target (change in victim), territorial (change in place), and functional (change in type of crime). Diffusion of benefits is defined as the unintended decrease in crimes following from a crime-reduction scheme, or the 'complete reverse' of displacement (Clarke & Weisburd, 1994).

Is CCTV or Improved Street Lighting More Effective?

Separate meta-analyses of the 19 CCTV evaluations and the 13 improved street-lighting evaluations provided evidence that both interventions were equally effective in reducing (total) crime. In the case of CCTV,

---

[3]This estimate of the variance is based on the assumption that total numbers of crimes (a, b, c, d) have a Poisson distribution. Thirty years of mathematical models of criminal careers (see, for example, Blumstein, Cohen, Roth & Visher, 1986; Piquero, Farrington, & Blumstein, 2003) have been dominated by the assumption that the commission of crimes can be accurately modelled by a Poisson process. For a more detailed discussion of the variance in this case, see Farrington and Welsh (2004, pp. 450–53). In the 32 evaluations, we empirically estimated the ratio of the variance to the mean, based on the before-and-after number of crimes in control areas. The average was 1.21, which is close to the Poisson figure of 1. (The geometric mean was used as an average because of the ratio variables.)

the weighted mean OR was 1.27 (95 per cent confidence interval 1.11–1.46, p = 0.0004). This means that crimes increased by 27 per cent after the installation of CCTV in control areas compared to experimental areas or, conversely, crimes decreased by 21 per cent in experimental areas compared to control areas. In the case of improved street lighting, the weighted mean OR was 1.28 (95 per cent confidence interval 1.11–1.48), which was also a highly significant effect (p = 0.0008). Again, this means that crimes increased by 28 per cent after improved street lighting in control areas compared with experimental areas or, conversely, crimes decreased by 22 per cent in experimental areas compared with control areas.[4]

Setting

All of the 19 CCTV evaluations and the 13 improved street-lighting evaluations were carried out in one of four settings: city centre, residential or public housing, car parks or public transportation (see Table 6.2). With the exception of CCTV in residential/public housing (only one study), all of the settings in which either CCTV or improved street-lighting schemes could be evaluated showed desirable effects on crime, as measured by the weighted mean OR. CCTV in car parks had the largest effect on crime, with an overall OR of 1.77 (95 per cent confidence interval 1.37–2.28, p < 0.0001). In city centres, improved street lighting (OR = 1.47, p = 0.022) was more effective than CCTV (OR = 1.15, ns).

Crime Type

Table 6.3 shows that CCTV and street lighting were more effective in reducing property crimes (OR for CCTV = 1.54, p < 0.0001; OR for lighting = 1.27, p = 0.019) than violent crimes (OR for CCTV = 1.05, ns; OR for lighting = 1.15, ns). Property crimes included burglary, vehicle crimes and theft, while violent crimes included robbery and assault. The effectiveness of CCTV in reducing property crimes was largely driven by its success in reducing vehicle crimes in car parks.

---

[4] These effect-size estimates are based on a random effects model that is appropriate when effect sizes are significantly heterogeneous (as here). Our previous meta-analyses were based on a fixed effects model. The random effects model eliminated the significant heterogeneity of effect sizes for the lighting meta-analysis (Q = 18.98, 12 df, ns). Hence, it was reasonable to regard all the lighting effect sizes as randomly distributed about the summary figure of 1.28. However, the random effects model did not eliminate the significant heterogeneity of effect sizes for the CCTV meta-analysis (Q = 29.33, 18 df, p = 0.044). Therefore, it is arguable how far it is reasonable to report a summary effect size of 1.27. It may be more reasonable only to report the CCTV effect sizes in different conditions (for example, settings or countries).

Table 6.2 Meta-analysis of CCTV and improved street-lighting evaluations by context of intervention

Context of Intervention	CCTV (N = 19)	Street Lighting (N = 13)
City Centre	OR = 1.15 (0.96–1.37) (n = 9; Newcastle, Birmingham, Airdrie, Doncaster, Burnley, Cambridge, Cincinnati N, Cincinnati H, Cincinnati F)	OR = 1.47* (1.06–2.04) (n = 5; Birmingham, Atlanta, Milwaukee, Kansas City, New Orleans)
Residential/ Public Housing	OR = 0.89 (0.42–1.91) (n = 1; New York)	OR = 1.22* (1.01–1.47) (n = 7; Bristol, Dudley, Stoke, Portland, Harrisburg, Fort Worth, Indianapolis)
Car Parks	OR = 1.77* (1.37–2.28) (n = 5; Guildford, Hartlepool, Bradford, Coventry, Sutton)	OR = 1.14 (0.62–2.08) (n = 1; Dover)
Public Transportation	OR = 1.30 (0.87–1.96) (n = 4; Underground S, Underground N, Underground C, Montreal)	n.a.

*$p < 0.05$.
Notes
OR = weighted mean odds ratio (and 95% confidence interval)
Cincinnati: N – Northside, H – Hopkins Park, F = Findlay Market; Underground: S = Southern sector, N = Northern line, C = Central; n.a. = not available.

Table 6.3 Meta-analysis of CCTV and improved street-lighting evaluations by crime type

Crime Type	CCTV	Street Lighting
Violent	OR = 1.05 (0.83–1.34) (n = 6; Airdrie, Burnley, Cambridge, Underground N, Underground C, Montreal)	OR = 1.15 (0.90–1.48) (n = 9; Bristol, Dudley, Stoke, Atlanta, Milwaukee, Portland, Kansas City, Harrisburg, New Orleans)
Property	OR = 1.54* (1.24–1.91) (n = 11; Newcastle, Airdrie, Burnley, Underground S, Underground C, Montreal, Guildford, Hartlepool, Bradford, Coventry, Sutton)	OR = 1.27* (1.04–1.55) (n = 11; Dover, Bristol, Birmingham, Dudley, Stoke, Atlanta, Milwaukee, Portland, Kansas City, Harrisburg, New Orleans)

*$p < .05$
Notes
OR = weighted mean odds ratio (and 95% confidence interval)
Underground: S = Southern sector, N = Northern line, C = Central
Cincinnati: N = Northside, H = Hopkins Park, F = Findlay Market, RC = Regional Commission, DIFL = Department of Intergovernmental Fiscal Liaison; SR = self-reports; PD = police department; 8/16 = 8 for experimental, 16 for control (in both pre- and post-)

Table 6.4 Meta-analysis of CCTV and improved street-lighting evaluations by country

County	CCTV	Street Lighting
United Kingdom	OR = 1.43* (1.18–1.74) (n = 14)	OR = 1.63* (1.26–2.12) (n = 5)
US and Canada	OR = 0.99 (0.95–1.02) (n = 5)	OR = 1.12 (0.97–1.27) (n = 8)
Total	OR = 1.27* (1.11–1.46) (N = 19)	OR = 1.28* (1.11–1.48) (N = 13)

*p < .05
Note
OR = weighted mean odds ratio (and 95% confidence interval)

Country Comparison

Of the 19 CCTV evaluations, 14 were from the UK and the other 5 from North America (4 from the US and 1 from Canada). Of the 13 improved street lighting evaluations, 8 were from the US and the other 5 were from the UK. As illustrated in Table 6.4, when the pooled meta-analysis results for each intervention were disaggregated by country, CCTV and improved lighting were more effective in reducing crime in the UK (OR for CCTV = 1.43, p = 0.0003; OR for lighting = 1.63, p = 0.0002) than in North America (OR for CCTV = 0.99, ns; OR for lighting = 1.12, ns).

Displacement of Crime and Diffusion of Crime-Prevention Benefits

Eleven of the 19 CCTV studies, and 12 of the 13 street-lighting studies measured displacement of crime, diffusion of crime-prevention benefits, or both. Across the CCTV studies, mixed results were found for territorial displacement and diffusion of benefits. For example, in the case of the seven city-centre CCTV studies that measured displacement, diffusion or both, four studies reported at least some evidence of territorial displacement, and three reported at least some evidence of diffusion of benefits. Different results were found for the street-lighting studies. Only three of these studies reported some, or possible, evidence of territorial displacement, and the other nine reported no evidence of displacement, with two of these (Birmingham and Stoke) also reporting at least some evidence of diffusion.

In order to investigate displacement of crime and diffusion of crime-prevention benefits, the minimum design should involve one experimental area, one adjacent area, and one non-adjacent comparable control area. If crime decreased in the experimental area, increased in the adjacent area, and stayed constant in the control area, this might be evidence of displacement. If crime decreased in the experimental and adjacent areas, and stayed constant or increased in the control area, this might be evidence of diffusion of benefits. Unfortunately, few CCTV or street-lighting studies used this minimum design. Instead, most had an adjacent control area and the remainder of the city as another (non-comparable) control area. Because of this, any conclusions about displacement or diffusion effects of CCTV and street lighting seem premature at this point in time.

DISCUSSION AND CONCLUSIONS

On the basis of the highest-quality research evidence available, both CCTV surveillance cameras and improved street lighting are effective situational measures for reducing crime. For city managers, business owners and others, this may be useful information if a decision needs to be made about implementing one or the other measure. Hopefully, as Moore (2002) argued for in another context, a cost-effectiveness analysis or comparative cost–benefit analysis would also be carried out to inform this decision.

What may be more helpful to practitioners and more useful for policy discussions is information about the specific conditions under which improved street lighting and CCTV are most effective in reducing crime. The present research showed that CCTV and improved street lighting were effective in reducing (total) crime, with one exception, in each of the four settings within which they were evaluated, with the largest effect on crime being for CCTV in car parks. And in the one setting (city centres) that CCTV could be compared with improved street lighting, the latter was found to be more effective in reducing (total) crime. This finding provides further direction for the allocation of scarce public resources.

Also of importance was evidence that showed that CCTV and improved lighting were more effective in reducing property crimes than in reducing violent crimes. Regular crime analysis by the police, such as that used by police department Compstat units in the US, could be used to identify those places that are at greatest risk of property crimes, particularly vehicle crimes, information which, in turn, could be used to guide the deployment of CCTV surveillance cameras or improved lighting. The advent of mobile and removable CCTV units may make this a more feasible and perhaps less costly option.

Another significant issue arising from the findings of the two situational crime-prevention measures is the potential benefit that may come from combining them. Both measures may reduce crime through a number of similar mechanisms; for example, by increasing offenders' perceived risks of committing a crime, or strengthening community cohesion and social control. However, this may be more effective with property crimes, as such crimes are usually more 'rational' than violent crimes. Arguably, there is no conflict in implementing these two measures alongside each other.[5] So, is there empirical support for combining the two interventions?

Five of the 19 CCTV evaluations (Underground N, Guildford, Bradford, Coventry and Sutton; see Table 6.1) used improved lighting as a secondary intervention. (None of the 13 improved street-lighting evaluations used CCTV as a secondary intervention.) A meta-analysis of these five evaluations provided evidence that the combination of CCTV and improved lighting can be highly effective in reducing crime, with a weighted mean OR of 1.65 (95 per cent confidence interval 1.24–2.21, $p = 0.0007$). A meta-analysis of the other 14 CCTV evaluations (4 of which used other interventions such as security officers and notices of CCTV) produced a lower weighted mean OR of 1.20 (95 per cent confidence interval 1.04–1.39, $p = 0.016$). From these results it can be seen that the combination of CCTV and improved lighting (as primary and secondary measures, respectively) was the more effective form of surveillance in reducing crime, and its superiority was significant ($p = 0.01$).[6] It is important to note, however, that four of these five evaluations took place in car parks and measured only the schemes' effect on vehicle crimes. Therefore, the powerful result evidenced from combining CCTV surveillance cameras and improved street lighting may be limited to targeting vehicle crimes in car parks.

Another interesting finding to emerge from the present research is that both forms of surveillance were found to be far more effective in reducing crime in the UK than in the US.[7] What might account for this? Or, more importantly, what lessons can be drawn from the UK studies to help improve the effectiveness of CCTV and improved street lighting in the US? There were some differences in key characteristics between the UK and US CCTV schemes, and between the UK and US improved street-lighting schemes, which may help to address these questions.

First, the average follow-up period of the five US CCTV schemes was substantially shorter than for the 14 UK CCTV schemes: 6.9 months

---

[5] Some may view the combination of CCTV surveillance cameras and street lighting as trivial, based on the notion that CCTV requires natural or artificial lighting to work. This is not the case. Technological innovations in CCTV cameras, such as infrared, allow cameras to work without other lighting. Thus, improved street lighting and CCTV should be viewed as distinct interventions. There may be a conflict between the two measures if improved lighting increases community cohesion and CCTV cameras give the impression that a place is unsafe, thus detracting from social cohesion because residents are afraid to go there.

[6] The significance of a difference between two ORs was tested by comparing LORs (natural logarithms of ORs). The formula for the variance of LOR, V(LOR) is given above. In this example, LOR for the five CCTV plus lighting evaluations = 0.50, SE = 0.15; LOR for the other 14 CCTV evaluations = 0.18, SE = 0.075. The pooled SE was 0.096, giving z = 0.32/0.096 = 3.3, p < 0.01. No other comparison of two ORs was statistically significant.

[7] Reference is hereafter made to the US because, with the exception of the Grandmaison and Tremblay (1997) CCTV evaluation, all of the CCTV and improved street lighting evaluations were conducted in either the UK or US.

versus 17.7 months. Four of the US evaluations had the shortest follow-up periods of all 19 CCTV evaluations, ranging from a low of 3 months to a high of 6 months. Because of the short follow-up periods in the US studies, it is possible that the CCTV schemes were not given enough time to produce a clear effect on crime, either desirable or undesirable (all five of the US studies showed evidence of either a null or uncertain effect on crime). Longer follow-up periods, as in the majority of the UK studies, seem to be warranted for future CCTV evaluations in the US. No difference was found in the average follow-up period for the UK and US improved street-lighting evaluations (14.4 months versus 13.6 months, respectively).

Second, and perhaps most importantly, not 1 of the 5 US CCTV evaluations used other interventions alongside CCTV, while 9 of the 14 British schemes used 1 or more other type of intervention, such as improved lighting or police patrols. It is possible that the absence of lighting, policing or other situational crime-prevention measures in the US CCTV schemes may be a contributing factor to their overall poor effect in reducing crime. CCTV on its own may not represent a sufficient deterrent in influencing an offender's decision-making process to commit a crime or not. No difference was found between the UK and US improved street lighting schemes.

Cultural context is an issue that may also be a contributing factor to the difference in effectiveness between the UK and US schemes, both for CCTV and improved street lighting. The UK has a high level of public support for the use of CCTV cameras to prevent crime in public settings (Norris & Armstrong, 1999, pp. 60–2; Phillips, 1999, pp. 139–40), while in the US the public is less accepting, and more apprehensive of Big Brother implications arising from this surveillance technology (Murphy, 2002). US resistance to the use of CCTV in public spaces also takes the form of legal action and constitutional challenges under the US Constitution's Fourth Amendment prohibition against unreasonable searches and seizures (Nieto, 1997, p. 1).

It could very well be the case that the poor showing of the US CCTV schemes was due in part to a lack of public support (and maybe even political support) for the schemes, which, in turn, may have resulted, for example, in cuts in programme funding, the police assigning lower priority to the schemes, or attempts to discourage desirable media coverage. Each of these factors could potentially undermine the effectiveness of CCTV schemes. In contrast, the Home Office, which has funded many of the UK evaluations, would have liked to find that CCTV was effective—in order to justify the massive government investment in this intervention.

While cultural context could play a role in the differential effectiveness of street lighting in the two countries (to our knowledge there have been no recent surveys of the public in either country), it is our opinion that this is not likely, mainly because this form of surveillance is generally viewed as having few harmful social consequences, unlike CCTV.

For improved street lighting, there may be something of a recency effect that has contributed to the difference in effectiveness between the UK and US schemes. With the exception of one of the eight US street-lighting evaluations, all were carried out at least 10 to 15 years earlier than the first UK street-lighting evaluation. Could it be that the UK street-lighting evaluations drew upon the knowledge gleaned from the individual US evaluations and the detailed review by Tien et al. (1979), and that this played some role in the effectiveness of the UK lighting schemes? This is quite possible, due to the great awareness of this US research, as evidenced in UK-based reviews of the literature (Painter, 1996; Ramsay & Newton, 1991) and in some of the UK lighting studies included here. Another factor that may have contributed to the difference in effectiveness between the US and UK street-lighting schemes is the possibility that offenders during the 1990s (in the case of the UK studies) may have been influenced by different factors compared to those over a decade ago.

Future research should begin with attention to the methodological rigour of the evaluation designs. The use of a comparable control group by all of the 32 included evaluations went some way towards ruling out some of the major threats to internal validity, such as selection, maturation, history and instrumentation. The effects of CCTV and street lighting on crime can also be investigated after controlling (for example, in a regression equation) not only for prior crime, but also for other community-level factors that influence crime, such as neighbourhood poverty and poor housing. A further possible research design is to match two areas and then to choose one, at random, as the experimental area. Ideally, several experimental areas and several comparable adjacent and control areas should be included. Adjacent and non-adjacent areas are needed to test hypotheses about displacement and diffusion of benefits.

Research is also needed on the monetary costs and benefits of CCTV and street-lighting programmes. As noted above, it would be useful to measure which of these two interventions is more cost-effective in preventing crime. It would also be useful to measure if a programme that combined both CCTV and street lighting was more cost-beneficial than either of the two implemented on its own. Though we had hoped to be able to examine these issues, this was not possible as only 3 of the 32 included studies (Painter & Farrington, 1997, 1999; Skinns, 1998) carried out a cost–benefit analysis. In each case, benefits from reduced crime substantially outweighed programme costs. Future cost–benefit analyses of CCTV and street-lighting programmes should take account of any displacement of crime or diffusion of crime-prevention benefits. While there remain a number of other issues pertaining to cost–benefit analysis of situational crime prevention that are in need of examination (see Roman & Farrell, 2002), our previous work (Welsh & Farrington, 1999, 2000) has shown that situational crime prevention generally is an economically efficient strategy.

REFERENCES

Armitage, R., Smyth, G. & Pease, K. (1999). Burnley CCTV evaluation. In K. Painter & N. Tilley (eds), *Surveillance of Public Space: CCTV, Street Lighting and Crime Prevention. Crime Prevention Studies* (Vol. 10). Monsey, NY: Criminal Justice Press.

Atlanta Regional Commission (1974). *Street Light Project: Final Evaluation Report*. Atlanta: Author.

Blumstein, A., Cohen, J., Roth, J.A. & Visher, C.A. (eds) (1986). *Criminal Careers and 'Career Criminals'* (Vol. 1). Washington DC: National Academy Press.

Braga, A.A. (2001). The effects of hot spots policing on crime. *Annals of the American Academy of Political and Social Science*, **578**, 104–25.

Brown, B. (1995). CCTV in town centres: Three case studies. *Crime Detection and Prevention Series Paper 68*. London: Home Office.

Burrows, J.N. (1980). The impact of closed circuit television on crime in the London Underground. In P. Mayhew, R.V.G. Clarke, J.N. Burrows, J.M. Hough & S.W.C Winchester (eds), Crime in Public View. *Home Office Research Study 49*. London: Home Office.

Clarke, R.V. & Homel, R. (1997). A revised classification of situational crime prevention techniques. In S.P. Lab (ed.), *Crime Prevention at a Crossroads*. Cincinnati: Anderson.

Clarke, R.V. & Weisburd, D. (1994). Diffusion of crime control benefits: Observations on the reverse of displacement. In R.V. Clarke (ed.), *Crime Prevention Studies* (Vol. 2). Monsey, NY: Criminal Justice Press.

Cook, T.D. & Campbell, D.T. (1979). *Quasi-Experimentation: Design and Analysis Issues for Field Settings*. Chicago: Rand McNally.

Department of Intergovernmental Fiscal Liaison (1974). *Final Report: Milwaukee High Intensity Street Lighting Project*. Milwaukee: Author.

Ditton, J. & Short, E. (1999). Yes, it works, no, it doesn't: Comparing the effects of open-street CCTV in two adjacent Scottish town centres. In K. Painter & N. Tilley (eds), *Surveillance of Public Space: CCTV, Street Lighting and Crime Prevention. Crime Prevention Studies* (Vol. 10). Monsey, NY: Criminal Justice Press.

Eck, J.E. (2002). Preventing crime at places. In L.W. Sherman, D.P. Farrington, B.C. Welsh & D.L. MacKenzie (eds), *Evidence-Based Crime Prevention*. London: Routledge.

Farrington, D.P., Gottfredson, D.C., Sherman, L.W. & Welsh, B.C. (2002). The Maryland scientific methods scale. In L.W. Sherman, D.P Farrington, B.C. Welsh & D.L. MacKenzie (eds), *Evidence-Based Crime Prevention*. London: Routledge.

Farrington, D.P. & Welsh, B.C. (2002a). Improved street lighting and crime prevention. *Justice Quarterly*, **19**, 313–42.

Farrington, D.P. & Welsh, B.C. (2002b). Effects of improved street lighting on crime: A systematic review. *Home Office Research Study 251*. London: Home Office.

Farrington, D.P. & Welsh, B.C. (2004). Measuring the effects of improved street lighting on crime: A response to Dr Marchant. *British Journal of Criminology*, **44**, 448–67.

Farrington, D.P., Bennett, T.H. & Welsh, B.C. (2005). The Cambridge Evaluation of the Effects of CCTV on Crime. In G. Farrell (ed), *Imagination for Crime Prevention*. Monsey, NY: Criminal Justice Press, in press.

Fleiss, J.L. (1981). *Statistical Methods for Rates and Proportions* (2nd edn). New York: Wiley.

Fleming, R. & Burrows, J.N. (1986). The case for lighting as a means of preventing crime. *Home Office Research Bulletin 22*, 14–17. London: Home Office.

Grandmaison, R. & Tremblay, P. (1997). Évaluation des effets de la télé-surveillance sur la criminalité commise dans 13 stations du Métro de Montréal. *Criminologie*, **30**, 93–110.

Harrisburg Police Department (1976). *Final Evaluation Report of the 'High Intensity Street Lighting Program.'* Harrisburg, PA: Planning and Research Section, Staff and Technical Services Division, Harrisburg Police Department.

Home Office Policing and Reducing Crime Unit (2001). *Invitation to Tender: Evaluation of CCTV Initiatives*. Unpublished. London: Author.

Inskeep, N.R. & Goff, C. (1974). *A Preliminary Evaluation of the Portland Lighting Project*. Salem, OR: Oregon Law Enforcement Council.

Koch, B.C.M. (1998). *The Politics of Crime Prevention*. Aldershot: Ashgate.

Lewis, E.B. & Sullivan, T.T. (1979). Combating crime and citizen attitudes: A case study of the corresponding reality. *Journal of Criminal Justice, 7*, 71–9.

Lipsey, M.W. & Wilson, D.B. (2001). *Practical Meta-Analysis*. Thousand Oaks, CA: Sage.

Mazerolle, L., Hurley, D. & Chamlin, M. (2002). Social behavior in public space: An analysis of behavioral adaptations to CCTV. *Security Journal, 15*, 59–75.

Moore, M.H. (2002). The limits of social science in guiding policy. *Criminology & Public Policy, 2*, 33–42.

Murphy, D.E. (2002). As security cameras sprout, someone's always watching. *New York Times,* 29 September.

Musheno, M.C., Levine, J.P. & Palumbo, D.J. (1978). Television surveillance and crime prevention: Evaluating an attempt to create defensible space in public housing. *Social Science Quarterly, 58*, 647–56.

Nieto, M. (1997). *Public Video Surveillance: Is it an Effective Crime Prevention Tool?* Sacramento: California Research Bureau, California State Library.

Norris, C. & Armstrong, G. (1999). *The Maximum Surveillance Society: The Rise of CCTV*. Oxford: Berg.

Painter, K. (1996). Street lighting, crime and fear of crime: A summary of research. In T.H. Bennett (ed.), *Preventing Crime and Disorder: Targeting Strategies and Responsibilities*. Cambridge Cropwood Series. Cambridge: Institute of Criminology, Cambridge University.

Painter, K. & Farrington, D.P. (1997). The crime reducing effect of improved street lighting: The Dudley project. In R.V. Clarke (ed.), *Situational Crime Prevention: Successful Case Studies* (2nd edn). Guilderland, NY: Harrow and Heston.

Painter, K. & Farrington, D.P. (1999). Street lighting and crime: Diffusion of benefits in the Stoke-on-Trent project. In K. Painter & N. Tilley (eds), *Surveillance of Public Space: CCTV, Street Lighting and Crime Prevention. Crime Prevention Studies* (Vol. 10). Monsey, NY: Criminal Justice Press.

Pease, K. (1999). A review of street lighting evaluations: Crime reduction effects. In K. Painter & N. Tilley (eds), *Surveillance of Public Space: CCTV, Street Lighting and Crime Prevention. Crime Prevention Studies* (Vol. 10). Monsey, NY: Criminal Justice Press.

Phillips, C. (1999). A review of CCTV evaluations: Crime reduction effects and attitudes towards its use. In K. Painter & N. Tilley (eds), *Surveillance of Public Space: CCTV, Street Lighting and Crime Prevention. Crime Prevention Studies* (Vol. 10). Monsey, NY: Criminal Justice Press.

Piquero, A.R., Farrington, D.P. & Blumstein, A. (2003). The criminal career paradigm. In M. Tonry (ed.), *Crime and Justice: A Review of Research* (Vol. 30). Chicago: University of Chicago Press.

Poyner, B. (1991). Situational crime prevention in two parking facilities. *Security Journal*, **2**, 96–101.

Poyner, B. (1993). What works in crime prevention: An overview of evaluations. In R.V. Clarke (ed.), *Crime Prevention Studies* (Vol. 1). Monsey, NY: Criminal Justice Press.

Poyner, B. & Webb, B. (1997). Reducing theft from shopping bags in city center markets. In R.V. Clarke (ed.), *Situational Crime Prevention: Successful Case Studies* (2nd ed.). Guilderland, NY: Harrow and Heston.

Quinet, K.D. & Nunn, S. (1998). Illuminating crime: The impact of street lighting on calls for police service. *Evaluation Review*, **22**, 751–79.

Ramsay, M. & Newton, R. (1991). The effect of better street lighting on crime and fear: A review. *Crime Prevention Unit Paper 29*. London: Home Office.

Reppetto, T.A. (1976). Crime prevention and the displacement phenomenon. *Crime & Delinquency*, **22**, 166–77.

Roman, J. & Farrell, G. (2002). Cost–benefit analysis for crime prevention: Opportunity costs, routine savings and crime externalities. In N. Tilley (ed.), *Evaluation for Crime Prevention. Crime Prevention Studies* (Vol. 14). Monsey, NY: Criminal Justice Press.

Sarno, C. (1995) Impact of CCTV on crime. In Bulos, M. (ed.), *Towards a Safer Sutton? Impact of Closed Circuit Television on Sutton Town Centre* (pp 4–32). London: London Borough of Sutton.

Sarno, C. (1996). The impact of closed circuit television on crime in Sutton town centre. In M. Bulos & D. Grant (eds), *Towards a Safer Sutton? CCTV One Year On*. London: London Borough of Sutton.

Shadish, W.R., Cook, T.D. & Campbell, D.T. (2002). *Experimental and Quasi-Experimental Designs for Generalized Causal Inference*. Boston: Houghton Mifflin.

Shaftoe, H. (1994). Easton/Ashley, Bristol: Lighting improvements. In S. Osborn (ed.), *Housing Safe Communities: An Evaluation of Recent Initiatives*. London: Safe Neighbourhoods Unit.

Sherman, L.W., Gottfredson, D.C., MacKenzie, D.L., Eck, J.E., Reuter, P. & Bushway, S.D. (1997). *Preventing Crime: What Works, What Doesn't, What's Promising*. Washington DC: National Institute of Justice, US Department of Justice.

Short, E. & Ditton, J. (1996). *Does Closed Circuit Television Prevent Crime? An Evaluation of the Use of CCTV Surveillance Cameras in Airdrie Town Centre*. Edinburgh: Central Research Unit, Scottish Office.

Skinns, D. (1998). *Doncaster CCTV Surveillance System: Second Annual Report of the Independent Evaluation*. Doncaster: Faculty of Business and Professional Studies, Doncaster College.

Sternhell, R. (1977). *The Limits of Lighting: The New Orleans Experiment in Crime Reduction: Final Impact Evaluation Report*. New Orleans, LA: Mayor's Criminal Justice Coordinating Council.

Tien, J.M., O'Donnell, V.F., Barnett, A. & Mirchandani, P.B. (1979). *Street Lighting Projects: National Evaluation Program. Phase 1 Report*. Washington DC: National Institute of Law Enforcement and Criminal Justice, US Department of Justice.

Tilley, N. (1993). Understanding car parks, crime and CCTV: Evaluation lessons from safer cities. *Crime Prevention Unit Series Paper 42*. London: Home Office.

Webb, B. & Laycock, G. (1992). Reducing crime on the London Underground: An evaluation of three pilot projects. *Crime Prevention Unit Paper 30*. London: Home Office.

Welsh, B.C. & Farrington, D.P. (1999). Value for money? A review of the costs and benefits of situational crime prevention. *British Journal of Criminology*, **39**, 345–68.

Welsh, B.C. & Farrington, D.P. (2000). Monetary costs and benefits of crime prevention programs. In M. Tonry (ed.), *Crime and Justice: A Review of Research* (Vol. 27). Chicago: University of Chicago Press.

Welsh, B.C. & Farrington, D.P. (2002). Crime prevention effects of closed circuit television: A systematic review. *Home Office Research Study 252*. London: Home Office.

Welsh, B.C. & Farrington, D.P. (2003). Effects of closed-circuit television on crime. *Annals of the American Academy of Political and Social Science*, **587**, 110–35.

Wilson, D.B. (2001). Meta-analytic methods for criminology. *Annals of the American Academy of Political and Social Science*, **578**, 71–89.

Wright, R., Heilweil, M., Pelletier, P., & Dickinson, K. (1974). *The Impact of Street Lighting on Crime*. Ann Arbor, MI: University of Michigan.

CHAPTER 7

Situational Burglary and Housing Interventions

TREVOR BENNETT

INTRODUCTION

This chapter reviews research on the effectiveness of situational crime-prevention initiatives in reducing burglary and other crimes against residences and businesses. The first section considers the research and policy context of the studies, the second discusses the methods and findings of the research included in the *UK review*, the third section updates the *UK review* by including additional studies and results, and the fourth section concludes with a discussion on the lessons learned for research and policy.

Theory Context

The programmes evaluated in this section are based mainly on the methods and principles associated with situational crime prevention. Situational crime prevention is based on the assumption that crime is caused by opportunities for crime and can be prevented by reducing these opportunities. This is typically done by increasing the effort and risks and reducing the rewards. Increasing the effort might be achieved by 'target hardening', such as the use of locks, safes or screens, or by making access to an area more difficult by fencing and road gates. Increasing risks might be achieved by entry or exit screening, which makes entry to an area more obvious, or by increasing surveillance, which increases the actual or perceived risks of detection. Reducing the rewards might be achieved by

Reducing Crime: The Effectiveness of Criminal Justice Interventions.
Edited by A. E. Perry, C. McDougall and D. P. Farrington. © 2006 John Wiley & Sons, Ltd.

removing potential targets such as prepayment gas and electricity coin meters from dwellings, or by making the item less attractive, for example, by property marking.

Situational crime prevention is also based on the assumption that offenders think more or less rationally and make decisions about offending. This idea was developed by Clarke (1980) who argued that crime could be conceived as the outcome of choices made by potential offenders in response to immediate situational opportunities. However, rational choice need not be viewed as a mathematical calculation. Instead, it can be conceived as a limited process in which both instrumental and non-instrumental factors (such as emotions) are taken into account (Clarke, 1992). Cornish (1993) broadened the concept of rationality by likening offender decision-making to following a 'script'. Offenders may carry with them a number of potential scripts of possible actions, and what actually happens in a particular situation depends on which of these scripts the offender chooses to follow and whether or not it is modified or abandoned during action. One of the aims of situational crime prevention is to influence the decision-making process to reduce the likelihood of a criminal outcome.

Research Context

A number of publications have summarised the results of evaluations of situational crime-prevention programmes. In 1987, Poyner conducted a large evaluation of 122 crime-prevention projects spanning situational, community and criminality prevention programmes (Poyner, 1993). Studies were selected if they were published in English, were accessible at the time of the review, and included results on outcome effectiveness. The selected studies were reviewed and grouped into six categories of crime prevention: 'campaigns and publicity', 'policing and other surveillance', 'environmental design or improvement', 'social and community services', 'security services' and 'target removal or modification'. Each study was given a numerical score depending on whether there was good evidence of a positive effect, some evidence of an effect, no evidence of an effect, or whether the evidence showed that crime actually increased. The highest score given was for target removal or modification programmes, and the lowest for social and community services interventions. Another review of evaluations of situational crime-prevention programmes was conducted by Graham and Bennett (1995). The research aimed to select a broad range of the initiatives currently being used. The review concluded that the results of the research were mixed. There were a number of studies that showed that situational crime prevention was effective in reducing crime and a number that generated negative or inconclusive results. Evaluations of access control, bus conductors, supervisors, receptionists, target removal and physical barriers were generally positive in their results. However, evaluations of steering-column locks, security campaigns, security surveys, preventative police patrol, CCTV, street lighting and property marking were generally negative or inconclusive.

Policy Context

The main policy context for the *UK review* is the government's Crime Reduction Programme (CRP) and, in particular, the Reducing Burglary Initiative (RBI). The CRP was launched in April 1999 and ran for three years. A combined total of £403 million was allocated to the programme, with the aim of obtaining evidence on the most effective means of tackling crime (Home Office, 2004). The main focus of the initiative was on crimes that were of most public concern, with a special emphasis on burglary, vehicle crime and anti-social behaviour. The RBI formed part of this programme and ran from 1999 to 2002. It aimed to reduce burglary nationally by targeting areas with higher-than-average burglary rates. In total, £25 million was invested in projects in areas with high burglary rates and a further £2 million in projects aimed at distraction burglary (for example, bogus callers). The project was divided into three rounds: in round one, 63 strategic development projects were funded; in round two, 161 projects were funded; and in round three, a further 23 projects were funded. An important principle of the programme was that all projects should be evaluated. The RBI schemes were to be evaluated at the individual level by the project teams as part of the monitoring process. The schemes were also to be evaluated at the aggregate level by three consortia of universities based at South Bank, Keele and Liverpool. Each consortia was commissioned to evaluate 21 projects.

It is relevant to note that in the discussion on the policy context of the CRP, there has been some recent debate about the overall effectiveness and value of the programme. In a recent paper by Maguire (2004), the author notes that the programme was initially intended to run for 10 years. However, it was instead brought to a premature end in 2002 as a result of practical problems associated with its implementation and evaluation. Maguire notes that few projects were implemented as planned, and that there was little conclusive evidence on whether any of the projects were effective. This was in part due to what he describes as an unrealistic timescale, slow-moving bureaucratic procedures and a shortage of capacity. There was also low commitment to project integrity and insufficient understanding among policy makers of the requirements of evaluative research. Maguire concludes that, while some useful outcomes can be claimed, the results of the CRP as a whole were unquestionably disappointing. It is beyond the remit of the current paper to engage in the politics of this debate. However, the results of the three main aggregate-level evaluations of the

RBI will be discussed in the update section and lessons for policy will be discussed in the conclusion.

DISCUSSION

This section looks at the results of two groups of evaluations on the effectiveness of situational crime-prevention interventions: burglary-reduction studies and housing studies. It includes eight studies on burglary-reduction interventions that evaluated six separate projects, and two studies on housing initiatives that evaluated two separate projects. The following overview has been divided into these two main sections. In addition, the section on burglary-reduction studies has been divided into five subsections ('Neighbourhood Watch', 'Repeat Burglary Prevention', 'Property Marking', 'Multiple Measures' and 'Small Business Initiatives'), and the section on housing studies has been divided into two subsections (the 'Secure By Design Project' and the 'Priority Estates Project').

Burglary-Reduction Studies

Neighbourhood Watch

One study looked at the effect of neighbourhood watch schemes on crime. See Table 9.18 in Chapter 9 for more details on the *What Works* classification system.

Barton (2000)
The study by Barton (2000) investigated neighbourhood watch in two areas in South Wales and Southwest England.

Description and methods
• *Research design.* The evaluation was based on a pre- to post design without controls. The selection of schemes was not discussed in the paper, apart from stating that the two schemes chosen for the research stood out from the other schemes in terms of their longevity and apparent success. The only information given on the selection of respondents was that the neighbourhood watch co-ordinators were identified through the police force of each area.
• *Research location.* The location of the neighbourhood watch schemes was somewhere within the broader study area of South Wales and Southwest England. Group A was described as a small hamlet just outside the main town, and Group B as a cul-de-sac. Both groups were located in an area of mainly terraced houses built at the turn of the century and included both owner-occupied and privately rented accommodation.

- *Programme description.* The main programme elements are not described in the paper. The only information given about the schemes is that Group A was the larger scheme based on more than 60 dwellings, and Group B was the smaller scheme based on 26 dwellings. It was also noted that both schemes had been running for longer than the other schemes in the area.
- *Data-collection methods.* The main data collection methods were personal interviews and self-completed questionnaire surveys of neighbourhood watch co-ordinators. The crime data were based on police-recorded crime.

Findings

A comparison of police crime statistics for burglary and car crimes in both areas indicated that over the two-year period covered by the study (1996 to 1998) both areas showed a decrease in crime. In 1996, Group A had an average of 5.8 burglaries per month, compared with 6.2 per month in Group B. In 1998, both rates were lower at 3.4 and 3.5 burglaries a month respectively. Results were also presented for vehicle crime (theft of, and theft from, vehicles). In 1996, Group A car crimes averaged 6.1 car crimes per month compared with Group B, which averaged 5.7 per month. In 1998, these rates fell to an average of 4.1 and 3.8 respectively. No further information is provided on the effect of the scheme on rates of crime.

Conclusion

The author concluded that the two groups were successful for a number of reasons. First, both had dynamic and upbeat co-ordinators who were younger than average. Second, both groups had a high concentration of established family units. Third, both groups had taken steps to implement their own crime-prevention measures.

Comment

The Barton (2000) publication was primarily concerned with describing the schemes and discussing the views of the neighbourhood watch co-ordinators. The results relating to crime reduction were presented in the conclusion to the paper mainly to demonstrate that the two schemes were fairly similar with respect to crime and changes in crime. As a result, the study included very little information on the methods used for selecting areas and little on the experimental design. There were no control groups and no attempts were made to guard against threats to internal validity.

Repeat-Burglary Prevention

Two studies looked at the effect of burglary-reduction strategies on repeat-burglary victimisation (Forrester, Frenz, O'Connor & Pease, 1990; Pease,

1992). Both were based on the Kirkholt burglary-reduction project. This study was widely publicised at the time, and there are a number of publications that provide information on it. The following overview summarises the main publication cited by Forrester et al. (1990), which gives the fullest account of the research and refers to the publication by Pease (1992) and other authors as appropriate. See Table 9.18 in Chapter 9 for more details on the *What Works* classification system.

Forrester et al. (1990) and Pease (1992)
The Kirkholt burglary-prevention programme began in 1987 and was implemented as a demonstration project for three years until 1990. The programme and its evaluation were divided into two phases. Phase one began in 1987 and ran for about one year. Phase two began in 1988 and ran until the end of the project.

Description and methods
• *Research design*. The evaluation design was not discussed in any detail by Forrester et al. (1990). However, it can be deduced from the results section that the main design was a pre- to post comparison repeated for each year of the project (one pre-measure and three post-measures). The study did not use a matched comparison area as part of the analysis, though other local areas were mentioned in other parts of the report, and some information was provided on the changes in crime in these areas over time. In terms of the results section, the main comparison was with the remainder of the police subdivision. The principal reasons given for the selection of the Kirkholt area were that it had a reputation for high crime and had well-defined boundaries that facilitated the evaluation (Forrester, Chatterton & Pease, 1988).
• *Research location*. Kirkholt is described as located two miles south of Rochdale town centre. It is a local-authority estate comprising 2,280 dwellings, bounded by four major roads. According to the authors, the rate of recorded residential burglary on the estate initially was more than double the national rate at the time.
• *Programme description*. The main programme elements of the first phase of the project were: (1) removal of prepayment fuel meters; (2) improved household security; (3) a community support team and (4) a cocoon neighbourhood watch. Cocoon neighbourhood watch is described as a scheme 'where close groupings of dwellings share information and support each other' (Forrester et al., 1988, p. 17). The main programme elements of the second phase of the project, which were added to the first phase elements, were: (5) probation group work programme; (6) a credit union; and (7) a project for schools.
• *Data-collection methods*. The data-collection methods included: (1) interviews with burglars; (2) interviews with burglary victims and their

neighbours; (3) informal contacts with key agencies and people; (4) police-recorded crime; and (5) a questionnaire for home watch participants. The interview schedule for victims included questions relating to the burglary, details about the victim and details of the victim's dwelling. Information from police crime reports included data on recorded burglaries for the period prior to the first phase of the project and for each year up to the end of the evaluation in 1990.

Findings
The results of the first phase of the Kirkholt project showed that burglary in the area fell to 40 per cent of its pre-initiative level within five months of the start of the programme. In the first report, the authors also note that burglaries on Kirkholt fell from 316 in 1986 to 147 in 1987 (comparing January to September each year; Forrester et al., 1988). We are also told that repeat victimisations fell to zero over the same period, and did not exceed two in any month thereafter.

The results of the second phase are presented in terms of average burglaries per year over the period of the evaluation. The results show that the annual number of residential burglaries fell from the pre-year to the first post-year by 38 per cent in the first year, 67 per cent by the end of the second year, and 72 per cent by the end of the third year (based on police-recorded data). The number of burglaries for the pre-year and the three subsequent years were 512, 317, 170 and 145. Hence, the study showed a regular year-on-year decline from the beginning of the project. The remainder of the police subdivision showed an increase in residential burglaries from the pre-year to the first post-year. However, residential burglaries then declined in the subdivision by 19 per cent in the next year and by 24 per cent in the year after that. Thus, the trend in burglaries was similar in both the experimental area and in the comparison areas, the main difference being the amount of reduction and the fact that the reduction occurred earlier in the Kirkholt area than in the subdivision as a whole.

The results relating to repeat victimisation are not presented in such detail. We are told that in 1986 (the base year), 34 per cent of victims who had lived at their current address for one year or less had been victimised more than once at that address. This percentage fell over each of the next two years. However, in the last year, repeat victimisation returned to almost the original figure at 33 per cent. No information is provided on changes in repeat victimisation in the rest of the subdivision.

Conclusion
The authors conclude that the Kirkholt burglary-prevention project resulted in a substantial reduction in burglaries over the three years of the project.

Comment
The Kirkholt burglary-prevention project was widely publicised at the time and is perhaps one of the best-known evaluations in the UK of a crime-prevention programme. There are a number of reasons for this, including the level of support the project received both from the Home Office and interest generated by the innovative nature of some of the programme elements implemented. It was also widely acclaimed as a result of its evaluation design and the methods used. However, the evaluation and the research design do have some weaknesses. The inclusion of the 'remainder of the subdivision' as a comparison area is not ideal as a result of lack of equivalence between the experimental and comparison areas. The presentation of results might also have been more extensive. Considering that the reduction in repeat victimisation was the principal research strategy, it is surprising that so little information was provided in the final report on changes in repeat-victimisation rates over time.

Property Marking

Laycock's (1991) study looked at the effect of property marking on crime. See Table 9.18 in Chapter 9 for more details on the *What Works* classification system.

Laycock (1991)
The 1991 publication by Laycock summarises the results of an evaluation originally published in Laycock (1985). The following discussion will include information from both publications. The property-marking scheme was launched in November 1983 in three areas in South Wales. The evaluation period lasted for one year and ran until the end of 1984.

Description and methods
• *Research design*. At the area level, the study was based on a pre- to post design with no comparison areas. At the individual level, the study was a pre- to post design with controls. In this case, the effect of the programme was determined for both participants and non-participants in the scheme. The method of selecting the area for the programme was based on a number of practical considerations. The author noted that the Home Office was interested at the time in launching a 'demonstration project' on property marking somewhere in the UK. It was also looking for an area in which the conditions for the scheme were optimal and where there was a good chance of success.
• *Research location*. The area chosen was part of the Caerphilly subdivision of the South Wales Constabulary. Three villages were selected in the areas with the highest concentrations of burglaries. Trethomas is a mixed area of detached, owner-occupied accommodation together with

an area of older housing, either local authority owned or owner-occupied. There were approximately 800 dwellings in the area. Graig-y-Rhacca is a local authority housing estate arranged as maisonettes or terraced houses comprising about 700 homes. Machen is an area of largely privately owned accommodation, also containing about 700 houses.

*   *Programme description.* Three methods were employed to achieve a reduction in burglary: (1) publicity at the launch; (2) door-to-door visits by the police or special constables; and (3) free property-marking equipment and door or window stickers. In addition, the chief constable sent a letter to all residents informing them of the launch. The launch included a press conference attended by the chief constable, Home Office officials and local television.

*   *Data-collection methods.* The main data used in the evaluation were police-recorded crime statistics. In addition, the police completed questionnaires at the time of each home visit. The first questionnaire was completed at the launch and recorded the name and age of all respondents. The second questionnaire was completed after one week, following the initial visit among those participating in the scheme, and recorded which goods were marked and whether a property-marking label had been displayed. The third questionnaire was completed approximately six months after the initial launch and recorded which houses were still displaying the property-marking window sticker.

Findings
In the 12-month period before the launch of the programme, 128 burglaries were reported to the police. In the 12-month period after the launch, 74 burglaries were reported (a reduction of 40 per cent). In the 1991 publication, Laycock also notes that the number of burglaries in the second 12-month period after the launch reduced even further, to 66. A comparison was also made of change in burglary among participants in the scheme and those not participating in the scheme. The results showed a reduction among participants from 91 in the year before the launch of the programme to 35 in the year following the launch. This compares with an increase among non-participants from 37 in the period before the launch to 39 in the period following the launch.

Conclusion
The author concludes that there were a number of positive results from the study (Laycock, 1991). First, the take-up rate of the programme was very high. This was explained by the advance publicity given to the programme, the use of home visits by the police, and the provision of free marking equipment. Second, the reduction in burglary in the first year was greater than expected. Third, the continuing reduction in burglary in the second

year was also higher than expected, which was explained in part by the continuing publicity given to this programme and the evaluation.

Comment
The research design is based on a pre- to post design with controls. However, this applies only at the individual level, as there were no controls at the area level. One problem with this design is that participants and non-participants are self-selecting and there may be differences between the two. In other words, there is a problem of non-equivalence between the experimental and control groups. It is possible that participants might be either more or less at risk of burglary than non-participants. The number of dwellings covered by the study was small and the number of burglaries committed even smaller. One problem of evaluations based on small areas is that the number of crimes committed will be small and may fluctuate widely year upon year. The final problem is that it is difficult to understand the mechanisms involved by which displaying a property-marking sticker in a window leads to a reduction in burglary. The author acknowledges this when she says that '... it was far from clear that the process underlying that reduction was as simplistic as marking property' (Laycock, 1991, p. 71). The finding that property marking works also sits uneasily with the results of other evaluations of property-marking schemes and the research findings on the decision-making of burglars.

Multiple Measures

This section has been called 'multiple measures' because the programmes discussed include a number of different kinds of crime-prevention interventions. It includes two publications covering a single evaluation of the Safer Cities CRP. See Table 9.18 in Chapter 9 for more details on the *What Works* classification system.

Ekblom et al. (1996) and Ekblom (1996)
Phase one of the Safer Cities CRP was funded and managed by the Home Office, and ran from 1988 to 1995. Some of the funds were allocated to evaluating the effectiveness of the programme as a whole.

Description and methods
• *Research design.* The programme covered 20 cities or (in the case of London) boroughs. At the time of the evaluation, 3,600 crime-reduction schemes had been started, 500 of which aimed to reduce residential burglary. From these 500 schemes, 300 were selected to be included in the evaluation covering 16 of the 20 cities or boroughs. They were selected on the grounds that they were fully implemented or completed at the time of the research. The evaluation comprised a pre- to post design with

comparison areas. Household surveys were conducted in 11 of the 16 areas in a period before the burglary-prevention action had started (late 1990) and again during a period after the action had been in place for some time (late 1992). Additional information was recorded on respondent characteristics, to be used as a statistical control for differences in equivalence of the samples obtained in the experimental and comparison areas.

- *Research location.* The 11 Safer City areas selected were: Birmingham, Bristol, Coventry, Hull, Rochdale, Salford, Sunderland, Middlesbrough and the London Boroughs of Lewisham, Tower Hamlets and Wandsworth. The eight comparison areas were: Manchester, North Tyneside, Wigan, Oldham, Leeds, Hackney, Southwark and Haringey.

- *Programme description.* The programmes evaluated covered a range of crime-prevention measures including target-hardening (for example, door and window improvements, entry systems, alarms and security lighting), community-oriented approaches (such as neighbourhood watch and property marking), and 'other activities' (for example, the distribution of leaflets and household surveys). Some projects focused on the city as a whole, while others focused on vulnerable groups or particular locations. Three-quarters of the projects were based on domestic target-hardening.

- *Data-collection methods.* The main methods of data collection were sample surveys of adult householders, and police-recorded crime figures. The surveys involved interviewing over 7,500 householders in 406 enumeration districts. Half of the interviews were conducted in September 1990, before the Safer Cities action had begun, and half in September 1992, after most of the projects had been implemented. The surveys covered crime victimisation, fear of crime, perceptions of crime and security-related behaviour. The police-recorded crime data were collected in 14 of the 16 Safer Cities covering 701 police beats. The data were collected for the entire period of the Safer Cities programme from 1987 (the year before the programme started) to 1992 (the final year of the programme). The data-collection methods were supplemented with geographic analysis using a geographic information system (GIS) and various qualitative methods including open-ended interviews with co-ordinators.

Findings

In all areas in which some action was taken, the prevalence of burglary reduced. The reductions were greater in the areas of higher-intensity action than in areas of lower-intensity action. The low-intensity areas experienced a reduction in burglary of 10 per cent, the medium-intensity areas showed a reduction of 22 per cent, and the high-intensity areas a reduction of 43 per cent. In the Safer City areas in which no action was taken, the proportion of households burgled once or more increased from 8.9 per cent to 10.2 per cent (a 15 per cent increase). In the comparison areas, burglary increased from 12 per cent to 12.4 per cent (a 3 per cent increase) from the before survey (1990) to the after survey (1992). However, police-recorded burglary data showed that burglary was reducing across all locations up to about 1990 in line with national trends. From 1990 onwards, burglary rates began to rise across all areas with the exception of the high-activity areas in which burglary continued to decline.

Conclusion
The study concludes that there was good evidence that Safer Cities schemes reduced the risk of burglary in the areas they covered. It also concludes that the more intense the burglary action, the greater the additional drop in risk. However, reducing burglaries in a scheme area sometimes led to burglaries being displaced to adjacent areas.

Comment
The evaluation design was strong in that a pre- to post design was used with comparison areas. The research also attempted to control for differences in respondents across surveys using multivariate techniques. The study was also fully documented in the main publication of the research, and most of the information needed to evaluate the research was available. The main problem lies in the interpretation of the results. The author concedes that the research was not set up to investigate causal mechanisms. However, it is difficult to know why the presence and intensity of a diverse range of actions might affect the decision making of local burglars. While the problem of identifying causality is a common problem with quasi-experimental designs, it can be ameliorated to some extent by including supplementary methods to monitor mediating and moderating factors. It is also possible to identify and reduce threats to internal validity.

Small Business Initiatives

Two studies examined the effectiveness of situational crime-prevention measures in reducing crimes against small businesses (Bowers, 2001; Tilley and Hopkins, 1998). See Table 9.18 in Chapter 9 for more details on the *What Works* classification system.

Bowers (2001)
The study by Bowers (2001) was an evaluation of an initiative aimed at reducing small business crime in Merseyside. The initiative was part of the Small Business Strategy (SBS) operated by the Safer Merseyside Partnership. The strategy aimed to reduce repeat burglaries against businesses in deprived neighbourhoods with fewer than 25 employees.

Description and methods
- *Research design.* The evaluation design was based on pre- and post surveys of the small businesses investigated. These were complemented with an analysis of police-recorded crime over the same periods. No control areas were used for the surveys. However, some comparisons were made between the scheme areas and other non-residential areas using police-recorded crime data. The businesses were selected in two stages. The first stage was based on stratified sampling, in which a total of 1,000 businesses were selected to receive a visit by an interviewer who assessed the crime risk of the property. The second stage was based on selecting those businesses that were scored as a high- or medium-risk on the survey. The businesses were asked whether they would like to be visited by a crime prevention officer (CPO). Of the 1,000 businesses visited, 470 surveys were completed and 140 businesses were visited by a CPO.
- *Research location.* The research was based on what were described as the most deprived neighbourhoods of Merseyside. The businesses were all located in residential areas and included some small corner-shops.
- *Programme description.* The programme comprised those initiatives recommended by the CPOs and taken up by the small businesses. The measures typically included situational measures such as burglar alarms, CCTV systems, roller shutters, window locks and detection devices, as well as advice on managing affairs and what was described as 'thoughtful' routine activities such as keeping limited amounts of money in the tills, being careful with keys and not disclosing information to strangers.
- *Data-collection methods.* The surveys of individual businesses were based on personal interviews. The area-level analysis was based on police-recorded crime. The surveys focused mainly on victimisation, but also included information on fear of crime and levels of satisfaction with the police.

Findings
A comparison of the victimisation rate at the baseline survey and at the follow-up survey showed that for all crime types investigated, with the exception of robbery, the number of businesses experiencing crime was lower in the evaluation period than in the baseline period. The reductions were largest for burglary, attempted burglary, shoplifting, fraud and forgery. The reductions were also more marked among those involved in the scheme. The reduction in the prevalence of burglary for the intervention group was 58.9 per cent compared with a reduction of 7.9 per cent among the non-intervention group. The evaluation also found that there was a reduction in repeat burglaries among businesses in the area (54.3 per cent in the baseline survey and 33.3 per cent in the evaluation survey). When the analysis was repeated for the intervention group and

non-intervention group, it was found that there had been a substantial reduction in repeat burglaries among the former, but no change among the
latter. The police-recorded data for Merseyside as a whole showed that
commercial burglaries generally decreased in both deprived residential
areas and in other areas during the course of the evaluation.

Conclusion
The paper concluded that levels of burglary had been significantly reduced
in the properties that were involved in the SBS intervention. The number
of burglary victims who experienced repeat victimisation was also substantially reduced in the intervention group.

Comment
The reduction of burglary against businesses in other areas not covered
by the scheme was explained by the author as a possible product of other
initiatives taking place or changes in reporting rates among businesses
owners. However, the reduction might also mean that commercial burglary
was declining anyway, and that the changes in the scheme areas were a
product of this general change. This highlights the problem of pre- to post
research designs without proper controls. It is hard to determine the effect
of extraneous factors on the outcome measure and it is difficult to know
what would have happened in the absence of the programme.

Tilley and Hopkins (1998)
The Small Business and Crime Initiative (SBCI) was a three-year demonstration project funded by the NatWest Bank Charitable Trust. The aim
of the initiative was to reduce crimes against small businesses.

Description and methods
• *Research design*. The evaluation design was a pre- to post design without controls, based on victimisation surveys. Police-recorded crime data
  were also collected covering the period of the evaluation for both the
  scheme area and other comparison areas. Within-group comparisons
  were also made based on the type of intervention received. Surveys were
  conducted of small businesses in the area before the implementation of
  the initiatives and again two years later. At the outset, 1,381 businesses
  were identified in the two scheme areas: 680 in one and 701 in the other.
• *Research location*. Two target areas in Leicester were selected for the
  initiative. The first, Belgrave, to the north of the city centre, comprised
  predominantly an Asian community and a major shopping area. The
  second, the West End, to the southwest of the city centre, was culturally
  and ethnically mixed. Both areas included a transient student population as well as longer-term local residents.

- *Programme description.* Measures were to be introduced among businesses thought to be at high risk of victimisation. These measures included temporary silent alarms with direct lines to the police, covert CCTV, forensic traps designed to obtain footwear marks, and a hidden movement detector that triggered an audible alarm.
- *Data-collection methods.* The main data-collection methods were victimisation surveys and police-recorded crime. The surveys mostly covered victimisation, but also included questions on losses incurred and fear of crime. The authors note that the police data might not be reliable as it did not distinguish commercial burglary from other non-dwelling burglary.

Findings
The findings from the survey analysis showed that both the incidence and prevalence of most crime categories investigated fell from the first to the second surveys. The incidence of burglary fell by 41 per cent and the prevalence by 36 per cent. The findings also show that repeat-burglary victimisation fell over the same period by 6 per cent. The findings from the police-recorded crime data analysis for the areas covered by the scheme also show an overall reduction of non-domestic burglary. Comparing the change in the project areas with the remainder of the division shows that in the case of the West End, the reduction in the scheme area was identical to the rest of the division (40 per cent in each case). In Belgrave, the reduction was greater in the scheme area than in the rest of the division (42 per cent compared with 18 per cent). Data for the county and the rest of England and Wales showed a general decline in non-domestic burglary, although not as great as in the scheme areas.

Conclusion
The authors concluded that crime affecting businesses decreased substantially in the target areas during the course of the SBCI. However, the evidence does not suggest that the work of the initiative played a significant part in causing this reduction.

Comment
The study suffers from the usual problem of quasi-experimental designs in that it is difficult to determine what might have happened in the target areas in the absence of the scheme. In other words, it is difficult to know whether the outcomes were caused by the interventions or by some other factors. The inclusion of police-recorded crime data for the general areas helped to some extent in determining more general trends. This data tended to show that burglaries might have fallen anyway. However, as the authors noted, the police data measured non-domestic burglary

rather than commercial burglary. Hence, it is not wholly clear whether the reductions were due to the programme or extraneous factors.

Housing Studies

The Secure By Design Project

One of the selected studies evaluated the Secure By Design (SBD) project (Armitage, 2000). See Table 9.20 (Chapter 9) for more details on the *What Works* classification system.

Armitage, 2000
The study by Armitage (2000) is an evaluation of the Secure By Design scheme implemented in West Yorkshire. The main element of the scheme was to encourage housing developers to design-out crime.

Description and methods
- *Research design*. This briefing note (four pages long) provides little information on the research design or the methods used. However, some information can be deduced from the results section. It is not stated how the SBD estates and non-SBD comparison estates were selected. However, it is likely that the newbuild estates were selected by purposive sampling from among those estates recently built. We are told that the non-SBD estates were selected by matched pair sampling. It is perhaps understandable that no information could be given on the pre-test conditions of the estates as they were newbuilds. Hence, the main research design appears to be a post-only design with matched controls. The trend analysis comprised multiple post-comparisons of experimental and control conditions. The main analysis is based on 25 SBD and 25 matched non-SBD estates comprising 660 and 522 dwellings respectively.
- *Research location*. The estates were all based in West Yorkshire and matched according to location, age, housing tenure and environmental risk factors.
- *Programme description*. The SBD scheme is based on a number of key characteristics built into dwelling design, including minimum standard of physical security, maximum natural surveillance, informal social control through a mix of dwellings, a minimum number of access points, and good management and maintenance policies.
- *Data-collection methods*. The main data used in the evaluation were police-recorded crimes.

Findings
The first part of the analysis comprises a comparison of crime rates of scheme and non-scheme estates at a point in time in the post period. We

are told that the prevalence rate for burglary offences was twice as high within the non-SBD sample as in the SBD sample, and that this difference was statistically significant. The incidence rate of burglary was also higher among the non-SBD estates than the SBD estates (0.42 compared with 0.24 per household). However, this difference was non-significant. The second part of the analysis involved comparing the difference in burglary rates of the SBD and non-SBD estates over successive post years. Specifically, this was a comparison of the burglary rates of SBD estates built over the period 1994 to 1998 expressed as a percentage of the burglary rates of their non-SBD matched pair for each year. In 1994, SBD estates had slightly higher burglary rates than their matched pairs. By 1998, SBD estates had less than half the burglary rates of the non-SBD estates.

Conclusion

The author concluded that the incidence of recorded crime was considerably lower among SBD housing estates than among the non-SBD counterparts. The paper also noted that it was unknown which specific factors contributed to the lower rates of burglary of SBD homes, and suggested that this might be a matter for further study.

Comment

It is unfortunate that the study was published as a briefing note rather than as a full Home Office study. As a result, little attention has been given to describing the research methods used. The use of a post-only design is generally regarded as weak, as it is unknown whether there were pre-existing differences between the experimental and comparison areas. Understandably, it is difficult to determine this when the evaluation is of newly built estates. However, it might have been possible to identify pre-existing differences in the general areas in which the homes were developed.

The Priority Estates Project

One of the studies included in the *UK review* evaluated the Priority Estates Project (Foster & Hope, 1993). See Table 9.20 in Chapter 9 for more details on the *What Works* classification system.

Foster & Hope, 1993

The Priority Estates Project is based on collaboration between local authorities and tenants and was implemented in some of the most difficult and run-down estates. Its aim was to improve the delivery of local housing services and management and to involve tenants in the day-to-day running of the estates.

Description and methods
* *Research design.* The authors describe the evaluation as a quasi-experimental research design in combination with detailed qualitative research. The research was based on a pre- to post design with matched control areas. The experimental areas were two new Priority Estate Project estates and the control areas were two paired comparison estates. The effect of the programme was determined by multivariate analysis in which the relative percentage change in outcome measures in the experimental area was compared with the relative percentage change in the outcome measures in the matched control areas.
* *Research location.* One experimental estate was located in the London Borough of Tower Hamlets and comprised two large blocks, a block of flats, a small number of three-storey houses and various other houses and flats. The other experimental estate was located in Hull and comprised part of a larger council housing development on the outskirts of the city. Half of the properties were houses and the remainder were four high-rise blocks of flats, three medium-rise blocks and a small number of three-storey town houses.
* *Programme description.* The programme elements were tailored to the particular area. In the case of the Hull project, the programme comprised environmental design modifications, changes in the method of managing the services on the estate, increased tenant-involvement in decision making, and a revised policy on tenant allocation to the estate.
* *Data-collection methods.* The main method of data collection was victimisation surveys conducted among residents on the estates. This information was supplemented with police-recorded crime statistics. In addition, the research included an independent qualitative study of the area.

Findings
In relation to the London estate, the results showed that the prevalence of burglary in the experimental area decreased over the period of the evaluation from 7.6 per cent to 2.1 per cent. In comparison, the prevalence of burglary in the control area decreased from 8.3 per cent to 2.7 per cent. The reductions were similar in both areas and as a result the relative percentage-change estimate was found not to be statistically significant. In relation to the Hull estate, the prevalence of burglary in the experimental area reduced from 10.3 per cent to 9.6 per cent. In comparison, the prevalence of burglary in the control area increased substantially from 6.1 per cent to 15.4 per cent. The relative percentage-change estimate in this case was found to be statistically significant. However, this result was brought about largely by an increase in burglary in the control area. The prevalence of burglary in the experimental area was virtually unchanged. The study also found that most of the reduction on the Hull estate occurred

in the small area of improved housing. The prevalence of burglary in the unimproved areas remained virtually constant, and the burglary rate in the tower blocks increased substantially.

Conclusion
The authors concluded that the crime-reduction effects of the programme were limited, occurring only in particular areas of the estate and among particular groups of residents. They also concluded that they were unable to give a precise answer to the question of whether the programme worked as a method of reducing crime. However, they expressed doubts about whether the Priority Estates Programme could be regarded as a method of crime prevention, bearing in mind that it provides no resources and focused mainly on giving advice.

Comment
This is perhaps one of the strongest evaluation designs in that it comprises the main elements of a quasi-experimental design and includes with it a detailed qualitative investigation of the potential causal mechanisms at work. This combined approach is generally recommended as a good method of dealing with threats to internal validity generated by quasi-experimental designs.

UPDATE

The main *UK review* includes UK evaluations published during the period 1990 to June 2002 and deemed to be eligible on grounds of methodological adequacy. The aim of this section is to update the review by looking at four categories of studies not included in the original:

(1) Studies published between 1990 and June 2002 and not eligible for inclusion.
(2) Studies published between 1990 and June 2002 and eligible for inclusion (that is, studies missed).
(3) Studies published from July 2000 to August 2004 and not eligible for inclusion.
(4) Studies published from July 2000 to August 2004 and eligible for inclusion.

Studies relevant to the first category were selected from those listed in the original report (Perry et al., 2003). Studies relevant to the second category were identified from studies known to the author. Studies relevant to the third and fourth categories were selected by systematically searching relevant databases such as ISI (BIDS), Criminal Justice Abstracts, PsycInfo,

PubMed, C2-SPECTR, NCJRS and the Home Office (RDS). The search terms were limited for simplicity and time to 'burglary', 'neighbourhood watch', and 'housing + crime'. The initial 'hits' were assessed and copies of the publications or the full abstracts were obtained for those that appeared relevant. These were then assessed as suitable for reporting in this update in either the third or fourth categories.

The search results across all databases were:

- 455 hits (231 for 'burglary', 23 for 'neighbourhood watch' and 201 for 'housing + crime')
- 11 studies selected (9 for 'burglary', 0 for 'neighbourhood watch', 2 for 'housing + crime')
- 7 of the selected studies were found not eligible on the grounds of methods (5 for 'burglary', 0 for 'neighbourhood watch', 2 for 'housing + crime'), and
- 4 of the selected studies were found to be eligible on the grounds of methods (4 for 'burglary', 0 for 'neighbourhood watch', 0 for 'housing + crime').

Studies Published Between 1990 and June 2002 and Not Eligible for Inclusion

These studies were not included in the original *UK review*. However, they were listed in the appendix of the report as relevant studies excluded on the grounds of methodological adequacy. They include:

Burglary-Reduction Studies

- Bennett and Durie (1999) conducted an evaluation of cocoon neighbourhood watch schemes operating in Cambridge as part of a larger burglary-reduction programme. The project found that there was a small reduction in burglary in the target area compared with a large reduction in the surrounding area.
- Knight (1994) investigated target-hardening methods for reducing burglaries and vandalism in Glasgow. The research showed a reduction in both burglary and vandalism.
- Chatterton and Frenz (1994) investigated the role of CCTV in reducing residential burglary. They found that the number of offences reduced in the 10-month follow-up period.
- Nation and Arnott (1991) looked at the effects of a burglary-offender victim mediation scheme in reducing offending. The study found that the vast majority of offenders did not reoffend in terms of burglary offences over the study period.

Housing Studies

- Davidson and Farr (1994) evaluated the effect of an estate-based management initiative on crime in the local area. The research showed an overall reduction in crime rate on the experimental site.
- Poyner (1994) summarised a study that evaluated the effect of the demolition of walkways between blocks of flats on a public-housing estate. The results showed that recorded crimes increased following the demolition.

Studies Published Between 1990 and June 2002 and Eligible for Inclusion

This section includes studies that were eligible but missed in the original review.

Burglary-Reduction Studies

Bennett (1990) conducted an evaluation of two neighbourhood watch schemes in London. The evaluation was based on a quasi-experimental design using pre- to post measures in scheme areas and comparison areas. Data were collected from interview surveys of residents and from police records. The results showed that household victimisation increased in the scheme areas and decreased in the comparison area. Residential burglary increased in one of the scheme areas and stayed more or less constant in the other scheme area. In comparison, residential burglary in the control area decreased during the evaluation. See Table 9.19 in Chapter 9 for more details on the *What Works* classification system.

Housing Studies

There were no additional housing studies.

Studies Published From July 2002 to August 2004 and Not Eligible for Inclusion

There have been some studies published since 2002 that would have been excluded from the *UK review* on the grounds of research designs. These include:

Burglary-Reduction Studies

Mawby (2004) evaluated a combined Help the Aged and Home Safe scheme for elderly residents in Plymouth. The research design was pre- to post only, with no controls, based on a postal survey of residents involved in the scheme. The study found that, in the four-year period preceding the scheme, burglary rates among the respondents ranged from 7 to 20 a year. In comparison, in the period since the security improvements were made, only three burglaries were reported.

Housing Studies

There were no additional housing studies.

Studies Published From July 2000 to August 2004 and Eligible for Inclusion

A number of studies published since 2002 would have been deemed eligible for inclusion in the *UK review*. See Table 9.19 in Chapter 9 for more details on the *What Works* classification system.

Burglary-Reduction Studies

- Bowers, Shane, Johnson and Hirschfield (2004) conducted an evaluation of 21 projects included in the Home Office Reducing Burglary Initiative. The evaluation aimed to determine whether there was an association between the intensity of the programme and changes in burglary rates before and after the schemes were implemented. The study was based on pre- and post measures of burglary rates that were compared for different levels of intensity of the schemes. The outcomes for the scheme areas were compared with the same outcomes measures for the police force area as a whole. It was found that output intensity (the amount of crime prevention implemented), but not input intensity (the amount of money spent of schemes), was significantly correlated with burglary reduction across the 21 projects.
- Hirschfield (2004) summarised the results of the evaluations of the 21 projects described above in Bowers et al. (2004), which comprised the northern consortium projects evaluated as part of the Home Office Reducing Burglary Initiative. The evaluation method was similar to that described above. Pre- and post-burglary rates were calculated for the two-year periods before and after the scheme implementation and then compared with changes in burglary rates in the police force areas covered by the schemes. The evaluation found that the change in the 21 scheme areas was 12 per cent lower than expected from changes in the police force areas (the difference was statistically significant).
- Millie and Hough (2004) conducted a similar evaluation of the 21 projects reviewed by the Southern consortium of the Reducing Burglary Initiative. There was sufficient data available to conduct pre- and post comparisons of 16 of the projects. Changes in the scheme areas were compared

against changes in the police basic command unit areas as a whole. The analysis showed that the change in burglary rates in the scheme areas reduced by a greater proportion than in the comparison areas. The study concluded that, on average, the schemes resulted in a reduction of 55 burglaries per area.

• Hope et al. (2004) provided similar results for the Midlands consortium on the Reducing Burglary Initiative. As with the other consortia, they were commissioned to investigate 21 projects. The evaluation design was similar to that used by the other consortia and was based on comparing expected and actual rates of burglary with changes in the basic command unit areas as a whole. The results showed that about one-third of the projects evaluated showed significantly greater reductions in burglary than would have been predicted by changes in the local burglary rates.

Housing Studies

There were no additional housing studies eligible for inclusion.

CONCLUSIONS

The chapter has shown that results of the reviewed studies were generally positive. The implementation of situational crime-prevention measures tended to be associated with reductions in crime. However, as a result of general weaknesses in the research designs, it was often impossible to determine whether these reductions were caused by the measures evaluated.

Summary of Findings

In relation to neighbourhood watch, the study by Barton (2000) showed a small reduction in burglary, but no information was given on burglary trends in other areas, and hence it is unknown whether burglaries would have dropped anyway. The additional study by Bennett (1990) listed in the update section concluded that there was no reduction in burglary that could be attributed to the programmes. The evaluation of schemes designed to reduce repeat victimisation showed some reductions in single and repeat burglaries in the scheme areas (Forrester et al., 1990; Pease, 1992). However, only limited information was provided on trends in single and repeat burglaries in similar areas. Research on property marking included just one study (Laycock, 1991). The evaluation showed that reductions in burglary were greater among scheme participants than non-participants. However, it was unknown whether there were pre-existing differences between participants and non-participants in burglary risk. No information was provided on comparison areas. The evaluation of the effect of multiple measures implemented as part of the Safer Cities CRP showed that there was a reduction in burglary in all areas, but this reduction was greatest in areas with high levels of activity (Ekblom, 1996; Ekblom et al., 1996). However, it was unknown whether the action caused the reduction. Research on schemes directed at small businesses also showed some positive results. The evaluation by Bowers (2001) showed a reduction in burglary among businesses that took action to improve their security. However, non-dwelling burglaries decreased in the scheme areas anyway. Tilley and Hopkins (1998) also showed a reduction in burglaries among businesses involved in the scheme. In one of the areas investigated, the reduction was the same as the prevailing trend, while in the other the reduction was greater than the prevailing trend. The authors doubted whether the initiative caused the reductions.

Similarly unclear results were obtained in the housing studies. The first of the two studies showed that crime was lower in the project areas than in comparison areas (Armitage, 2000). However, it was based on a post-only design and it is unknown whether the scheme and non-scheme areas were equivalent at outset. The second study (Foster & Hope, 1993) found that changes in burglary were similar in the scheme area and non-scheme area in the first comparison, but greater in the scheme area than the non-scheme area in the second comparison. However, the positive effect was produced mainly by a substantial increase in crime in the control area.

The results of evaluative research on situational crime prevention are clearly unsatisfying. While there is some indication that situational crime prevention might be effective in reducing burglary, the research methods are often insufficiently strong to generate conclusive findings. The most important problem in terms of research design is determining whether actual crime rates were better or worse than expected.

Implications for Research

The first conclusion that can be drawn for research is that there are relatively few good-quality UK evaluations of programmes designed to reduce residential burglary. It is important that there is a substantial body of rigorous evaluations to enable systematic reviews of the evidence. The second conclusion concerns research design. The most common evaluation design is a pre- to post design with no controls (or no effective controls). This is unfortunate as the absence of controls means that it is unknown whether any changes were caused by extraneous factors. Without a comparison, it is not possible to determine whether the experimental group performed better or worse than might have been expected in the absence of the intervention. The third conclusion concerns the problem of potential non-equivalence of experimental and comparison groups. It is accepted that it is impossible to find completely identical areas; nevertheless, some attempt should be made to select comparable areas. This could be done by random allocation. However, when random allocation is not possible, then some other method should be used to ensure equivalence. Using the rest of the division or rest of the force as a comparison is not wholly adequate as the areas might be different. Similarly, non-participants might not be equivalent to participants as they are likely to be different in terms of pre-existing crime risks.

The fourth conclusion is concerned with the problem of causal mechanisms. This is a problem for both experimental and quasi-experimental designs. The research often concludes that despite favourable results, it cannot be determined conclusively whether the changes were a result of the intervention. In part, this is a problem of research design, but it is also a problem of lack of information on likely causal mechanisms. It is usually considered good practice to include in the research, design methods for determining the effects of mediating and moderating factors that might influence causal processes. Additional information on potential intermediary causal mechanisms might also help indicate the effect of the intervention.

The fifth point is the problem of disaggregation of findings by subgroups. In many of the studies reviewed, the major findings relate to the sample as a whole. While demographic factors are sometimes included in regression analysis, many studies do not break down the findings by subgroups in a way that would demonstrate a differential programme effect. It would be useful to know whether the programme affected only certain kinds of individual or certain kinds of property. It would also be useful to disaggregate the findings by type of programme. It is possible that some versions of a programme are more effective than others.

The final problem is research co-ordination. Apart from a few major Home Office initiatives, research on the effectiveness of burglary-reduction programmes is largely uncoordinated, with different research teams exploring different outcomes, among differing populations, over different time periods, using different methods. Drawing conclusions from such a variable body of studies is difficult. There might be some gains in adopting greater consistency across research studies in terms of research methods that might facilitate systematic reviews. One way of doing this is to encourage a research culture similar to that of the scientific community, which works to agreed standards of research design. While this has been tried in the past, the agreed standards have not necessarily been high enough. There may be something to be gained in specifying more rigorous guidelines for evaluative research. The development of systematic reviews and the presence of overseeing bodies such as the Campbell Collaboration might help in this respect.

Implications for Policy

In the discussion on the UK government's Crime Reduction Programme at the beginning of the chapter, it was noted that there was some concern about the quality of research projects implemented and the quality of the research that was set up to evaluate them. One of the underlying problems was seen as the desire for quick results. This meant that projects and their evaluations were often rushed. These comments were directed mainly at the recent government CRP, but can also be applied to the wider policy context. Policy makers might learn from recent experiences and try to better balance the need for urgent action against the need for effective action.

Another finding relevant to policy is that a number of the evaluations have indicated that the more intense the activity, the greater the crime-reduction effects. It is possible that both the quantity and quality of the programme might be important in determining outcomes. If so, this would suggest that some benefits may be made in promoting good-quality versions of these programmes. It is also possible that the type of programme implemented might be significant. This might apply not only to the broad project types (such as whether to implement neighbourhood watch or target hardening), but also to the different kinds of projects (for example, whether to implement one type of neighbourhood watch scheme or another). A similar argument can be applied to the potential victim. It has been frequently argued that some programmes might be more suitable for some offenders than others. This same argument could be applied to burglary-prevention programmes and their suitability for different areas; some programmes might be more effective in some areas and against some victims rather than others. This suggests that those responsible for national and local crime-prevention policy might encourage better matching of projects to targets. In order for policy to proceed along this route, it is important that evaluation research does the same, which would mean not only that studies improve their research designs, but also that they pay more attention to disaggregating their results by programme and target characteristics.

REFERENCES

Armitage, R. (2000). An evaluation of secure by design housing within West Yorkshire. *Home Office Briefing Note 7/00*. London: Home Office.

Barton, A. (2000). A tale of two projects: The growth and development of two neighbourhood watch schemes in South Wales. *Crime Prevention and Community Safety: An International Journal*, 2(3), 7–16.

Bennett, T.H. (1990). *Evaluating Neighbourhood Watch*. Aldershot: Gower.

Bennett, J. & Durie, L. (1999). Preventing residential burglary in Cambridge: From crime audits to targeted strategies. *Crime Detection and Prevention Series Paper 182*. (Police Research Group). London: Home Office.

Bowers, K.J. (2001). Small business crime: The evaluation of a crime prevention initiative. *Crime Prevention and Community Safety: An International Journal*, **7**, 23–42.

Bowers, K.J., Shane, D., Johnson, S.D. & Hirschfield, A.F.G. (2004). The measurement of crime prevention intensity and its impact on levels of crime. *British Journal of Criminology*, **44**(3), 419–40.

Chatterton, M.R. & Frenz, S.J. (1994). Closed circuit television: Its role in reducing burglaries and the fear of crime in sheltered accommodation for the elderly. *Security Journal*, **5**(3), 133–39.

Clarke, R.V.G. (1980). Situational crime prevention: Theory and practice. *British Journal of Criminology*, **20**, 136–47.

Clarke, R.V.G. (ed.) (1992). *Situational Crime Prevention: Successful Case Studies*. New York: Harrow and Heston.

Cornish, D. (1993). Crime as scripts. In D. Dolling & T. Feltes (eds), *Comparative Aspects of Community-Oriented Police Work*. Holzkirchen: Felix-Verlag.

Davidson, J. & Farr, J. (1994). Mitchell Hill estate: Estate-based management (concierge) initiative. In S. Osborn (ed.), *Housing Safe Communities: An Evaluation of Recent Initiatives*. London: Safe Neighbourhoods Unit.

Ekblom, P. (1996). Safer cities and residential burglary: A summary of evaluation results. *European Journal on Criminal Policy and Research*, **4**, 22–52.

Ekblom, P., Law, H. & Sutton, M. (1996). Safer cities and domestic burglary. *Home Office Research Study 164*. London: Home Office.

Forrester, D., Chatterton, M. & Pease, K. (1988). The Kirkholt Burglary Prevention Project, Rochdale. *Crime Prevention Unit Paper 13*. London: Home Office.

Forrester, D., Frenz, S., O'Connor, M. & Pease, K. (1990). The Kirkholt Burglary Prevention Project: Phase II. *Crime Prevention Unit Paper 23*. London: Home Office.

Foster, J. & Hope, T. (1993). Housing, community and crime: The impact of the Priority Estates Project. *Home Office Research Study 131*. London: Home Office.

Graham, J. & Bennett, T.H. (1995). *Crime Prevention Strategies in Europe and North America*. Helsinki, Finland: HEUNI.

Hirschfield, A. (2004). The impact of the Reducing Burglary Initiative. *Home Office Online Report 40/04*. London: Home Office.

Home Office (2004). *The Reducing Burglary Initiative*. London: Home Office. www.crimereduction.gov.uk/bri.htm. Accessed September 2004.

Hope, T., Bryan, J., Crawley, E., Crawley, P., Russell, N. & Trickett, A. (2004). Strategic Development Projects in the Yorkshire and the Humber, East Midlands and Eastern regions. *Home Office Online Report 41/04*. London: Home Office.

Knight, B. (1994). Fossil park estate security scheme. In S. Osborn (ed.), *Housing Safe Communities: An Evaluation of Recent Initiatives*. London: Safe Neighbourhoods Unit.

Laycock, G. (1985). Property marking: A deterrent to domestic burglary? *Crime Prevention Unit Paper 3*. London: Home Office.

Laycock, G. (1991). Operation identification or the power of publicity? *Security Journal*, **2**(2), 67–72.

Maguire, M. (2004). The Crime Reduction Programme in England and Wales: reflections on the vision and the reality. *Criminal Justice* **4**(3), 213–37.

Mawby, R. (2004). Reducing burglary and fear among older people: An evaluation of a Help the Aged and Homesafe Initiative in Plymouth. *Social Policy and Administration*, **38**(1), 1–20.

Millie, A. & Hough, M. (2004). Assessing the impact of the Reducing Burglary Initiative in southern England and Wales. *Home Office Online Report 42/04*. London: Home Office.

Nation, D. & Arnott, J. (1991). House burglars and victims. *Probation Journal*, **38**(2), 63–7.

Pease, K. (1992). Situational crime prevention: Preventing burglary on a British public housing estate. In R.V.G. Clarke (ed.), *Successful Case Studies*. New York: Harrow & Heston.

Perry, A., McDougall, C., Swaray, R., Murphy, T., Harris, R. & Bjornsson, H. (2003). *The Effectiveness of Criminal Justice Interventions in Reduction of Crime: A Review of the Literature*. (Report to Home Office). York: University of York.

Poyner, B. (1993). What works in crime prevention: An overview of evaluations. In R.V.G. Clarke (ed.), *Crime Prevention* Studies. (Vol. 1). New York: Criminal Justice Press.

Poyner, B. (1994). Lessons from Lisson Green: An evaluation of walkway demolition on a British housing estate. In R.V.G. Clarke (ed.), *Crime Prevention Studies* (Vol. 3). Monsey, NY: Criminal Justice Press.

Tilley, N. & Hopkins, M. (1998). Business as usual: An evaluation of the Small Business and Crime initiative. *Policy Research Series Paper 95*. London: Home Office.

CHAPTER 8

Economic Methodology and Evaluations: The Costs and Benefits of Criminal Justice Interventions

RAYMOND SWARAY[1]

INTRODUCTION

Public resources to prevent crimes and increase public safety are in limited supply and, even in wealthy countries, compete with the allocation of resources to other areas such as education and health. Therefore, choices must be made as to how the limited resources (that is, people, facilities, equipment and knowledge) are to be allocated among competing

[1] Author's note: A significant part of this chapter is reproduced from the following article: Swaray, R., Bowles R. & Pradiptyo, R. (2005). The application of economic analysis to criminal justice interventions: A review of the literature. *Criminal Justice Policy Review* (in press). Reproduced by permission of Sage Publications, Inc.

A large proportion of this work was undertaken when I was employed as a research fellow at the Centre for Criminal Justice Economics and Psychology, University of York. I would like to thank my former colleagues there for contributing in many ways to the success of the project. In particular, I would like to thank Cynthia McDougall, Roger Bowles, Rimawan Pradiptyo, Amanda Perry, Mark Cohen, Matt McGovern, Rochelle Harris, Hedinn Bjornsson, Judith Jackson and Zoe Cooke for their assistance in conducting this piece of research. I would also like to thank the Home Office for financial support to the Centre for Criminal Justice Economics and Psychology. The views expressed in this document are those of the author. The Home Office, University of York and the University of Hull do not take any responsibility for the contents.

Reducing Crime: The Effectiveness of Criminal Justice Interventions.
Edited by A. E. Perry, C. McDougall and D. P. Farrington. © 2006 John Wiley & Sons, Ltd.

uses. Decision makers are therefore repeatedly faced with the option of meticulously scrutinising crime-reduction programmes and earmarking resources on the basis of *What Works*, and at *What Cost* (see McGuire, 2001; McGuire & Priestley, 1995).

Economic analysis brings a consistent and logical approach to choosing the best possible deployments of public resources in criminal justice. HM Treasury recently published a blueprint for appraisal and evaluation of public-sector projects on the basis of value for money (HM Treasury, 2003).

Cost–benefit evaluations have become increasingly popular in government departments. Nevertheless, there are notable disparities in the quality of economic analysis available to policy makers in the criminal justice field. DiIulio (1996) points to the varying backgrounds of scholars and practitioners who have come to dominate the criminal justice field as the main cause of the shortcomings. According to DiIulio, most of these scholar-practitioners have neither the 'quantitative' nor 'formal modelling' skills required to add new ideas to the debates, nor the ability to provide 'analytically compelling answers to methodologically complicated questions' on crime and public policy. He solicits 'help' from economists to tackle the field of crime. Although economists have not given crime and criminal justice the same levels of attention they have given to healthcare and health policy over the last two decades, they have not totally neglected crime and public policy. The literature on crime has benefited immensely from a myriad of extensions to Becker's (1968) seminal model. These include work on gangs and illicit drugs markets (Akerlof & Yellen, 1994) and Levitt's (1997) work on electoral cycles and policing budget allocation.

This chapter will examine the application of cost–benefit analysis to criminal justice interventions. The first section presents the findings from the *UK review* conducted by Perry et al. (2003) on the effectiveness of criminal justice interventions in the UK. The review found a paucity of studies that comprehensively measured the costs, cost-effectiveness (Armitage, 2000; Bottoms, 1995; Dodgson et al., 2001; Ekblom, 1996; Ekblom, Law & Sutton, 1996; Miers, Maguire, Goldie, Sharpe & Hale, 2001; Oldfield, 1997) and cost–benefit (Farrington et al., 2002; Painter & Farrington, 1997, 1999a, 1999b, 1999c, 2001a, 2001b) of criminal justice interventions.

The second section of the chapter develops the *UK review*, looking at the international literature and presenting a synthesis of studies that contain rigorous examination of the costs and benefits (that is, monetised outcomes) of criminal justice interventions, and identifying the methodological problems and gaps that still remain in the literature. The chapter also draws on examples of published studies to highlight what is known about cost and benefit evaluation of criminal justice interventions. See Tables 9.1 to 9.20 in Chapter 9 for more details on the *What Works* classification system.

ECONOMIC METHODOLOGY OF CRIMINAL
JUSTICE INTERVENTIONS

Recent advances in modelling crime and criminal justice policies have not displaced traditional methods of cost–benefit analysis (CBA) and cost-effectiveness analysis (CEA) from the prime spot of policy analysis. CEA and CBA hold the key to simplicity, user-friendliness and non-technical ways of applying complex tools of economic analysis to policies in the criminal justice field.

In light of the evidence, criminal justice policy-makers and practitioners are increasingly relying on common staples in the economist's tool-kit to assess the efficiency and effectiveness of policy interventions, making choices between alternative uses of resources, or alternative ways of distributing resources among competing users.

The UK Home Office has produced guidelines to help evaluators assess the costs and benefits of the Crime Reduction Programme (CRP) (Dhiri & Brand, 1999). The Treasury's 'Green Book' provides guidelines on appraising and evaluating public-sector projects (HM Treasury, 2003), and literature on the National Institute of Justice website provides a parallel source for the US.

Methodologically, practical CBA and CEA use similar procedures to identify the scope of the problem and to measure the effects of an intervention. However, CBA progresses to further stages of monetising a stream of programme costs and outcomes, and subjects the estimates to a sensitivity analysis; that is, CBA examines the totality of all costs and benefits of a given intervention. Barnett and Escobar (1987) describe CEA as an 'incomplete' version of CBA. The lack of an attempt to monetise programme effects and the focus on programme costs (resources) makes CEA seem like an incomplete CBA exercise. Thus, cost-effectiveness evaluations neglect some important ingredients of a full economic analysis that are relevant to understanding the total impact of a criminal justice intervention.

On the contrary, a cost–benefit evaluation monetises and compares all costs and outcomes of policy interventions. In fact, a full cost–benefit evaluation should go a stage further to address the question of time preference for money, by discounting a programme's costs and benefits. Welsh and Farrington (2000a) enumerate six steps that are akin to a full economic analysis: (1) defining the scope of analysis (problem); (2) obtaining estimates of programme effects (outcomes); (3) estimating the monetary value of programme costs and benefits; (4) calculating the present value of costs and benefits and assessing profitability; (5) description of the distribution of programme costs and benefits (that is, involving the assessment of those who gain and those who fail under the programme; for example, programme participants, crime victims, government/taxpayers); and, finally, (5) conducting a sensitivity analysis for understanding changes in underlying assumptions. A full cost–benefit analysis will follow all the six steps listed above, while cost-effectiveness evaluations usually omit steps (3) and (6).

In addition to embracing the six steps outlined above, the authenticity of cost–benefit and cost-effectiveness evaluations are equally determined by the quality of the study design. Welsh and Farrington (2000a) noted that the economic analysis of programmes in criminal justice and related fields can be viewed as an extension of 'outcome evaluation, and is only as defensible as the evaluation on which it is based' (p. 310). Moreover, Cohen (2000) stressed that when improperly used, cost-effectiveness and cost–benefit analyses in crime and justice programmes 'become nothing but rhetorical ammunition in an ideological debate' (p. 266). Therefore, it is vital that the programmes under evaluation have a clearly defined experimental design. Weimer and Friedman (1979) recommended the use of 'experimental or strong quasi-experimental design' for correctional intervention programmes (p. 264). And Farrington (1983) further suggests a randomised experimental design as the 'gold standard' for evaluation of crime-prevention programmes.

The Sherman et al. (1997) and Sherman, Farrington, Welsh and MacKenzie (2002) Scientific Methods Scale has frequently been used to assess the validity of research designs in criminal justice (see Welsh & Farrington, 2000b). The scale lists five scores that help researchers to assess the methodological quality of studies in criminal justice and related fields. The Sherman et al. (1997, 2002) scoring system ranks study designs in ascending order of quality standard. It assigns a score of one to interventions with the lowest methodological quality standard (studies based on correlational evidence), and a score of five to a randomised experimental design, depicting a gold standard (see Chapter 2 for further details on the scale).

A thorough assessment of the costs and benefits (outcomes) of a criminal justice intervention will provide an invaluable input into the process of making choices between alternative uses of resources or alternative distributions of services (Knapp, 1997). It will also enable decision makers to identify feasible alternatives in the decision-making processes. Like most forms of economic analysis, the concept of efficiency is vital to cost–benefit evaluation of criminal justice interventions. A common way to measure efficiency is to aggregate all the 'gains and losses from a programme in such a way that the net gain from the programme can be compared to that of an alternative' (Barnett & Escobar 1987, p. 389). Analysts can then proceed to use the aggregation technique to rank programmes on the basis of economic efficiency.

To achieve logical aggregate values of costs and benefits, analysts often convert programme cost and benefits into monetary values. However, it is sometimes difficult, or logically impossible, to translate some intangible elements of costs and benefits into equivalent monetary units. For example, the intangible costs of pain and suffering for a victim of crime are problematic to quantify, thus the strength and policy relevance of a cost–benefit evaluation is largely dependent on the extent to which it logically and consistently monetises intangible costs and benefits of interventions.

McDougall, Cohen, Swaray and Perry (2003) developed a cost–benefit validity scale that can help policy makers and researchers to understand the depth of cost–benefit information in studies on sentencing interventions. Emphasis was placed on the extent of monetisation of (tangible and intangible) costs and (tangible and intangible) benefits of sentencing options, quality of cost–benefit analysis, and the validity of the benefit–cost ratio.

The present *UK review* focuses on the methodological quality and comprehensiveness of cost–benefit studies on criminal justice intervention, and presents the findings using the Drummond 11-point economic checklist (Drummond, O'Brien, Stoddart & Torrance, 1997) followed by the wider international cost–benefit literature.

ECONOMIC ANALYSIS OF CRIMINAL JUSTICE INTERVENTIONS: THE CURRENT *UK REVIEW*

UK Cost- and Cost-Effectiveness Studies

The following section focuses on the economic findings from the current *UK review* (for which the methodology is outlined in Chapter 2). Seven studies contained some cost- and cost-effectiveness information, but did not contain comprehensive CBA, as described below. The studies include Armitage (2000), Bottoms (1995), Dodgson et al. (2001), Ekblom (1996), Ekblom et al. (1996), Miers et al. (2001) and Oldfield (1997). A more detailed description of these studies, including the *What Works* classification, is shown in Tables 9.1 to 9.20 in Chapter 9.

The studies by Ekblom (1996) and Ekblom et al. (1996), scoring 8 out of a possible 11 on the Drummond checklist in the *UK review*, discussed the overall and marginal costs associated with residential burglary prevention programmes using estimates and data from other studies. The authors estimated the overall cost and marginal costs of preventing burglary using estimates from recorded crime data and comparing these to equivalent cost estimates from the survey.

In neighbourhoods where risks are high (that is, 20 incidents per 100 households in a year), the estimated costs of the Safer Cities programme were about £360 (£200) overall, and slightly over £1,300 (£900) at the margin. The costs figures in brackets are estimates of equivalent costs from the survey in neighbourhoods with 'burglary and other action only'.

In areas with 10 recorded burglary incidents per 100 households in a year, the overall cost of a burglary was about £550 (£400), and a little over £2,000 (£1,500) at the margin. These figures go up to over £1,400 (£1,400) overall, and about £4,700 (£4,800) at the margin for areas where the risk of recorded burglary was 3 per 100 households. The estimates for both the overall and marginal cost of the Safer Cities burglary prevention programme generally show that less expenditure was required to prevent burglaries in areas where the incidence of recorded burglaries was high, compared to areas where it was rare. The methodology for these studies is discussed in Chapter 7.

The Armitage (2000) study scored 5 out of a possible 11 on the Drummond checklist in the *UK review*. It used post only, with matched controls design, to evaluate the crime-reducing impact of Secure By Design (SBD) housing in West Yorkshire, England. This SBD housing scheme aims to 'encourage housing developers to design out crime' in general, and burglary in particular, at the planning stage of the estate. The report puts the additional cost of constructing an SBD building at £1,250 per property for a three-bedroom property, but the average additional cost figure for West Yorkshire was £440. However, the cost of refurbishing estates to SBD standard was estimated at approximately £600 per dwelling. Overall, there were 26 per cent fewer crime events per dwelling in the intervention area. Within the control areas, the prevalence rates of burglary offences was twice as high before the intervention compared with after. The methodology for this study is discussed in Chapter 7.

Knapp and Fenyo, as part of a study by Bottoms (1995), scoring 8 out of a possible 11 on the Drummond checklist in the *UK review*, used a cohort sample to examine cost and cost-effectiveness of intermediate treatment orders compared to custody. They enumerated the average weekly costs of four main intermediate treatment (IT) programmes: Heavy End IT (HEIT), Other IT (OIT), custody and supervision orders. The primary outcome was reoffending. The report found no cost differences between custody and HEIT after standardising for individual characteristics. In addition, no significant cost difference was found between HEIT and OIT, but OIT was significantly more costly than supervision orders. The findings from the cost analysis showed that the cost of treatment varied according to the type of treatment and the individual characteristics of the participants. The report notes that average direct and indirect costs can be much higher for young offenders (YOs) with personal and social problems convicted of more serious crimes.

Dodgson et al. (2001) scored 7 out of 11 on the Drummond checklist in the *UK review*, and used a cohort design to examine the cost-effectiveness analysis of a Home Detention Curfew (HDC) scheme across England and Wales. The evaluation focused on financial costs and resource savings (benefits) of the HDC over a 12-month and a 16-month period of operation. The main components of cost examined were prison staff costs, probation service costs, contractor costs, and cost of the sentence enforcement unit. Prison places saved and long-term resource savings that would result from reduction in the prison population were treated as the main benefits of the scheme. The results of a cost–benefit analysis, excluding start-up costs, show that the scheme generated a net benefit of £36.7 million and £49.2 million after 12 and 16 months of operation respectively.

The Oldfield (1997) study scored 5 out of 11 on the Drummond checklist in the *UK review*. The study examined the impact of probation interventions on probationers' reconvictions, compared to custody reconvictions. The intervention sample consisted of all individuals who commenced probation orders in Kent in 1991. The cost comparison in this study of the probation intervention and the prison reconviction rate gives only partial information. The paper did not present detailed costs of probation reconvictions. It estimated the cost of prison as approximately £2,000 per month compared to £105 per month for probation, and noted that the 'more expensive, less successful option does not work' in terms of impact on reconvictions. The methodology of this study is discussed in Chapter 4 of this book.

The Miers et al. (2001) study scored 7 out of a possible 11 on the Drummond checklist in the *UK review*. The study calculated the cost per case using information on levels of input, unit costs and cost per outcome over a period of two years. In calculating the cost of achieving a unit of outcome, the researchers divided the cost per case by the number of prevented offences per case. Since information about individual cases was limited, researchers used expected costs based on the characteristics of the interventions. Direct and indirect costs of the schemes were linked to levels of staff activity. The results showed that one adult scheme was cost-effective. The methodology of this study is discussed in Chapter 5 of this book.

All the studies examined here used the gross-costing approach to estimate the costs of interventions (see Manning, 1999; Murray, Evans, Acharya & Baltuseen, 2000). The gross-cost technique involves estimates of aggregate costs of imprisonment, for example, rather than costing the individual elements such as incarceration, staffing and services performed during imprisonment (that is, micro costing). The main advantages of the gross-costing method are simplicity, practicability and robustness to variation. However, its principal disadvantage is that scant attention is paid to the smaller details that contribute to cost (Gold, Siegel, Russell & Weinstein, 1996).

UK Cost–Benefit Studies

From the current *UK review*, five studies contained a degree of CBA. The studies include Farrington et al. (2002) and Painter and Farrington (1997, 1999b, 2001a, 2001b).

The Farrington et al. (2002) study scored 8 out of 11 on the Drummond checklist in the *UK review*. It conducted a cost–benefit analysis of two intensive regimes for YOs, one in the north of England and the other in the south. The report examined the costs associated with the YO regime including: cost to society per offence and cost to society of reconvictions (programme cost, paid staff, travel and subsistence, crime cost, social cost). The authors used data from Brand and Price (2000) to estimate the total costs of juvenile crimes and reconvictions for the crimes.

A cost–benefit analysis of the High Intensity Training (HIT) reconvictions data showed that 'crime savings from the HIT regime recouped its extra costs' (p. 27). When undetected offences were taken into account, the benefit–cost ratio of the HIT was at least 5:1. A further cost–benefit analysis of the Military Corrective Training Centre (MCTC) programme using two-year reconviction data showed that, although YOs in the control group on average committed more crimes than those in the experimental group, the average cost to society of crimes committed by YOs in the experimental group was more than that committed by YOs in the control group. Cost–benefit findings from the MCTC reconviction data show that 'for each extra £1 invested, at least an additional 89 pence would have been lost' (p. 59). This result, however, did not take 'non-crime benefits' into account. The methodology for this study is discussed in Chapter 5.

The Painter and Farrington (1999b, 2001b) studies scored 8 and 6 respectively out of a possible 11 on the Drummond checklist in the *UK review*. They examined the benefits and costs of improved street lighting in Stoke-on-Trent and Dudley (Painter & Farrington, 1997, 2001a, 2001b).

The Stoke-on-Trent project focused on the costs of various crimes committed in the experimental, control and adjacent areas before and after the implementation of the project. The main annual costs incurred in the project included capital costs, maintenance costs, electrical energy costs, and the increased costs after improvement. The project's benefits were mainly in the form of cost savings from reduced loss of property and tangible losses. The benefit–cost ratio for the project was 1.3:1 after one year, or 12:1 after one year if capital cost repayment was spread over 20 years. The Dudley project showed that savings from reduced crimes exceeded the financial costs by between 2.2 and 9.4 times after one year. The methodology of this study is discussed in Chapter 6 of this book.

Summary from UK Literature

The findings from the *UK review* on the cost, cost-effectiveness and cost–benefits of criminal justice interventions show a great paucity in the amount of research that has been conducted in this area. Generally cost- and cost-effectiveness studies are easier to conduct, and require less rigorous study designs and calculations; they are therefore more apparent in the literature. For those few cost–benefit studies that have been conducted, the following methodological limitations are noted:

- The lack of discounting, or inappropriate treatment of depreciation.
- The lack of up-to-date information on monetary values of intangible costs and consequences of interventions examined.
- Inadequate or inappropriate choice of outcome measure.

Following our brief assessment of cost, cost-effectiveness and cost–benefits within criminal justice interventions, relating to the *UK review*, the next section will attempt to describe the findings from the international literature.

REVIEW OF THE ECONOMIC ANALYSIS FROM AN INTERNATIONAL REVIEW

The following section expands on the *UK review* to include rigorous cost–benefit studies from the international literature that focus on the reduction of criminal activity. The section will include information about how the review was conducted, its scope, methodology, search processes and findings.

Scope and Methodology

The international review examined both published and unpublished ('grey') literature containing cost–benefit analysis of criminal justice interventions. The criminal justice interventions examined include, but are not limited to, the following: crime-prevention programmes involving young offenders; situational crime-prevention methods such as CCTV; neighbourhood watch; policing methods; early release on parole; electronic monitoring (electronic surveillance); treatment programmes and correctional interventions (that is, imprisonment, probation, community sentences, fines, and so on).

The review screened two main sources of bibliographic information, including online databases and 'thumb referencing' relevant publications. The online search focused on the following sources: the National Criminal Justice Reference Service (NCJRS); Manchester Information & Associated Services (MIMAS); Educational Resources Information Clearinghouse; Psychological Abstracts (PsycINFO); World Wide Web (mainly Google); UK Universities Theses Index; EconLit; Bath Information and Data Services (BIDS); and the National Bureau of Economic Research (NBER).

Three simple criteria were used in the selection of studies for the review: first, studies must have been published after the year 1979; second, they should focus on at least one criminal justice intervention; and third, they should contain some form of economic and financial evaluation,

Table 8.1 Descriptive statistics of screening and review phases

Search records	No. or %
Total number of studies identified in searches of databases	9919
Number of studies selected at the1st screening phase	2105
Selection at 1st screening (as % of total records found)	21%
Discharge at 1st screening phase (as % of total records found)	79%
Number of records selected at the 2nd screening phase	748
Selection at 2nd screening (as % of records selected at 1st screening)	36%
Discharge at 2nd screening phase (as % of records at selected 1st screening)	64%
Number of studies reviewed	154
Reviewed (as age of records at 2nd screening)	20%
Discharge (as age of records selected at 2nd screening)	80%

Note: All figure percentages are rounded to the nearest 100.

specifically cost–benefit analysis. Bibliographic records from all searches, consisting of journal articles, evaluation reports, research and conference papers that were uncovered from the bibliographic sources listed above, were downloaded or entered into an electronic EndNote® database. The database contained a library of 9,919 records.

The EndNote® software search facility was used to screen records in the database. Table 8.1 presents descriptive statistics of the screening and review phases. The first screening phase used a combination of keywords and phrases (such as 'crime', 'corrections' and 'sentencing cost analysis') to identify bibliographic records pertaining to criminal justice interventions. It identified a bibliography of 2,105 records from the total 9,919 records in the database.

Many of the studies that were discarded after the first screening stage examined relevant criminal justice interventions, but failed to focus on economic and/or financial analysis, or were not produced after 1979. The second screening stage examined the 2,105 prescreened records from the first stage. This stage utilised keywords and phrases such as 'cost', 'cost effectiveness' and 'costs benefits') to whittle down the records to 748. The remaining 1,357 records that failed to make it through the second screening phase were not considered further.

Although the process of searching, screening and selecting bibliographic records was similar to a full-scale systematic review, the intention was neither to conduct a systematic review nor to perform a traditional-style literature review on the topic. The preliminary stages used appropriate keywords and phrases to run extensive search routines on the aforementioned databases, and followed the path of a systematic review because they utilised search routines that could be repeated by independent researchers for the purposes of verifying and/or updating the findings in this document.

A full-scale systematic review study was not attempted here for two reasons. First, the broad scope of the project, including the requirement to cover most proactive and reactive criminal justice interventions, made it difficult, if not impossible, to devise selection criteria that would be uniform, logical and consistent with the goals of the interventions. Farrington and Welsh (2002) highlighted the need for 'explicit eligibility criteria' in systematic review studies. Second, the Sherman et al. (1997, 2002) Scientific Method Scale and NHS CRD (2001) guidelines that are frequently used to guide social science researchers on study design and methodological rigour did not provide guidance on the quality of economic analysis in any detail.

An economic analysis rating scale that helps researchers to judge the quality of costs and benefits information in the literature was developed in McDougall et al. (2003). This study examines application of cost–benefit analysis to criminal justice interventions. A related study by Swaray, Bowles and Pradiptyo (2004) attempts to cover all common applications of economic analysis to criminal justice interventions. Therefore, this study could be viewed as a 'hybrid' between the more structured and rigorous methodology required in a systematic review study, and the less rigorous yet critical approach used in traditional literature reviews. Traditional literature reviews usually aim to provide an overview of research in a particular field, but are not commonly constrained by the need for consistent and unbiased collection of information. Unlike a systematic review, traditional literature reviews do not necessarily require two or more researchers to systematically 'summarise, appraise, and communicate the results and implications of otherwise unmanageable quantities of research' (NHS CRD, 2001).

The Search Process

The project began with a composition of keywords and phrases that were likely to identify relevant literature from the databases suggested above. To ensure a thorough search of the databases, the keywords and phrases were placed in three non-mutually exclusive, but by no means exhaustive, categories based on: (1) type of economic analysis, namely costs analysis, cost-effectiveness analysis and cost–benefit analysis; (2) types of criminal justice interventions; and (3) keywords and phrases to depict methodological rigorousness of an economic analysis.

The next stage involved the utilisation of keywords and phrases in (1) to (3). Due to differences in the type of bibliographic information held in the databases, and the level of coverage, the search routines were tailored to the requirements of the database. For example, specialised databases, like NCJRS and PsycINFO, primarily focus on information on criminal justice systems and psychological literature, while EconLit and NBER cover the broad subject area of economics and related fields. In addition, more versatile and diversified database services like MIMAS and BIDS have the capacity to hold multiple information including bibliographic references, electronic journals, scientific and socio-economic datasets.

The third, and final, stage of the search procedure involved compilation of an EndNote® database[2] of all the bibliographic information uncovered in the searches. The EndNote® bibliographic referencing software is equipped with many different types of import filters, some of which are compatible with MIMAS and PsycINFO, but incompatible with NCJRS, NBER and BIDS, and Internet-based search engines such as Google. Therefore, the process of entering bibliographic records into the EndNote® library from incompatible sources was carried out on a record-by-record basis. Once the EndNote® library was compiled, the bibliographic records were screened for the criteria relevant for the review.

The 748 bibliographic records that emerged from the two screening phases were obtained from the following sources: downloading from authors' and/or publishers' web pages on the Internet; photocopying the articles available in the University of York Library; retrieving articles held in the Centre for Criminal Justice Economics and Psychology Library; photocopying from the British Reference Library; and ordering copies of documents through the Inter-library Loans service operated by the University of York Library. Perhaps the exclusive focus on English language-based databases and bibliographic sources could be a potential bias in this study because relevant foreign-language publications that are not available in the English language are likely to be left out. However, the criteria used to assess studies uncovered in the search process can guide researchers on the suitability of studies published in other languages.

Findings from the International Literature

This section summarises the main findings of studies that were selected for rigorous applications of CBA to criminal justice interventions. Two studies were selected from 154 that were subsequently reviewed in the project, which constitutes 1.3 per cent of the number of papers reviewed, and 0.3 per cent of the studies that qualified after the second screening. Data from all 154 studies reviewed were entered in a specially designed Microsoft Access® database.

The above statistics clearly show the paucity of rigorous applications of CBA to interventions in criminal justice. While the two studies selected could not be classed as gold standard CBAs, they nevertheless distinguished themselves from other studies in so far as they rigorously applied CBA to the interventions that were studied, and clearly set themselves

---

[2]EndNote® is a bibliographic software tool developed by ISI ResearchSoft.

apart from the rest in attempting to monetise intangible costs and benefits of the interventions, and executing good-quality study designs.

Table 8.2 contains details of the two studies summarised under the following headings: (a) author(s) and publication date; (b) concepts and domains; (c) study design; (d) method(s) of cost calculation; and (e) method(s) of benefit valuation (outcomes). To avoid misinterpretation of the original study findings, we made little or no attempt to identify additional costs, outcomes and benefits of intervention(s) beyond those stated by the authors of the selected papers. Likewise, there were no attempts to, retrospectively, impute monetary values for costs and outcomes beyond those reported in the studies. In fact, the vast differences among the studies in terms of study settings, methodologies and study design made it very difficult, if not impossible, to use standard monetary metrics to make retrospective calculations meaningful.

Many studies left out of the selection were conceptually sound, but were judged to be less rigorous at utilising CBA for the purposes of this review. Some contained methodologically rigorous applications of other traditional methods of evaluation in criminal justice and social policy—specifically CEA. For example, some methodologies focused on cost analysis of methadone treatment interventions (Anglin, Speckart, Booth & Ryan, 1989; Deschenes, Anglin, and Speckart, 1991); community punishment (Knapp, Robertson & McIvor, 1992), and in-prison treatment of paedophiles (Shanahan & Donato, 2001). In addition, Griffith, Hiller, Knight and Simpson (1999) contains detailed cost-effectiveness evaluation of therapeutic communities in the prison environment.

Unlike costs analysis and CEA, CBA places more emphasis on monetisation of all costs and outcomes (benefits) of the intervention. This is mainly because expressing costs and benefits in monetary terms can enable analysts to directly compare the programme's incremental costs with its incremental benefits in the same unit of measurement, and facilitates a calculation of cost–benefit ratios. The two studies selected for rigorous applications of CBA to criminal justice interventions were: Hakim, Rengert and Shachmurove (1996) and Prentky and Burgess (1990). In theory, this can be achieved by comparing the discounted future streams of a programme's incremental benefits with its incremental costs; and differences between the benefit and cost streams are viewed as a net social benefit of the intervention (Drummond et al., 1997, p. 203). In practice, however, none of the two studies thoroughly discounted incremental costs and incremental benefits. Summaries of the methods used to calculate costs and value benefits are presented in Table 8.2.

The first study, by Hakim et al. (1996), used survey data on house owners in the Tredyffrin Township, Pennsylvania, US to estimate the social costs and social benefits associated with ownership of residential electronic security devices. The cost of police response to false alarm activations,

Table 8.2 Cost–benefit analysis of criminal justice interventions

Author(s), Year	Concepts and Domains	Study Design	Method(s) of Cost Calculation	Method (s) of Benefit Valuation
Hakim, Rengert & Shachmurove (1996)	Burglary, residential electronic security	Cohort study	The social cost of residential alarm was calculated as the sum of installation cost, monthly service costs and the costs of response to false activations. The costs of responding to false activations were the product of: the hourly cost of a police officer; number of officers who responded to alarm activation, and average response time. The cost per hour of an officer = police budget yearly ÷ (number of officers number of days' service number of hours' service per day). The annual cost to all alarm owners = (installation cost of one unit × number of alarms owners × capital recovery rate).	The value of violent crimes avoided as a result of burglar alarms was estimated as the 'difference between the probability of residential break-ins without and with an alarm, multiplied by the number of homes with alarms'. This figure was then multiplied by the average cost of crime estimated by Cohen (1988) and the change in the Consumer Price Index was used to update the estimates from 1988 to 1990.
Prentky & Burgess (1990)	Rehabilitation	Cohort study	Cost estimates were obtained from the programme studied as well as other programmes. Costs were generally approximated from secondary data. Social costs figures were based on hypothetical estimations.	Programme benefits were calculated by comparing recidivism rates for treated and untreated offenders.

and the costs of crimes (that is, burglary, assault and rape) that may be prevented were the main components of costs included. The paper discusses conditions under which public resources can be allocated to private alarm owners and suggests ways of internalising external costs that alarm owners impose on their communities, and on the society at large.

Secondly, Prentky and Burgess (1990) conducted a cost–benefit analysis of a rehabilitation programme for child molesters. The cost–benefit comparison was made between groups of subjects who underwent rehabilitation treatments and a group that did not undergo treatment. It shows that the recidivism rate of the treated group (that is, 25 per cent) is lower than that of the untreated group. The cost of treatment was substantially higher in this study, but given the expected cost of reoffending, this study shows that rehabilitative treatment produces higher net benefits than the no-treatment option. The basic analysis assumed that the subjects committed one reoffence, and the sensitivity analysis in the paper was based on the assumption that subjects committed multiple reoffences and had multiple victims. A notable drawback of the method is that it was not possible to quantify psychological costs in the analysis.

It should be noted that the selection of the two studies does not necessarily mean that they met the gold standard of research design, or that they offered a detailed and exhaustive quantification of the intangible costs and benefits associated with interventions examined.

Summary of the International Literature

Worldwide cost–benefit analysis is limited in its technique and methodology, with only two studies being identified. A larger number of cost and cost-effectiveness studies were identified, partly because these types of studies are easier to conduct than a full cost–benefit analysis. However, the limitations of such studies are apparent when trying to assess the relative benefits associated with the cost of an intervention.

CONCLUSIONS

This chapter has presented findings from the *UK review* and international literature focusing on the cost, cost-effectiveness and cost–benefit analysis of criminal justice interventions. The *UK review* results show a paucity of methodologically rigorous study design and cost–benefit evaluation. Only one of the studies selected was based on a quasi-experimental design that is generally superior to 'controlled observational' study designs often used to evaluate the effectiveness of criminal justice interventions. In addition, the quality ratings using the Drummond checklist ranged from a score of 5 to 8 out of a possible 11. These shortcomings are similar to those of the international literature reviewed. This trend generally indicates a serious lack of experimentally rigorous evaluation of criminal justice policies. In addition, although the quality of CBA in the two selected papers is clearly better than the rest, they nevertheless left specific gaps that need to be addressed in future research. Both studies generally stop short of discounting interventions costs and benefits, and appropriately accounting for overhead costs in the analysis.

IMPLICATIONS FOR POLICY AND PRACTICE

From a policy perspective, CBA is potentially a useful tool at various stages in what might be termed the 'project lifecycle'. In other fields of public-sector decision making, such as the transport sector, it is often used as a method for supporting project appraisal ex ante. In the criminal justice sphere, as our review of studies suggests, it is more often used as a method of developing an ex post evaluation of an intervention. From an economics perspective, the danger of using it as an ex post tool is that criminal justice interventions often have a rather complex structure, with multiple objectives and poorly articulated outcome measures.

An even greater danger is that much of the 'evaluation' work on criminal justice interventions is commissioned shortly after a project has begun. However, this does not present a problem if the analysis is well-informed and the analyst recognises that a distinction needs to be made between costs and benefits incurred prior to an 'intermediate evaluation' and those not yet experienced at the time of investigation. Such a distinction plays a central role in guidelines on how to conduct evaluations (for example, Dhiri & Brand, 1999), but is much less in evidence in the scores of evaluations conducted by non-economists: for further discussion, see Bowles, Harris and Pradiptyo (2003) and Bowles and Pradiptyo (2003).

A comprehensive review of studies on criminal justice interventions has revealed that policy-relevant findings are generally based on less rigorous economic analysis and methodology. This occurs during a decade when decision makers are looking for *What Works* at *What Cost* in many areas of criminal justice policy, and at a time when some commonly transferable methods of economic analysis—such as cost analysis, CEA and CBA—have been rigorously developed and applied to healthcare interventions.

These trends call for improvement in the methodological standards of study and data collection in projects that seek policy-relevant answers from economic analysis. All stakeholders in such projects should a priori recognise the conceptual and methodological demands of a good economic evaluation exercise and deploy adequate resources to address such demands at the conception stage of the project cycle.

A better understanding of the impact of criminal justice interventions could be achieved with a greater appreciation of the weaknesses in the understanding of cost–benefit and evaluation methodology. The fact that the quality of much of the work reviewed in this paper falls short of the highest standards is an indication that criminal justice represents a field ripe for more refined application of appraisal and evaluation techniques.

REFERENCES

Akerlof, G. & Yellen, J. (1994). Gang behaviour, law enforcement and community values. In H.J. Aaron, T.E Mann & T. Taylor (eds), *Values and Public Policy*. Washington: Brookings Institution.

Anglin, M D., Speckart, G.R, Booth, M.W. & Ryan, T.M. (1989). Consequences and costs of shutting off methadone. *Addictive Behaviors*, **14**(3), 307–26.

Armitage, R. (2000). An evaluation of secure by design housing within West Yorkshire. *Home Office Briefing Note 7/00*, 1–4. London: Home Office.

Barnett, W.S. & Escobar, C.M. (1987). The economics of early educational intervention: A review. *Review of Educational Research*, **57**, 387–414.

Becker, G.S. (1968). Crime and punishment: An economic approach. *Journal of Political Economy*, **76**, 169–217.

Bottoms, A.E. (1995). *Intensive Community Supervision for Young Offenders: Outcomes, Process and Cost*. Cambridge: Institute of Criminology.

Bowles, R., Harris, R. & Pradiptyo R. (2003). Assessment of economic evaluations of the crime reduction programme, *mimeo*. York: Centre for Criminal Justice Economics and Psychology, University of York.

Bowles, R. & Pradiptyo R. (2003). Reducing burglary initiative: An analysis of costs and benefits, *mimeo*. York: Centre for Criminal Justice Economics and Psychology, University of York.

Brand, S. & Price, P. (2000). The economic and social costs of crime. *Home Office Research Study 217*. London: Home Office.

Cohen, M.A. (1998). The monetary value of saving a high-risk youth. *Journal of Quantitative Criminology*, **14**(1), 5–33.

Cohen, M.A. (2000). Measuring the costs and benefits of crime and justice. In D. Duffee, *Measurement and Analysis of Crime and Justice* (Vol. 4) (pp 263–316). Washington DC: National Institute of Justice, US Department of Justice.

Deschenes, E.P., Anglin, M.D. & Speckart, G. (1991). Narcotics addiction: Related criminal careers, social and economic costs. *Journal of Drug Issues*, **21**(2), 383–411.

Dhiri, S. & Brand, S. (1999). *Analysis of Costs and Benefits: Guidance to Evaluators. Crime Reduction Programme Guidance Note 1*. London: Home Office.

DiIulio, J. J. Jr. (1996). Help wanted: Economists, crime and public policy. *Journal of Economic Perspectives*, **10**(1), 3–24.

Dodgson, K., Goodwin, P., Howard, P., Llewellyn-Thomas, S., Mortimer, E., Russell, N. & Weiner, M. (2001). Electronic monitoring of released prisoners: An evaluation of the Home Detention Curfew Scheme. *Home Office Research Study 222*. London: Home Office.

Drummond, M.F., O'Brien, B., Stoddart, G.L. & Torrance, G.W. (1997). *Methods for the economic evaluation of Health Care Programmes* (2ndedn). Oxford: Oxford University Press.

Ekblom, P. (1996). Safer cities and residential burglary: A summary of evaluation results. *European Journal on Criminal Policy and Research*, **4**, 22–52.

Ekblom, P., Law, H. & Sutton, M. (1996). Safer cities and domestic burglary. *Home Office Research Study 164*. London: Home Office.

Farrington, D.P. (1983). Randomized experiments on crime and justice. In M. Tonry & N. Morris (eds), *Crime and Justice: An Annual Review of Research* (Vol. 4) (pp 257–308). Chicago: University of Chicago Press.

Farrington, D.P., Ditchfield, J., Hancock, G., Howard, P., Jolliffe, D., Livingston, M.S. & Painter, K.A. (2002). Evaluation of two intensive regimes. *Home Office Research Study 239*, 1–70. London: Home Office.

Farrington, D.P. & Welsh, B.C. (2002). Effects of improved street lighting on crime: a systematic review. *Home Office Research Study 251*. London: Home Office.

Gold, M.R., Siegel, J.E., Russell, L.B. & Weinstein, M.C. (1996).*Cost-Effectiveness in Health and Medicine*. New York: Oxford University Press.

Griffith, J.D., Hiller, M.L, Knight, K. & Simpson, D.D. (1999). A cost effectiveness analysis of in-prison therapeutic community treatment. *Prison Journal*, **79**(3) 352–65.

Hakim, S., Rengert, G.F. & Shachmurove, Y. (1996). Estimation of net benefits of residential electronic security. *Justice Quarterly*, **13**(1), 153–70.

HM Treasury (2003). The Green Book: Appraisal and evaluation in central government. *Treasury Guidance*. London: TSO.

Knapp, M. (1997). Economic evaluations and intervention for children and adolescents with mental health problems. *Journal of Child Psychology and Psychiatry*, **38**, 3–25.

Knapp, M., Robertson, E. & McIvor, G. (1992). The comparative costs of community service and custody in Scotland. *The Howard Journal*, **31**(1), 8–30.

Levitt, S. (1997). Using electoral cycles in police hiring to estimate the effect of police on crime. *American Economic Review*, **87**(3), 270–90.

Manning, W.G.J. (1999). Panel on cost-effectiveness in health and medicine recommendations: Identifying costs. *Journal of Clinical Psychiatry*, **60**(3), 54–8.

McDougall, C. Cohen, M. Swaray, R. & Perry, A. (2003). The cost and benefits of sentencing: A systematic review. *The Annals of the American Academy of Political and Social Science*, **587**, 160–77.

McGuire, J. (2001). What works in correctional interventions? Evidence and practical implications. In G.A. Bernfeld, D.A. Farrington, D.A. & A.W. Leschied (eds), *Offender Rehabilitation in Practice: Implementing and Evaluating Effective Programs* (pp 25–43). Chichester: John Wiley & Sons Ltd.

McGuire, J. & Priestley, P. (1995). Reviewing 'What works': Past, present and future. In J. McGuire (ed.), *What Works: Reducing Re-Offending: Guidelines From Research and Practice* (pp 3–34). Chichester: John Wiley & Sons Ltd.

Miers, D., Maguire, M., Goldie, S., Sharpe, K. & Hale, C. (2001). Exploratory evaluation of restorative justice schemes. *Crime Reduction Research Paper* **9**, 113. London: Home Office.

Murray, C.J., Evans, D.B. Acharya, A. & Baltuseen, R. M. (2000). Development of WHO guidelines on generalized cost-effectiveness analysis. *Health Economics*, **9**, 235–51.

NHS CRD (2001). *Undertaking Systematic Reviews of Research on Effectiveness, CRD's Guidance for those Carrying Out or Commissioning Reviews* (Paper 4), (2nd edn). York: University of York.

Oldfield, M. (1997). What worked? A five year study of probation reconvictions. *Probation Journal*, **44**(1), 2–10.

Painter, K.A. & Farrington, D.P. (1997). The crime reducing effect of improved street lighting: The Dudley project. In R.V Clarke (ed.), *Situational Crime Prevention: Successful Case Studies.* Albany, NY: Harrow and Heston.

Painter, K.A. & Farrington, D.P. (1999a). Improved street lighting: Crime reducing effects and cost-benefit analysis. *Security Journal,* **12**(4), 17–32.

Painter, K.A. & Farrington, D.P. (1999b). Street lighting and crime: Diffusion of benefits in the Stoke-on-Trent project. In K.A Painter & N. Tilley (eds), *Surveillance of Public Space: CCTV, Street Lighting and Crime Prevention: Crime Prevention Studies* (pp 77–122). Monsey, NY: Criminal Justice Press.

Painter, K.A. & Farrington, D.P. (1999c). Improved street lighting: Crime reducing effects and cost-benefit analysis. *Security Journal,* **12**(4), 17–32.

Painter, K.A. & Farrington D.P. (2001a). Evaluating situational crime prevention using a young people's survey. *British Journal of Criminology,* 4(2), 266–84.

Painter, K.A. & Farrington, D.P. (2001b). The financial benefits of improved street lighting, based on crime reduction. *Lighting Research Technology,* **331**(1), 3–12.

Perry, A.E., McDougall, C., Swaray, R., Murphy, T., Harris, R. & Bjornsson, H. (2003). *The Effectiveness of UK Criminal Justice Interventions in the Reduction of Crime: A Review of the Literature.* York: The Centre for Criminal Justice Economics and Psychology, University of York.

Prentky, R. & Burgess, A.W. (1990). Rehabilitation of child molesters: A cost–benefit analysis. *American Journal of Orthopsychiatry,* **60**, 108–17.

Shanahan, M. & Donato, R. (2001). Counting the cost: Estimating the economic benefit of paedophile treatment program. *Child Abuse and Neglect,* **25**, 541–55.

Sherman L.W., Gottfredson, D., MacKenzie, D., Eck, J., Reuler, P. & Bushay, S. (1997). *Preventing Crime: What Works, What Doesn't, What's Promising: A Report to the United States Congress.* (www.cjcentral.com/sherman/sherman.htm).

Sherman, L.W., Farrington, D.P., Welsh, B.C. & MacKenzie, D.L. (2002). *Evidence-Based Crime Prevention.* London: Routledge.

Swaray, R., Bowles, R. & Pradiptyo, R. (2005). The application of economic analysis to criminal justice interventions: A review of the literature. *Criminal Justice Policy Review* **16**, 141–163.

Weimer, D.L. & Friedman, L.S. (1979). Efficiency considerations in criminal justice rehabilitation research: Costs and consequences. In L. Sechrest, S.O. White & E.D. Brown (eds), *The Rehabilitation of Criminal Offenders: Problems and Prospects* (pp 251–72). Washington DC: National Academy of Sciences.

Welsh, B.C. & Farrington, D.P. (2000a). Monetary costs and benefits of crime prevention programs. *Crime and Justice: A Review of Research,* **27**, 305–62.

Welsh, B.C. & Farrington, D.P. (2000b). Correctional intervention programs and cost benefit analysis. *Criminal Justice and Behaviour,* **27**(1), 115–33.

CHAPTER 9

Overview of Effectiveness of Criminal Justice Interventions in the UK

CYNTHIA MCDOUGALL, AMANDA E. PERRY AND DAVID P. FARRINGTON

The preceding chapters have fully described the evidence of *What Works, What Doesn't, What's Promising* and *What's Unknown* from the UK effectiveness studies included in the *UK review*, completed in 2002. The authors have updated the information by describing more recent research, and positioned this research within the wider international research evidence-base and within policy contexts. This chapter seeks to summarise the evidence, its strengths in terms of the quality of the methodology, the gaps in the research, and identifies future directions. Tables summarise studies that have included control or comparison groups.

ALCOHOL AND DRUG INTERVENTIONS

Studies on interventions to reduce alcohol and drug-misuse (Table 9.1) are described in Chapter 3. Only two of the studies on alcohol-related interventions reported a significant effect on crime. One of these (Singer, 1991) did not have a control group, so although a significant effect on reconvictions was observed at the 12-month follow-up after an alcohol education course, it is not certain that the effect was solely due to the effectiveness of the course. The other study that found a significant effect on crime was by Baldwin et al. (1991). This intervention study of an alcohol education

Reducing Crime: The Effectiveness of Criminal Justice Interventions.
Edited by A. E. Perry, C. McDougall and D. P. Farrington. © 2006 John Wiley & Sons, Ltd.

Table 9.1 Alcohol treatment studies

Classification	Intervention — Description, SMS score & study details	With Whom? — Gender	Adult	YO	Juvenile	Age Range/ Mean	Ethnicity	In What Setting?	Effective in Reducing? — Criminal activity outcome, source, effectiveness	Follow-up (months)	At What Cost? £/$
What's Promising	Alcohol education programme (I) vs control (C) SMS = 5 [Baldwin et al., 1991]	100% male	–	✓	–	17–22 Mean 19.4	N/R	Secure establishment	Property offences (#) (self-report) Positive indication Rule offences (#) (self-report) Positive indication	Mean 14 Range 9–21	N/R
What's Unknown	Alcohol self-help manual (I) vs group intervention (I1) vs control (C) SMS = 4 [McMurran & Boyle, 1990]	100% male	–	✓	✓	15–21 Mean N/R	N/R	Secure establishment	Conviction (%) (official) No difference	15	N/R

164

What's Unknown									
Hospital-referred psychiatric nurse aftercare for alcohol dependence (I) vs standard outpatient care (C) SMS = 3 [Patterson et al., 1997]	100% male	✓ ✓ –	16–70 Mean 36.8	100% white	Community	Conviction (%) (self-report) No difference	60	N/R

Key
Positive indication: Result favours intervention group
Negative indication: Result favours comparison group
No difference: No difference between the groups
Within: Measures were within groups (no between-group comparisons)
N/R: Not reported
SMS: Scientific Methods Score
YO: Young offender
Official: Data collected from official sources (e.g., national databases)
Victim survey: Questionnaires distributed to victims
Self-report: Reports by offenders
N/A: Not applicable
✓ : Participants fall into this category
– : Participants do not fall into this category
% : Dichotomous measure (individual)
# : Continuous measure (population)

course for 17- to 22-year-olds did have a control group with random allocation to treatment and control groups, and showed a significant reduction
in drinking, numbers of property offences and offences against rules and
regulations. Studies by McMurran and Boyle (1990) on the use of a 'self-
help manual' for young male offenders, and Patterson, Macpherson and
Brady (1997) on community psychiatric nurse aftercare found no significant reduction in offending in the treatment groups when compared to
control groups, although the Patterson study found that a greater number
of the aftercare treatment group was abstinent at a five-year follow-up.
In reviewing the studies, McMurran observes that all of the interventions
described were of short duration and would not be considered sufficient in
duration by current accreditation standards.

Within the drug treatment studies, a larger proportion were effective,
with studies by Martin and Player (2000), McCusker and Davies (1996),
Parker and Kirby (1996), (Table 9.2), and Hough, Clancy, McSweeney and
Turnbull (2003) (Table 9.3) reporting a significant impact on crime. The
studies (Table 9.2) met the criterion for inclusion in the review, scoring at
least three on the Maryland Scientific Methods Scale. Three studies additionally cited in Chapter 3 did not have a comparison group (Coid, Carvell,
Kittler, Healey & Henderson, 2000; Keen, Rowse, Mathers, Campbell &
Seivewright, 2000; Haynes, 1998). Two of these showed a significant impact on crime, but the third study had mixed results. McMurran gives a
critical analysis of the quality of the studies in general, identifying baseline methodological flaws, and problems of missing data and choice of
outcome measures. In her summary, McMurran makes recommendations
on methods to be employed to minimise errors related to research design
in alcohol- and drug-related studies.

DIVERSION FROM COURT AND EFFECTIVE SENTENCING

Hedderman and Hough in Chapter 4 have highlighted the particular
difficulties of applying rigorous research design in the court environment.
They state that, although the ideal would be for sentencers to apply randomised control procedures in evaluating court decisions on sentencing,
in their view this is unlikely to be adopted in the near future. Hence
Hedderman and Hough have widened the range of studies included in
their discussion.

It is clear that the study by Cooke (1991) (Table 9.4) had a rigorous design and identified benefits in diversion from court; however, other findings are less than obvious. In the case of probation sentences, there are
conflicting results (Home Office, 1993; Oldfield, 1997) (Table 9.15), as in
some cases probation with an order was effective whilst in others probation without an order was effective. Until it is defined and established
what is implied by 'an order', then such conflicting results will arise. As

Table 9.2 Drug treatment studies

Classification	Intervention — Description, SMS score & study details	With Whom? — Gender	Adult	YO	Juvenile	Age Range/ Mean	Ethnicity	In What Setting?	Effective in Reducing? — Criminal activity outcome, source, effectiveness	Follow-up (months)	At What Cost? £/$
What's Promising	Methadone treatment clinic (I) vs heroin and poly-drug users in the community not receiving methadone (C) SMS = 4 [Parker & Kirby, 1996]	63% male	✓	✓	–	15–71 Mean 29.7	94% white	Community	Acquisitive crime (%) (self-report) Positive indication	1	The cost of the drugs bill per year for the (C) group was 5 times that of the (I) group [Parker & Kirby, 1996]

(*Continued*)

Table 9.2 Drug treatment studies (*Continued*)

Classification	Intervention: Description, SMS score & study details	With Whom? Gender	Adult	YO	Juvenile	Age Range/ Mean	Ethnicity	In What Setting?	Effective in Reducing? Criminal activity outcome, source, effectiveness	Follow-up (months)	At What Cost? £/$
What's Promising	Prison drug treatment programme (I) vs treatment dropouts (I1) vs non-starters control (C) SMS = 3 [Martin & Player, 2000]	100 % male	✓	–	–	21–62 Mean 32	74% white	Secure establishment	Conviction (%) (multiple sources) [I was significantly less likely than I1 & C to be reconvicted] Positive indication	13	N/R
What's Promising	Pharmaceutical heroin (I) vs methadone treatment (I1) in a community drug clinic SMS = 3 [McCusker & Davies, 1996]	86% male	✓	–	–	Age range N/R Mean 28.9	N/R	Secure establishment	Days engaged in illegal activity in past 30 days (#) (self-report) Positive indication Legal status (on probation/ awaiting trial) (%) (self-report) No difference	6 6	N/R

What's Unknown

Injectable heroin (I) vs injectable methadone (II) in a community drug clinic SMS = 3 [Metrebian et al., 2001]	72% male	✓	–	–	Age range 24–29 Median I: 38 I1: 36 Mean N/R	84% white	Secure establishment	Criminal activity by Opiate Index Treatment scores (#) (self-report) No difference (Reductions within each group; no difference between)	12	N/R

Table 9.3 Drug treatment studies (literature in addition to the *UK review*)

| | Intervention | With Whom? | | | | | | In What Setting? | Effective in Reducing? | | At What Cost? |
| | | | | | | | | | Criminal activity outcome, source, effectiveness | Follow-up (months) | |
Classification	Description, SMS score & study details	Gender	Adult	YO	Juvenile	Age Range/ Mean	Ethnicity				£/$
What's Unknown	Drug treatment and testing order (DTTO) completers (I) vs non-completers (11) SMS = 2 [Hough et al., 2003]	N/R	N/R	N/R	N/R	N/R	N/R	Community	Conviction (%) (official) Positive indication	24	N/R

Key
Positive indication: Result favours intervention group
Negative indication: Result favours comparison group
No difference: No difference between the groups
Within: Measures were within groups (no between-group comparisons)
N/R: Not reported
SMS: Scientific Methods Score
YO: Young offender
Official: Police-recorded data
Victim survey: Questionnaires distributed to victims
Self-report: Reports by offenders
N/A: Not applicable
✓ : Participants fall into this category
– : Participants do not fall into this category
% : Dichotomous measure (individual)
# : Continuous measure (population)

Table 9.4 Court and police referral schemes

Classification	Intervention — Description, SMS score & study details	With Whom? Gender	Adult	YO	Juvenile	Age Range/ Mean	Ethnicity	In What Setting?	Effective in Reducing? — Criminal activity outcome, source, effectiveness	Follow-up (months)	At What Cost? £/$
What's Promising	Police-referred psychiatric diversion scheme (I) vs no diversion scheme (C) SMS = 3 [Cooke, 1991]	52% male	✓	✓	✓	16–50+	N/R	Sentencing & the courts	Conviction (%) (official) Positive indication	23–34	N/R
What's Unknown	Court-referred behavioural alcohol education course (I) or talk-based (I1) SMS = 4 [Baldwin et al., 1991]	100% male	✓	✓	–	17–24 Mean 20.0	N/R	Sentencing & the courts	Offending behaviour (#) (court data) No difference Offending behaviour (#) (police data) No difference Conviction (#) (self-report) [within only] No difference	12 12 12	N/R

(Continued)

Table 9.4 Court and police referral schemes (Continued)

Classification	Intervention: Description, SMS score & study details	With Whom? Gender	Adult	YO	Juvenile	Age Range/Mean	Ethnicity	In What Setting?	Effective in Reducing? Criminal activity outcome, source, effectiveness	Follow-up (months)	At What Cost? £/$
What's Unknown	Court-referred psychiatric diversion to hospital (I) vs community hospital admission to hospital (C) SMS = 3 [James et al., 2002]	85% male	✓	N/R	N/R	Range N/R Mean 35.1	59% white	Sentencing & the courts	Conviction (%) (official) Negative indication Conviction (#) (official) [within only] Positive indication Sentencing occasions (#) (official) [within only] Positive indication	24 24 24	N/R

Key

Positive indication: Result favours intervention group
Negative indication: Result favours comparison group
No difference: No difference between the groups
Within: Measures were within groups (no between-group comparisons)
N/R: Not reported
SMS: Scientific Methods Score
YO: Young offender
Official: Police-recorded data
Victim survey: Questionnaires distributed to victims
Self-report: Reports by offenders
N/A: Not applicable
✓ : Participants fall into this category
− : Participants do not fall into this category
% : Dichotomous measure (individual)
# : Continuous measure (population)

Hedderman and Hough point out, the situation is likely to become even more unclear following the full implementation of the new Criminal Justice Act (2003), which requires a range of mixed sentences. They do, however, point out that within these sentencing structures there may be scope for more rigorous testing of outcomes. The pitfalls in using 'raw' reconviction data, and the biases inherent in the criminal justice processes, are outlined. Whilst concluding that, due to these biases, it is difficult to determine which sentences work for whom, the authors support Effective Practice initiatives to aid sentencing in meeting its objectives.

POLICE AND SECURITY INTERVENTIONS

Seven police and security interventions were identified in the *UK review* completed in 2002. They included a repeat victimisation strategy in residential areas, a retail theft initiative, situational shoplifting prevention, use of aerosol incapacitation, use of police decoy vehicles in crime prevention, a motor vehicle theft scheme, and targeting vendor sales of alcohol to underage adolescents. Three of the studies (see Table 9.5), covering two interventions (Anderson, Chenery & Pease, 1995; Chenery, Holt & Pease, 1997; McCulloch, 1996) reported a significant reduction in reconvictions of the intervention group when compared to a control group.

The strategy to combat repeat victimisation (Anderson et al., 1995; Chenery et al., 1997) was based on research evidence that victimisation predicts further victimisation, and that by concentrating police resources on repeat victims, crime can be reduced. The Huddersfield project (Anderson et al., 1995; Chenery et al., 1997) recorded a reduction in domestic burglary of 30 per cent and vehicle crime of 20 per cent, reduced levels of repeat burglary, and increased arrests due to the implementation of temporary alarms. The third study to report positive results in reducing reconvictions (McCulloch, 1996) was of a retail theft initiative in which first-offence shoplifters were given either a caution and referred to a retail theft education programme, or a caution alone. The Farrington et al. (1993) study (Table 9.5) of situational shoplifting prevention showed mixed results. The prevention methods adopted were electronic tagging, store redesign, and the presence of a uniformed guard. Electronic tagging of items was found to be the most successful prevention method, causing a lasting decrease in shoplifting. Store redesign had an immediate impact on shoplifting, but the effect wore off in six weeks. Positioning a uniformed guard in the store had no effect on shoplifting. Two studies that showed no difference between the intervention group and the control group were by Rix and Kock (1997), and Willner, Hart, Binmore, Cavendish and Dunphy (2000). The use of aerosol incapacitation did not reduce the number of assaults on police officers (Rix & Kock, 1997), though police-officer perception

Table 9.5 Police and security intervention studies

Classification	Intervention Description, SMS score & study details	With Whom? Gender	Adult	YO	Juvenile	Age Range/ Mean	Ethnicity	In What Setting?	Effective in Reducing? Criminal activity outcome, source, effectiveness	Follow-up (months)	At What Cost? £/$
What's Promising	Repeat victimisation strategy in residential areas in Huddersfield Police Force Area (I) vs rest of Police Force Area (C) vs displacement Police Force Area (C1) SMS = 3 [Chenery et al., 1997; Anderson et al., 1995]	N/A	N/A	N/A	N/A	N/A	N/A	Crime prevention	Domestic burglary (official) [I vs C & C1] Positive indication Vehicle crime (official) [I vs C & C1] Positive indication Repeat burglary (official) Positive indication Arrests from temporary alarms (official) [within only] Positive indication	14 14 14 14	N/R
What's Promising	Retail theft initiative & caution (I) vs caution only (C) SMS = 3 [McCulloch, 1996]	N/R	N/R	N/R	N/R	N/R	N/R	Crime prevention	Offending (%) Positive indication	2–24	N/R

What's Unknown	Situational shoplifting prevention using electronic tagging (I) vs store redesign (I1) vs uniformed guard (I2) vs no prevention strategy (C) SMS = 3 [Farrington et al., 1993]	N/A	N/A	N/A	N/A	N/A	Crime prevention	Shoplifting (% of goods stolen) (official) [I was most effective; I1 had short mixed effects & I2 was not effective] Mixed results	0.25; 0.75; 1.5	N/R
What's Unknown	Vehicle theft schemes in intervention areas (I) vs control areas (C) SMS = 3 [Honess et al., 1993]	N/A	N/A	N/A	N/A	N/A	Crime prevention	Monthly vehicle theft (# converted to % change) (official) Inconclusive	12	N/R
What's Unknown	CS gas aerosol incapacitation by the police in intervention area (I) vs control area (C) SMS = 4 [Rix & Kock, 1997]	N/A	N/A	N/A	N/A	N/A	Crime prevention	Assaults on police officers (#) (official) No difference	6	N/R
What's Unknown	Police decoy vehicles (I) vs control area (C) SMS = 4 [Sallybanks, 2001]	N/A	N/A	N/A	N/A	N/A	Crime prevention	Monthly total vehicle theft (#) (official) Monthly transit vehicle theft (#) (official) Mixed results	20 20	N/R

(Continued)

Table 9.5 Police and security intervention studies (*Continued*)

Classification	Intervention — Description, SMS score & study details	With Whom? — Gender	Adult	YO	Juvenile	Age Range/ Mean	Ethnicity	In What Setting?	Effective in Reducing? — Criminal activity outcome, source, effectiveness	Follow-up (months)	At What Cost? £/$
What's Unknown	Targeting vendors of alcohol to underage adolescents (I) vs control areas (C) SMS= 4 [Willner et al., 2000]	N/A	N/A	N/A	N/A	N/A	N/A	Crime prevention	Successful purchases of alcohol (% of purchase attempts; recorded at time of attempt) No difference	2	N/R

Key
Positive indication: Result favours intervention group
Negative indication: Result favours comparison group
No difference: No difference between the groups
Within: Measures were within groups (no between-group comparisons)
N/R: Not reported
SMS: Scientific Methods Score
YO: Young offender
Official: Police-recorded data
Victim survey: Questionnaires distributed to victims
Self-report: Reports by offenders
N/A: Not applicable
✓ : Participants fall into this category
– : Participants do not fall into this category
% : Dichotomous measure (individual)
# : Continuous measure (population)

was that the incapacitation was effective in reducing assaults. Similarly, targeting vendors of alcohol to underage drinkers (Willner et al., 2000) did not reduce numbers of underage alcohol sales, except in the short term. Two schemes to reduce vehicle theft, one using decoy vehicles in high vehicle theft areas as 'bait' for offenders (Sallybanks, 2001), and the other a vehicle watch scheme (Honess, Maguire & Chapman, 1993), had mixed or inconclusive results. Although in one or two study areas there was an effect in the first few months, this diminished over time. The evidence seems to suggest that a number of police interventions make short-term gains, but consideration needs to be given to how these effects can be maintained. These conclusions find support in the international literature that prevention effects tend to fade out over time without modification and renewal of police practices (Sherman & Eck, 2002).

Similarly, the UK studies that have shown effectiveness in preventing crime are supported by the conclusions of Sherman and Eck (2002) that the more focused police interventions are most likely to prevent crime; see the Huddersfield Project (Anderson et al., 1995; Chenery et al., 1997).

PRISON AND PROBATION INTERVENTIONS

Studies conducted in prison and probation were reviewed by Friendship and Debidin in Chapter 5.

There were promising significant results (Table 9.6) from a UK therapeutic prison establishment (Marshall, 1997; Taylor, 2000), and similar findings have been reported in the international literature (Lees, Manning & Rawlings, 1999). A Christian-centred therapeutic community project in a prison, however, did not show a significant effect on reconvictions when compared to a control group (Burnside et al., 2001). Friendship and Debidin noted that the number of offenders involved in the Christian-centred community was not large, and that the study may therefore have lacked sufficient power to detect any small effect size.

A study of High Intensity Training (HIT) and a Military Corrective Training Centre (MCTC) for young offenders (Farrington, Hancock, Livingston, Painter & Towl, 2000; Farrington et al., 2002) was identified (Table 9.7). In these studies, there was a significant effect on reconvictions at the end of one year for the HIT regime, but this effect was no longer evident at the two-year follow-up. The MCTC did not have a significantly different impact on reconvictions when compared with a comparison group at the one- or two-year stage. This finding, that high-intensity type regimes do not have a long-term impact on reconvictions, is supported by a systematic review of intensive regimes in the international literature (MacKenzie, Wilson & Kiders, 2001).

Table 9.6 Therapeutic community studies

Classification	Intervention Description, SMS score & study details	With Whom? Gender	Adult	YO	Juvenile	Age Range/ Mean	Ethnicity	In What Setting?	Effective in Reducing? Criminal activity outcome, source, effectiveness	Follow-up (months)	At What Cost? £/$
What's Promising	HMP Grendon therapeutic community (I) vs waiting list control (C) vs general prison population (C1) SMS = 4 [Marshall, 1997; Taylor, 2000]	100% male	✓	N/R	N/R	20+ Mean N/R	N/R	Secure establishment	Violent conviction (%) (official) Positive indication	48	N/R
									Conviction for sexual offence (%) (official) Positive indication	48	
									Conviction for sexual/violent offence (%) (official) Positive indication	48	
									Any conviction (%) (official) Positive indication	84	
									Conviction for violent offence (%) (official) Positive indication	84	
									Conviction for sexual offence (%) (official) Positive indication	84	
									Custodial sentence (%) (official) Positive indication	84	

What's Unknown	Christian-centred therapeutic community (I) vs control (C) SMS = 3 [Burnside et al., 2001]	I: 82% male C: N/R	N/R	N/R	N/R	N/R	Secure establishment	Conviction (%) (official) No difference	12 (from discharge)	N/R

Key
Positive indication: Result favours intervention group
Negative indication: Result favours comparison group
No difference: No difference between the groups
Within: Measures were within groups (no between-group comparisons)
N/R: Not reported
SMS: Scientific Methods Score
YO: Young offender
Official: Police-recorded data
Victim survey: Questionnaires distributed to victims
Self-report: Reports by offenders
N/A: Not applicable
✓ : Participants fall into this category
– : Participants do not fall into this category
% : Dichotomous measure (individual)
# : Continuous measure (population)

Table 9.7 Intensive regime studies

Classification	Intervention: Description, SMS score & study details	With Whom? Gender	Adult	YO	Juvenile	Age Range/Mean	Ethnicity	In What Setting?	Effective in Reducing? Criminal activity outcome, source, effectiveness	Follow-up (months)	At What Cost? £/$
What's Unknown	High Intensity Training (HIT) (I) vs YO institution without HIT (C) Military Corrective Training (MCTC) (I1) vs YO institution without MCTC (C1) SMS = 4 [Farrington et al., 2000; 2002]	100% male	–	✓	–	18–21	N/R	Secure establishment	Actual & predicted conviction (%) (official) No difference Offences (#) (official) Mixed results	12; 24 12; 24	Cost savings from HIT outweighed the extra cost of the regime (benefit–cost ratio 5:1) Benefit–cost analysis found MCTC committed fewer crimes but they were more costly.

180

At least 89p was lost for every extra £1 spent on the regime [Farrington et al., 2000; Farrington et al., 2002] Drummond rating 8/11

Key
Positive indication: Result favours intervention group
Negative indication: Result favours comparison group
No difference: No difference between the groups
Within: Measures were within groups (no between-group comparisons)
N/R: Not reported
SMS: Scientific Methods Score
YO: Young offender
Official: Police-recorded data
Victim survey: Questionnaires distributed to victims
Self-report: Reports by offenders
N/A: Not applicable
✓ : Participants fall into this category
– : Participants do not fall into this category
% : Dichotomous measure (individual)
# : Continuous measure (population)

Conclusions from studies on the effectiveness of cognitive behavioural programmes are rapidly evolving, as more and more reconviction data is becoming available (Tables 9.8, 9.9). At the time of the *UK review* (2002), Reasoning & Rehabilitation (R&R) and Enhanced Thinking Skills (ETS) programmes were included in the *What's Promising* category as a consequence of evaluation of both prison and probation programmes (Friendship, Blud, Erikson & Travers, 2002; also reported by the National Probation Service, 2002). Since then, however, two large-scale studies have been conducted on prison R&R and ETS programmes that have produced contrary results, with no significant difference being found between treated offenders and a comparison group (Cann, Falshaw, Nugent & Friendship, 2003; Falshaw, Friendship, Travers & Nugent, 2003). Friendship and Debidin discuss the programme-integrity risks in large-scale ongoing programmes and the need for closer examination of targeting and motivational factors. Whilst awaiting further research, they conclude that it is premature to say that R&R and ETS programmes *Don't Work*, but at this stage should be classified as *What Has Worked* or *What Sometimes Works*; these programmes have therefore been classified as *What's Unknown*. These latest results go against a large body of international literature on the effectiveness of cognitive behavioural programmes in reducing crime (Pearson, Lipton, Cleland & Yee, 2002).

A more positive evaluation was found for prison-based sex offender treatment programmes. A study conducted more recently (Friendship, Man & Beech, 2003a), described in Chapter 5, found a reduction in sexual and violent reconvictions combined for a sex offender treatment group, when compared to a matched comparison group.

Three studies (Table 9.10) of sex offender treatment programmes in the community (Allam, 1998; Hedderman & Sugg, 1996; Proctor, 1994), with control groups, found significant reductions in sexual and violent offences, leading to a *What Works* categorisation in the review. Although there are mixed conclusions in the international literature pertaining to sex offender treatment, MacKenzie (2002) assessed that the research evidence supported the effectiveness of cognitive behavioural interventions in non-prison programmes, and that prison-based programmes were 'promising' in reducing sexual offending. In Chapter 5, Friendship and Debidin give a critical analysis of the UK studies, and raise issues of caution in interpretation and in linking evaluations of studies with different kinds of sex offender treatment methods.

The National Probation Service (2002) report (Table 9.10) describes outcomes from a number of different cognitive behavioural studies, including the sex offender programme by Allam (1998) already described. It also includes outcomes of studies on R&R, aggression replacement training (ART), and the South Yorkshire drink impaired drivers course (DIDC). Since these are not primary studies, it has not always been possible to

Table 9.8 Cognitive behavioural programmes—prison

Classification	Intervention — Description, SMS score & study details	With Whom? Gender	Adult	YO	Juvenile	Age Range/ Mean	Ethnicity	In What Setting?	Effective in Reducing? — Criminal activity outcome, source, effectiveness	Follow-up (months)	At What Cost? £/$
What's Unknown [previously classified as What's Promising: see Table 9.9 for updated evidence]	Reasoning and Rehabilitation (R&R) or Enhanced Thinking Skills (ETS) programmes (I) vs retrospective control (C) SMS = 4 [Friendship et al., 2002] (Also reported by National Probation Service, 2002)	100% male	✓	–	–	–	N/R	Secure establishment	Expected & observed conviction (%) (official) Positive indication	24	Based on the number of prisoners expected to complete ETS and R&R in 2002–2003, this represents a saving of 21,000 crimes [Friendship et al. 2002]

Key
Positive indication: Result favours intervention group
Negative indication: Result favours comparison group
No difference: No difference between the groups
Within: Measures were within groups (no between-group comparisons)
N/R: Not reported
SMS: Scientific Methods Score
YO: Young offender
Official: Police-recorded data
Victim survey: Questionnaires distributed to victims
Self-report: Reports by offenders
N/A: Not applicable
✓ : Participants fall into this category
– : Participants do not fall into this category
% : Dichotomous measure (individual)
# : Continuous measure (population)

Table 9.9 Cognitive behavioural programmes—prison (literature in addition to the *UK review*)

Classification	Intervention: Description, SMS score & study details	With Whom? Gender	Adult	YO	Juvenile	Age Range/ Mean	Ethnicity	In What Setting?	Effective in Reducing? Criminal activity outcome, source, effectiveness	Follow-up (months)	At What Cost? £/$
What's Unknown	Reasoning and Rehabilitation (R&R) or Enhanced Thinking Skills (ETS) programmes (I) *vs* retrospective matched control (C)	100% male	✓	–	–	Range N/R Mean N/R	N/R	Secure establishment	Expected & observed conviction (%) (official) Positive indication	24	N/R
	1. [Friendship et al., 2002] (Identified in the *UK review*; also reported by National Probation Service, 2002) SMS = 3	100% male	✓	–	–	Range N/R Mean N/R	N/R	Secure establishment	Expected & observed conviction (%) (official) No difference	24	N/R
	2. [Falshaw et al., 2003] (Also reported in Falshaw et al., 2004) SMS = 3	100% male	✓	–	–	Range N/R Mean N/R	N/R	Secure establishment	Expected & observed conviction (%) (official) No difference	12; 24	N/R
	3. [Cann et al., 2003] (Two evaluations) SMS = 3	N/R	–	–	–	Range N/R Mean 34.0	N/R	Secure establishment	Expected & observed conviction (%) (official) No difference	12; 24	N/R

What's Promising	Sex Offender Treatment Programme (SOTP) for sex offenders (I) vs retrospective control (C) [Friendship et al., 2003a] (Also reported in Friendship et al., 2003b) SMS = 3	100% male	✓	–	–	Range N/R Mean 40.2	N/R	Secure establishment	Conviction for a sexual offence (%) (official) No difference	24	N/R
									Conviction for a sexual/violent offence (%) (official) Positive indication	24	
									Conviction for any offence (%) (official) No difference	24	

Key
Positive indication: Result favours intervention group
Negative indication: Result favours comparison group
No difference: No difference between the groups
Within: Measures were within groups (no between-group comparisons)
N/R: Not reported
SMS: Scientific Methods Score
YO: Young offender
Official: Police-recorded data
Victim survey: Questionnaires distributed to victims
Self-report: Reports by offenders
N/A: Not applicable
✓ : Participants fall into this category
– : Participants do not fall into this category
% : Dichotomous measure (individual)
# : Continuous measure (population)

Table 9.10 Cognitive behavioural programmes – probation

Classification	Intervention — Description, SMS score & study details	With Whom? Gender	Adult	YO	Juvenile	Age Range/ Mean	Ethnicity	In What Setting?	Effective in Reducing? — Criminal activity outcome, source, effectiveness	Follow-up (months)	At What Cost? £/$
What Works	Cognitive behavioural programmes for sex offenders (I) vs control (C)								Conviction for sexual offence (#) (official)	12; 24; 36	N/R
	1. [Allam, 1998] SMS = 3	100% male	N/R	N/R	N/R	N/R	N/R	Community	Positive indication		
									Conviction for violent offence (#) (official)	12; 24; 36	
									Positive indication		
									Conviction for other offence (#) (official)	12; 24; 36	
									Positive indication		
	2. [Hedderman & Sugg, 1996] SMS = 3	N/R	✓	–	–	N/R	N/R	Community	Conviction for sexual offence (%) (official)	24	N/R
									Positive indication		
									Conviction for non-sexual offence (%) (official)	24	
									Positive indication		
									Conviction for any offence (%) (official)	24	
									Positive indication		
									Actual & predicted (%) (official)	24	
									Positive indication		

								Measure / Outcome		
3. [National Probation Service, 2002] Review Prison and probation sex offender treatment programme. Aggression Replacement Therapy. ETS in prisons. R&R in the National Probation Service and prison. Impaired Drivers Course. DTTO.	N/R	N/R	N/R	N/R	N/R	Community		Conviction for any offence (%) (official) Positive indication	24	N/R
								Conviction for sexual offence (%) (official) Positive indication	24	
								Conviction for violent offence (%) (official) Positive indication	24	
								Conviction for other offence (%) (official) Positive indication	24	
4. [Proctor, 1994] SMS = 3	100% male	N/R	N/R	N/R	N/R	Community		Conviction for sexual offence (%) (N/R) Positive indication	Mean 30	N/R

Key

Positive indication: Result favours intervention group
Negative indication: Result favours comparison group
No difference: No difference between the groups
Within: Measures were within groups (no between-group comparisons)
N/R: Not reported
SMS: Scientific Methods Score
YO: Young offender
Official: Police-recorded data
Victim survey: Questionnaires distributed to victims
Self-report: Reports by offenders
N/A: Not applicable
✓ : Participants fall into this category
− : Participants do not fall into this category
% : Dichotomous measure (individual)
# : Continuous measure (population)

Table 9.11 Cognitive behavioural programmes—probation (literature in addition to the *UK review*)

Classification	Intervention Description, SMS score & study details	With Whom? Gender	Adult	YO	Juvenile	Age Range/ Mean	Ethnicity	In What Setting?	Effective in Reducing? Criminal activity outcome, source, effectiveness	Follow-up (months)	At What Cost? £/$
What's Unknown	Community-based cognitive behavioural programme completers (I) vs treatment dropouts (I1) vs retrospective control (C) Data was pooled across 5 Pathfinder programmes: Think First; Reasoning and Rehabilitation (R&R); Enhanced Thinking Skills (ETS); Priestley One-to-One; Addressing Substance-Related Offending (ASRO) SMS = 3 [Hollin et al., 2004]	85.6% male	✓	–	–	Range N/R Mean 28.2	N/R	Community	Conviction (%) (official) [The programmes were found to be effective when comparing (I) to (I1) and (C), however this effect was not found when results were pooled for the programme completers (I) and dropouts (I1) & compared to (C)]	I mean: 19.3 I1 mean: 18.6 C mean: 27.0 Pooled mean: 23.3	N/R

| *What's Unknown* | Community-based Think First completers (I) vs non-completers (I1) vs non-starters (I2) SMS = 3 [Stewart-Ong et al., 2004] | 90% male | ✓ | N/R | N/R | Range N/R Mean 27 | 98% white | Community | Conviction (%) (official) [I is more effective than I2; I1 is least effective] Positive indication | 6; 9; 12 | N/R |

Key
Positive indication: Result favours intervention group
Negative indication: Result favours comparison group
No difference: No difference between the groups
Within: Measures were within groups (no between-group comparisons)
N/R: Not reported
SMS: Scientific Methods Score
YO: Young offender
Official: Police-recorded data
Victim survey: Questionnaires distributed to victims
Self-report: Reports by offenders
N/A: Not applicable
✓ : Participants fall into this category
− : Participants do not fall into this category
% : Dichotomous measure (individual)
# : Continuous measure (population)

evaluate whether they meet the methodology criteria for inclusion as *Promising* in the review. The methodologies of the studies are also discussed in detail by Friendship and Debidin.

More recently, the National Probation Service has published findings from evaluation of the Think First programme, one of the general offending cognitive behavioural programmes (Stewart-Ong et al., 2004), and an evaluation of Pathfinder programmes (Think First, R&R, ETS, Priestley One-to-One, Addressing Substance-Related Offending—ASRO) in the probation service (Hollin et al., 2004) (Table 9.11). Although, in both studies, no significant difference in reduced reconvictions was found between intervention and comparison groups, different results were obtained when non-completers of the programme were examined separately from completers. Those offenders who completed a programme showed significantly lower reconviction rates than both those who failed to complete and the untreated comparison group. These studies are discussed in detail by Friendship and Debidin.

Only one study (Table 9.12) on the impact of employment projects on reconviction rates was identified (Sarno, Hearnden & Hedderman, 2001) and showed a significant effect in reducing reconvictions in the intervention group when compared to a comparison group.

A probation motoring offending project (Wilkinson, 1995, 1997; Wilkinson & Morgan, 1995) (Table 9.13) was found to significantly reduce reconvictions when compared to a matched comparison group.

Restorative justice (RJ) (Table 9.14) was found to be effective in reducing reconvictions in one adult group when compared with a comparison group (Miers, Maguire, Goldie, Sharpe & Hale, 2001), but the RJ process had no impact on reconviction rates of a juvenile intervention group when compared with a comparison group (Miers et al., 2001). There are some encouraging results from international research about the effectiveness of restorative justice in reducing crime; however, as with many study areas, the research methodologies have been criticised. Latimer and Kleinknecht (2000), in reviewing recidivism research on RJ, commented that studies rarely used randomised control groups, and where random assignment was used the treatment groups were to some extent self-selected, being volunteers, and hence not comparable with less willing participants. Latimer and Kleinknecht did state, however, that findings that were available tended to indicate a slight reduction in recidivism rates for RJ programmes. A randomised control study of RJ is currently being conducted in the UK, but outcomes are not available at the time of going to print.

There have been a number of evaluation studies that examine court-mandated sentences, and comparisons between various community penalties connected with probation or other treatments (Table 9.15). Although listed as *Promising* or *Unknown*, there are some contradictory results that point to the need for more systematic research comparing different

Table 9.12 Probation employment projects

Classification	Intervention — Description, SMS score & study details	With Whom? — Gender	Adult	YO	Juvenile	Age Range/ Mean	Ethnicity	In What Setting?	Effective in Reducing? — Criminal activity outcome, source, effectiveness	Follow-up (months)	At What Cost? £/$
What's Promising	Probation employment scheme ASSET (I) vs non-attenders (C) SMS = 3 [Sarno et al, 2000; 2001; reporting data from one project]	87% male	✓	✓	✓	Range 16–25 Mean 20.3	32% white	Community	Conviction (%) (official) Positive indication	12	There was no specific cost information but both projects had funding of £1m over a 3-year period [Sarno et al, 2000]

Key
Positive indication: Result favours intervention group
Negative indication: Result favours comparison group
No difference: No difference between the groups
Within: Measures were within groups (no between-group comparisons)
N/R: Not reported
SMS: Scientific Methods Score
YO: Young offender
Official: Police-recorded data
Victim survey: Questionnaires distributed to victims
Self-report: Reports by offenders
N/A: Not applicable
✓ : Participants fall into this category
– : Participants do not fall into this category
% : Dichotomous measure (individual)
# : Continuous measure (population)

Table 9.13 Motoring offending projects

Classification	Intervention: Description, SMS score & study details	With Whom? Gender	Adult	YO	Juvenile	Age Range/ Mean	Ethnicity	In What Setting?	Effective in Reducing? Criminal activity outcome, source, effectiveness	Follow-up (months)	At What Cost? £/$
What's Promising	Motor Project (I) vs control (C) SMS = 4 [Wilkinson, 1995, 1997; Wilkinson & Morgan, 1995; reporting data from one project]	100% male	✓	✓	N/R	Range N/R Mean 18.9	84% white	Community	Offending (%) (official) Positive indication Motoring offences (#) (official) Positive indication	12; 24; 36 12; 24; 36	N/R

Key
Positive indication: Result favours intervention group
Negative indication: Result favours comparison group
No difference: No difference between the groups
Within: Measures were within groups (no between-group comparisons)
N/R: Not reported
SMS: Scientific Methods Score
YO: Young offender
Official: Police-recorded data
Victim survey: Questionnaires distributed to victims
Self-report: Reports by offenders
N/A: Not applicable
✓ : Participants fall into this category
– : Participants do not fall into this category
% : Dichotomous measure (individual)
# : Continuous measure (population)

Table 9.14 Restorative justice studies

Classification	Intervention Description, SMS score & study details	With Whom? Gender	Adult	YO	Juvenile	Age Range/ Mean	Ethnicity	In What Setting?	Effective in Reducing? Criminal activity outcome, source, effectiveness	Follow-up (months)	At What Cost? £/$
What's Promising	1. Restorative justice adult scheme 1 (I) vs retrospective control (C)	92% male	✓	✓	–	Range 18–60 Mean 25.7	N/R	Community	Conviction (%) (official) Positive indication	≤24	Adult scheme 1 was shown to be cost effective
	2. Restorative justice adult scheme 2 (I1) vs retrospective control (C1) SMS = 4 [Miers et al., 2001]	N/R	✓	✓	–	Range 19–28 Mean 24.4	N/R	Community	Conviction (%) (official) No difference	≤24	Data was not available for adult scheme 2 [Miers et al., 2001] Drummond rating 7/11

(Continued)

Table 9.14 Restorative justice studies *(Continued)*

Classification	Intervention Description, SMS score & study details	With Whom? Gender	Adult	YO	Juvenile	Age Range/ Mean	Ethnicity	In What Setting?	Effective in Reducing? Criminal activity outcome, source, effectiveness	Follow-up (months)	At What Cost? £/$
What's Unknown	Restorative justice juvenile scheme (I2) vs retrospective control (C2) SMS = 4 [Miers et al., 2001]	84% male	–	–	✓	Range 10–17 Mean 13.8	N/R	Community	Conviction/caution (%) (official) No difference	≤24	N/R

Key
Positive indication: Result favours intervention group
Negative indication: Result favours comparison group
No difference: No difference between the groups
Within: Measures were within groups (no between-group comparisons)
N/R: Not reported
SMS: Scientific Methods Score
YO: Young offender
Official: Police-recorded data
Victim survey: Questionnaires distributed to victims
Self-report: Reports by offenders
N/A: Not applicable
✓ : Participants fall into this category
– : Participants do not fall into this category
% : Dichotomous measure (individual)
# : Continuous measure (population)

Table 9.15 Sentencing intervention studies

Classification	Intervention — Description, SMS score & study details	With Whom? — Gender	Adult	YO	Juvenile	Age Range/ Mean	Ethnicity	In What Setting?	Effective in Reducing? — Criminal activity outcome, source, effectiveness	Follow-up (months)	At What Cost? £/$
What's Promising	Probation & cognitive behavioural skills training (I) vs traditional probation (C) SMS = 5 [Deering et al., 1996]	N/R	N/R	N/R	N/R	N/R	N/R	Probation sentencing	Conviction (%) (official) Positive indication	12	N/R
What's Promising	Court-mandated programmes for domestic violence (I) vs other sentencing sanctions (C) SMS = 4 [Dobash et al., 1996, 1999; Dobash & Dobash, 1996]	100% male	N/R	N/R	N/R	N/R	N/R	General sentencing	Any violence (%) (self-report) Positive indication Frequent violence (%) (self-report) Positive indication	3; 12 3; 12	N/R
What's Promising	Probation order & day centre treatment & 4A requirement (I) vs probation orders & no requirement (I1) vs community service (I2) SMS = 3 [Home Office, 1993]	N/R	✓	✓	N/R	Range <21– 30+ Mean N/R	N/R	Probation sentencing	Conviction (%) (official) [I1 is most effective in comparison to I2 & I] Positive indication	24	N/R

(Continued)

Table 9.15 Sentencing intervention studies (Continued)

Classification	Intervention — Description, SMS score & study details	With Whom? Gender	Adult	YO	Juvenile	Age Range/Mean	Ethnicity	In What Setting?	Effective in Reducing? — Criminal activity outcome, source, effectiveness	Follow-up (months)	At What Cost? £/$
What's Promising	Probation only (I) vs probation with requirement (I1) vs community service (I2) vs combination orders (I3) SMS = 3 [May, 1999a, 1999b]	N/R	✓	✓	N/R	Range 17+ Mean N/R	N/R	Probation sentencing	Conviction (%) (official) [I2 is most effective] Positive indication	24	N/R
What's Promising	Enforcement action (I) vs minimal enforcement action (I1) vs no enforcement action (C) SMS = 3 [May & Wadwell, 2001]	N/R	N/R	N/R	N/R	N/R	N/R	General sentencing	Actual & predicted conviction (%) (official) [I is effective in reducing reconviction rates. I & C are not compared for level of significance] Positive indication	24	N/R

What's Promising	Probation order with no requirement (I) vs probation order with requirement (I1) vs probation order with day centre requirement (I2) vs prison only (I3) SMS = 3 [Oldfield, 1997]	N/R	✓ ✓ –	Range 17–30+ Mean N/R	N/R	Probation sentencing	Conviction (%) (official) [I1 was found to be more successful than I, I2 & I3] Positive indication	60	Estimated costs for probation is ≥105 per month vs prison £2,000 per month [Oldfield, 1997] Drummond rating 5/11
What's Promising	Probation order with requirement of group work (I) vs adult care team (I1) vs community probation project (I2) vs group work & intensive probation supervision (I3) SMS = 4 [Williams & Creamer, 1997]	N/R	✓ ✓ ✓	Range 16–30+	N/R	Probation sentencing	Actual & predicted custodial rates (%) (official) [Most marked proportionate decrease is displayed in I2] Positive indication	12	N/R

(Continued)

Table 9.15 Sentencing intervention studies (*Continued*)

Classification	Intervention — Description, SMS score & study details	With Whom?				Age Range/ Mean	Ethnicity	In What Setting?	Effective in Reducing? — Criminal activity outcome, source, effectiveness	Follow-up (months)	At What Cost? £/$
		Gender	Adult	YO	Juvenile						
What's Unknown	Intensive supervision orders of Heavy End Intermediate Treatment (I) vs other Intermediate Treatment (I1) vs supervision orders (I2) vs custody (I3) SMS = 3 [Bottoms, 1995]	100% male	–	✓	✓	Range 10–17 Mean 15.7	98% white	Probation Sentencing	Conviction by offence type (%) (official & self-report) [Comparison of I vs I3 & I1 vs I2 showed no difference on official data] No difference	14	Heavy End Intermediate Treatment (HEIT) was no more or less cost-effective than custody. A supervision order without intermediate treatment was more cost-effective than other intermediate treatment, HEIT or custody [Bottoms, 1995] Drummond rating 8/11

| What's Unknown | Electronic monitoring of released prisoners (I) vs retrospective control (C) SMS = 3 [Dodgson et al., 2001] | N/R | ✓ | ✓ | – | Range 18–50+ | N/R | Sentencing & the courts | Conviction (%) (official) No difference | 6 | At 16 months the net benefit to prison resources was £49.2m. The number of prison places saved was 2,600 [Dodgson et al., 2001] Drummond rating 7/11 |

Key

Positive indication: Result favours intervention group
Negative indication: Result favours comparison group
No difference: No difference between the groups
Within: Measures were within groups (no between-group comparisons)
N/R: Not reported
SMS: Scientific Methods Score
YO: Young offender
Official: Police-recorded data
Victim survey: Questionnaires distributed to victims
Self-report: Reports by offenders
N/A: Not applicable
✓ : Participants fall into this category
– : Participants do not fall into this category
% : Dichotomous measure (individual)
# : Continuous measure (population)

types of sentences, to define *What Works* and *For Whom*. When comparing the main community penalties, studies show effectiveness, for example, for probation with a requirement (Oldfield, 1997), probation without a requirement (Home Office, 1993), and community service orders in comparison with probation with and without requirements (May, 1999a, 1999b). One study found group work with intensive supervision to be effective (Williams & Creamer, 1997), while another found no difference in reconvictions between intensive supervision and standard supervision (Bottoms, 1995). This latter finding, that intensive supervision does not impact significantly more than standard supervision on reconvictions, is strongly supported in the international literature (MacKenzie, 2002). In contrast, it is interesting that enforcement action during probation supervision was found in one study to be more effective than minimal, or no, enforcement (May & Wadwell, 2001). The contradictory results overall on the comparative effectiveness of different community penalties may relate to differences in research design, or more probably to the lack of specificity in what is meant by 'a requirement' and the possible variety in types of supervision. Friendship and Debidin comment in their conclusions on the limitations of prison and probation research due to variation in a range of aspects of research design.

Court-mandated programmes for domestic violence were found to impact on self-report of domestic violence (Dobash, Cavanagh & Lewis, 1996; Dobash & Dobash, 1996; Dobash, Dobash, Cavanagh & Lewis, 1999). Such programmes for domestic violence, to the editors' knowledge, have not been replicated in international research.

Electronic monitoring was found not to impact on reconviction rates when compared to those released from prison without electronic monitoring (Dodgson et al., 2001). This finding has support in the international literature (Bonta, Wallace-Capretta & Rooney, 2000).

CCTV AND STREET-LIGHTING INTERVENTIONS

Results from UK studies on the effectiveness of CCTV are mixed (Table 9.16), as reported in a systematic review of CCTV (Welsh & Farrington, 2002). Three studies identified in the UK reported a positive effect on crime after the installation of CCTV. Eight studies reported either inconclusive or mixed results, with effectiveness frequently dependent on the type of offence. One study reported no difference between the intervention and control group.

The Welsh and Farrington (2002) review concluded that CCTV reduces crime to a small degree. It is most effective when used in car parks, but has little effect in city centres or on transport systems.

Table 9.16 CCTV intervention studies

Classification	Intervention Description, SMS score & study details	With Whom? Gender	Adult	YO	Juvenile	Age Range/ Mean	Ethnicity	In What Setting?	Effective in Reducing? Criminal activity outcome, source, effectiveness	Follow-up (months)	At What Cost? £/$
What Works	Car parks with CCTV (I) vs comparison car parks without CCTV (C) [Welsh & Farrington, 2002]	N/A	N/A	N/A	N/A	N/A	N/A	Crime Prevention	Varying measures of recorded crime (official) Positive indication	Varied	N/R
	Selection of 3 UK studies from the systematic review: Poyner, 1991; Tilley, 1993 (3 evaluations); Sarno, 1996	N/A	N/A	N/A	N/A	N/A	N/A	Crime Prevention	Positive indication	Varied	N/R
What Doesn't Work	City centres or public housing with CCTV (I) vs comparison areas (C) [Welsh & Farrington, 2002]	N/A	N/A	N/A	N/A	N/A	N/A	Crime Prevention	Varying measures of recorded crime (official & victim survey) Negative indication	Varied	One study reported that criminal justice benefits from fewer prosecutions and sentences were greater than running costs of CCTV by more than three times (benefit–cost ratio: 3.5:1) [Skinns, 1998]

(Continued)

Table 9.16 CCTV intervention studies *(Continued)*

Classification	Intervention Description, SMS score & study details	With Whom?						In What Setting?	Effective in Reducing?		At What Cost? £/$
		Gender	Adult	YO	Juvenile	Age Range/ Mean	Ethnicity		Criminal activity outcome, source, effectiveness	Follow-up (months)	
	Selection of 8 UK studies from the systematic review: Brown, 1995 (2 evaluations); Ditton & Short, 1999; Farrington, Bennett & Welsh, 2002; Sarno, 1996; Short & Ditton, 1995; 1996; Skinns, 1996; Armitage, Smyth & Pease, 1998; 1999 SMS = 3	N/A	N/A	N/A	N/A	N/A	N/A	Crime Prevention	Negative indication	Varied	N/R

What Doesn't Work									
Public transportation with CCTV (I) vs comparison public transportation (C) [Welsh & Farrington, 2002]	N/A	N/A	N/A	N/A	N/A	Crime Prevention	Varying measures of recorded crime (official) Negative indication	Varied	N/R
Selection of 2 UK studies from the systematic review: Burrows, 1979; Webb & Laycock, 1992 (2 evaluations)	N/A	N/A	N/A	N/A	N/A	Crime Prevention	Negative indication	Varied	N/R

Key
Positive indication: Result favours intervention group
Negative indication: Result favours comparison group
No difference: No difference between the groups
Within: Measures were within groups (no between-group comparisons)
N/R: Not reported
SMS: Scientific Methods Score
YO: Young offender
Official: Police-recorded data
Victim survey: Questionnaires distributed to victims
Self-report: Reports by offenders
N/A: Not applicable
✓ : Participants fall into this category
− : Participants do not fall into this category
% : Dichotomous measure (individual)
# : Continuous measure (population)

Table 9.17 Street lighting studies

Classification	Intervention — Description, SMS score & study details	With Whom? — Gender	With Whom? — Adult	With Whom? — YO	With Whom? — Juvenile	With Whom? — Age Range/Mean	With Whom? — Ethnicity	In What Setting?	Effective in Reducing? — Criminal activity outcome, source, effectiveness	Effective in Reducing? — Follow-up (months)	At What Cost? £/$
What Works	Area with street lighting (I) vs area without street lighting (C)										
	1. [Farrington & Welsh, 2002] Systematic review	N/A	N/A	N/A	N/A	N/A	N/A	Crime prevention	Recorded crime: Total crime (#) Violent crime (#) Property crime (#) (victim survey) Positive indication	Varied	N/R
	2. [Painter & Farrington, 1997; 2001a] SMS = 4	N/A	N/A	N/A	N/A	N/A	N/A	Crime prevention	Total offences (#) (self-report) Positive indication	12	The financial savings from reduced crimes exceeded the financial costs by between 2.2 and 9.4 times after one year. 9.4 times after one year. [Painter & Farrington, 1997; 2001a]
									Vandalism crimes (#) (self-report) Positive indication	12	
									Dishonesty crimes (#) (self-report) Positive indication	12	
									Total offences (#) (victim survey) Positive indication	12	Drummond rating 8/11
									Burglary offences (#) (victim survey) Positive indication	12	Drummond rating 8/11
									Vehicle offences (#) (victim survey) Positive indication	12	
									Violent offences (#) (victim survey) Positive indication	12	

Study								Measure		Comment
3. [Painter & Farrington, 1999b, 2001b] SMS = 4	N/A	N/A	N/A	N/A	N/A	N/A	Crime Prevention	Crime (%) (victim survey) Positive indication	12	Improved street lighting provided benefits in terms of the savings to the public from crimes prevented, which greatly outweighed the costs [Painter & Farrington, 1999b; 2001b] Drummond rating 8/11 Drummond rating 6/11
								Crime (#) (victim survey) Positive indication	12	
								Burglary offences (#) (victim survey) Positive indication	12	
								Vehicle offences (#) (victim survey) Positive indication	12	
								Vehicle offences (#) (victim survey) Positive indication	12	
4. [Pease, 1999] Literature review	N/A	N/A	N/A	N/A	N/A	N/A	Crime Prevention	Recorded crime Crime (#) (official) [within only] Positive indication	12	N/R
								Recorded crime (victim survey) Positive indication	12	

Key

Positive indication: Result favours intervention group
Negative indication: Result favours comparison group
No difference: No difference between the groups
Within: Measures were within groups (no between-group comparisons)
N/R: Not reported
SMS: Scientific Methods Score
YO: Young offender
Official: Police-recorded data
Victim survey: Questionnaires distributed to victims
Self-report: Reports by offenders
N/A: Not applicable
✓ : Participants fall into this category
− : Participants do not fall into this category
% : Dichotomous measure (individual)
# : Continuous measure (population)

205

Four studies identified in the UK reported a positive effect of improved street lighting on crime (Farrington & Welsh, 2002; Painter & Farrington, 1997, 1999a, 2001a, 2001b; Pease, 1999). The most comprehensive evidence is generated from a systematic review (Farrington & Welsh, 2002). The review concluded that street lighting led to a significant (30 per cent) decrease in crime.

In Chapter 6, Welsh and Farrington have taken the systematic reviews further, performing meta-analyses on studies of CCTV and street lighting, comparing the relative effectiveness of the two interventions. The systematic reviews incorporate international studies of CCTV and street lighting, and interestingly found differences between the results from UK studies and those from the US, with both CCTV and street lighting being more effective in reducing crime in the UK than in the US. Reasons for these differences are discussed in the chapter.

BURGLARY-REDUCTION INTERVENTIONS

The burglary-reduction studies (Barton, 2000; Bowers, 2001; Ekblom, 1996; Ekblom, Law & Sutton, 1996; Forrester, Frenz, O'Connor & Pease, 1990; Laycock, 1991; Pease, 1992; Tilley & Hopkins, 1998; Table 9.18) all met the criteria for inclusion in the review, and in all cases showed a significant decrease in offences. Bennett, in Chapter 7, has identified three additional studies published since July 2002 (Bowers, Shane, Johnson & Hirschfield, 2004; Hirschfield, 2004; Hope et al., 2004; Millie & Hough, 2004) that similarly meet the criteria for inclusion (Table 9.19), two of which record statistically significant impacts on crime, and one that reported mixed results (Hope et al., 2004). In summary, Bennett comments that the reviewed studies were generally positive and that implementation of situational crime-prevention measures tend to be associated with reductions in crime. Bennett adds, however, that 'as a result of general weaknesses with the research designs, it was often impossible to tell whether these reductions were caused by the measures evaluated'. In Chapter 7, the designs of the studies are clearly described, and where there are reasons for caution in interpretation of the results, Bennett gives a full explanation. Recommendations are given on how research designs in situational studies can be improved, and implications for policy are defined.

HOUSING STUDIES

A Secure by Design (SBD) housing project and a Priority Housing Estate (PEP) project were identified as meeting the criteria in the systematic review of UK effectiveness studies (Table 9.20). The SBD study (Armitage,

Table 9.18 Burglary-reduction studies

Classification	Intervention Description, SMS score & study details	With Whom? Gender	Adult	YO	Juvenile	Age Range/ Mean	Ethnicity	In What Setting?	Effective in Reducing? Criminal activity outcome, source, effectiveness	Follow-up (months)	At What Cost? £/$
What's Unknown	Neighbourhood watch scheme using a social/ situational approach (focusing on reducing opportunistic crime) (I) vs neighbourhood watch scheme using a situational approach (installing CCTV cameras) (II) [Barton, 2000] SMS = 4	N/A	N/A	N/A	N/A	N/A	N/A	Crime prevention	Burglary offences (#) (police data) [within groups only] Positive indication Theft of and from cars (#) (police data) [within groups only] Positive indication	24 24	N/R

(Continued)

Table 9.18 Burglary-reduction studies *(Continued)*

Classification	Intervention — Description, SMS score & study details	With Whom? — Gender	Adult	YO	Juvenile	Age Range/ Mean	Ethnicity	In What Setting?	Effective in Reducing? — Criminal activity outcome, source, effectiveness	Follow-up (months)	At What Cost? £/$
What Works	Residential burglary prevention schemes in geographic areas (I) vs comparison sites (C) [Ekblom et al., 1996; Ekblom, 1996] Summary review of evaluation projects	N/A	N/A	N/A	N/A	N/A	N/A	Crime Prevention	Burglary (% and #) (police data & victim survey) [Effective in areas classified as 'high action' with high levels of burglary at the start of the programme] Positive indication	Each 12 months for up to 6 years	Overall the cost of burglary was diminished where burglary was more common [Ekblom 1996; Ekblom et al., 1996] Drummond rating 8/11
What's Unknown	Repeat victimisation and burglary initiative in a housing estate (I) vs adjacent areas (C) SMS = 3 [Forrester et al., 1990; Pease, 1992]	N/A	N/A	N/A	N/A	N/A	N/A	Crime Prevention	Burglary (#) (official & victim survey) Positive indication	36	The cost savings of the project at the end of the 3 year period indicated a balance of cost savings of £1.2 million [Forrester et al. 1990; Pease, 1992]

What's Unknown								
Houses participating in an operation identification scheme aimed at reducing domestic burglary (I) vs houses that did not receive the intervention or display stickers/decals (C) SMS = 3 [Laycock, 1991]	N/A	N/A	N/A	N/A	N/A	Crime Prevention	Burglary (%) (official) Positive indication	12	N/R
							Burglary (#) (official) [within groups only] Positive indication	12; 24	
Crime prevention and target-hardening measures in small businesses (I) vs control areas (C) SMS = 4 [Bowers, 2001]	N/A	N/A	N/A	N/A	N/A	Crime Prevention	Burglary and other crime by offence type (#) (victim survey) [within groups only] Positive indication	N/R	N/R

(Continued)

Table 9.18 Burglary-reduction studies (*Continued*)

Classification	Intervention: Description, SMS score & study details	With Whom? Gender	With Whom? Adult	With Whom? YO	With Whom? Juvenile	With Whom? Age Range/ Mean	Ethnicity	In What Setting?	Effective in Reducing? Criminal activity outcome, source, effectiveness	Effective in Reducing? Follow-up (months)	At What Cost? £/$
What's Unknown	Areas with intervention tackling repeat victimisation in small business crime (I & II) vs comparison areas without intervention (C) [Tilley & Hopkins, 1998] SMS = 3	N/A	N/A	N/A	N/A	N/A	N/A	Crime Prevention	Commercial burglary (% and #) (official & survey) Positive indication	24	Monetary losses from crime are reported. [Tilley & Hopkins, 1998]

Key
Positive indication: Result favours intervention group
Negative indication: Result favours comparison group
No difference: No difference between the groups
Within: Measures were within groups (no between-group comparisons)
N/R: Not reported
SMS: Scientific Methods Score
YO: Young offender
Official: Police-recorded data
Victim survey: Questionnaires distributed to victims
Self-report: Reports by offenders
N/A: Not applicable
✓ : Participants fall into this category
− : Participants do not fall into this category
% : Dichotomous measure (individual)
# : Continuous measure (population)

Table 9.19 Burglary-reduction studies (literature in addition to the *UK review*)

	Intervention	With Whom?								In What Setting?	Effective in Reducing?		At What Cost?
	Description, SMS score & study details	Gender	Adult	YO	Juvenile	Age Range/ Mean	Ethnicity				Criminal activity outcome, source, effectiveness	Follow-up (months)	£/$
Classification													
What's Unknown	Evaluation of projects reporting a range of interventions in Reducing Burglary Initiative scheme areas (I) vs police force areas (C) in the North of England												
	1. [Hirschfield, 2004] SMS = 3	N/A	N/A	N/A	N/A	N/A	N/A			Crime Prevention	Burglary (#) (official) Positive indication	24	Input costs were £2.9 million; cost of burglaries saved was £2.5 million. Overall cost–benefit ratio was 0.89 [Hirschfield, 2004]

(Continued)

Table 9.19 Burglary-reduction studies (literature in addition to the *UK review*) (*Continued*)

Classification	Intervention Description, SMS score & study details	With Whom? Gender	Adult	YO	Juvenile	Age Range/ Mean	Ethnicity	In What Setting?	Effective in Reducing? Criminal activity outcome, source, effectiveness	Follow-up (months)	At What Cost? £/$
	2. [Bowers et al., 2004] SMS = 3	N/A	N/A	N/A	N/A	N/A	N/A	Crime Prevention	Burglary (#) (official) Positive indication Output intensity was significantly correlated with burglary reduction	N/R	Input intensity (amount of money spent on schemes) was not correlated with burglary reduction [Bowers et al. 2004]
What's Unknown	Neighbourhood watch schemes in 2 geographic areas (I & II) vs comparison sites (C1 & C2) SMS = 3 [Bennett, 1990]	N/A	N/A	N/A	N/A	N/A	N/A	Crime prevention	Household offences (#) (official and victim survey) Negative indication	12	Nominal salary costs for (I) were £1,727 and £2,118 for (II) for the first year of operation. Non-salary costs for (I) were £308 and £254 for (II) during the same period [Bennett, 1990]
									Household offences (%) (official and victim survey) Negative indication	12	
									Personal offences (#) (official and victim survey) Negative indication	12	
									Personal offences (%) (official and victim survey) Negative indication	12	

| *What's Unknown* | Evaluation of 21 projects reporting a range of interventions in Reducing Burglary Initiative scheme areas (I) vs police basic command unit areas (C) in the Midlands of England [Hope et al., 2004] SMS = 3 | N/A | N/A | N/A | N/A | N/A | N/A | Crime Prevention | Burglary (#) (official) Mixed results (Approximately one third of the projects showed (I) to be effective) | ≤34 | Limited cost data was presented. |

(Continued)

Table 9.19 Burglary-reduction studies (literature in addition to the *UK review*) (*Continued*)

	Intervention	With Whom?						In What Setting?	Effective in Reducing?		At What Cost?
	Description, SMS score & study details	Gender	Adult	YO	Juvenile	Age Range/ Mean	Ethnicity		Criminal activity outcome, source, effectiveness	Follow-up (months)	£/$
Classification											
What's Unknown	Evaluation of 21 projects reporting a range of interventions in Reducing Burglary Initiative scheme areas (I) vs police basic command unit areas (C) in the South of England [Millie & Hough, 2004] SMS = 3	N/A	N/A	N/A	N/A	N/A	N/A	Crime Prevention	Burglary (#) (official) Positive indication (Based on data from 16 projects)	12	Cost of projects ranged between £63,000 and £609,000 [Mallender et al., 2002]

Key
Positive indication: Result favours intervention group
Negative indication: Result favours comparison group
No difference: No difference between the groups
Within: Measures were within groups (no between-group comparisons)
N/R: Not reported
SMS: Scientific Methods Score
YO: Young offender
Official: Police-recorded data
Victim survey: Questionnaires distributed to victims
Self-report: Reports by offenders
N/A: Not applicable
✓ : Participants fall into this category
– : Participants do not fall into this category
% : Dichotomous measure (individual)
# : Continuous measure (population)

Table 9.20 Housing studies

<table>
<tr>
<th rowspan="3"></th>
<th>Intervention</th>
<th colspan="7">With Whom?</th>
<th rowspan="3">In What Setting?</th>
<th colspan="2">Effective in Reducing?</th>
<th rowspan="3">At What Cost?</th>
</tr>
<tr>
<th rowspan="2">Description, SMS score & study details</th>
<th rowspan="2">Gender</th>
<th rowspan="2">Adult</th>
<th rowspan="2">YO</th>
<th rowspan="2">Juvenile</th>
<th rowspan="2">Ethnicity</th>
<th colspan="2">Age Range/ Mean</th>
<th>Criminal activity outcome, source, effectiveness</th>
<th>Follow-up (months)</th>
</tr>
<tr>
<th></th>
<th></th>
<th></th>
<th>£/$</th>
</tr>
<tr>
<td>Classification</td>
<td></td>
<td></td>
<td></td>
<td></td>
<td></td>
<td></td>
<td></td>
<td></td>
<td></td>
<td></td>
<td></td>
<td></td>
</tr>
<tr>
<td>*What's Unknown*</td>
<td>Secure By Design (SBD) housing (I) vs control housing estate (C)

SMS = 3
[Armitage, 2000]</td>
<td>N/A</td>
<td>N/A</td>
<td>N/A</td>
<td>N/A</td>
<td>N/A</td>
<td>N/A</td>
<td>N/A</td>
<td>Crime prevention</td>
<td>Total crime per house recorded (#)
Positive indication
Total crime (%) (victim survey)
Positive indication
Burglary offences per household (#) (victim survey)
Positive indication
Vehicle crime (#) (victim survey) [within only]
Burglary (%) (victim survey)
Positive indication</td>
<td>Estate completion until 01/03/2000</td>
<td>Average cost based on Registered Social Landlords (RSL), quantity surveyors and builders was £440 more per SBD dwelling than a housing estate without SBD. Refurbishment of an estate to SBD standard was estimated at £600, as opposed to newly built SBD dwellings. [Armitage, 2000] Drummond rating 5/11</td>
</tr>
</table>

(Continued)

Table 9.20 Housing studies (*Continued*)

Classification	Intervention Description, SMS score & study details	With Whom? Gender	Adult	YO	Juvenile	Age Range/ Mean	Ethnicity	In What Setting?	Effective in Reducing? Criminal activity outcome, source, effectiveness	Follow-up (months)	At What Cost? £/$
What's Unknown	Priority Housing Estate Project (PEP) (I & I1) vs control housing estate (C & C1) SMS = 3 [Foster & Hope, 1993]	N/A	N/A	N/A	N/A	N/A	N/A	Crime prevention	Crime by offence type (#) (official) No difference	12	N/R

Key
Positive indication: Result favours intervention group
Negative indication: Result favours comparison group
No difference: No difference between the groups
Within: Measures were within groups (no between-group comparisons)
N/R: Not reported
SMS: Scientific Methods Score
YO: Young offender
Official: Police-recorded data
Victim survey: Questionnaires distributed to victims
Self-report: Reports by offenders
N/A: Not applicable
✓ : Participants fall into this category
− : Participants do not fall into this category
% : Dichotomous measure (individual)
# : Continuous measure (population)

216

2000) reported a reduction in the incidence of burglary and total recorded crime in SBD housing estates. The PEP project (Foster & Hope, 1993) did not have a significant effect on burglary rates.

Bennett, in Chapter 7, comments on the research designs for such project evaluations, and praises the PEP project design in combining quantitative evaluation with qualitative investigation of potential causal mechanisms at work.

ECONOMIC ASSESSMENT

A number of UK studies included cost information, and in most cases this greatly helped consideration of the value of the intervention. Some studies (Armitage, 2000; Bottoms, 1995; Dodgson et al., 2001; Ekblom, 1996; Ekblom et al., 1996; Farrington et al., 2002; Miers et al., 2001; Oldfield, 1997; Painter & Farrington, 1999 a, 1999b; Sarno et al., 2001) provided comprehensive information on the cost, cost-effectiveness or costs and benefits of the interventions. The topic areas that included economic analyses were housing strategies to prevent crime, intensive supervision orders, electronic monitoring, burglary-reduction strategies, intensive regimes, adult restorative justice, probation versus prison, CCTV, street lighting, and probation employment projects. It is encouraging that some authors now consider research to be incomplete without the inclusion of cost and benefit information. In addition to describing the methodologies adopted in the UK studies, Swaray, in Chapter 8, goes on to review how economic analysis is applied internationally to studies of effectiveness in criminal justice.

SUMMARY OF THE FINDINGS FROM THE SYSTEMATIC REVIEW OF UK STUDIES ON EFFECTIVENESS IN REDUCING CRIME

The chapters in this book have incorporated studies identified in a systematic review of UK effectiveness completed in 2002, together with updated evidence of subsequent research. Those studies which met the inclusion criteria for the review and subsequential studies of similar standard have been summarised in tables throughout Chapter 9, and described fully in the preceding chapters.

A wide range of subject areas met the review's inclusion criteria. Many of the studies evaluated cognitive behavioural programmes and community rehabilitation projects, situational crime-prevention and situational crime-reduction projects. Clear gaps in the range of studies were interventions for specific groups, that is, young offenders, women offenders and ethnic minority offenders. Not surprisingly, there were few early childhood and school interventions, as these mainly would not include offence and reconviction data, which was the main criterion for inclusion in the review. However, neither were there any rigorous studies on the impact on offending of basic educational or vocational skills training, which might have been expected.

A number of studies looked at the impact of selected sentences on offenders, and in some cases produced contradictory findings, possibly due to the use of different methodologies and different implementations of interventions with similar titles. Some comparisons were unreliable as a result of the baseline differences in risk between offenders given custodial and community sentences. A more strategic view of the sentencing framework would be helpful to examine the effectiveness of the range of sentences in a consistent way. An update on the Lloyd, Mair & Hough (1994) cohort study comparing prison with a number of community sentences would be valuable.

The *UK review* found no studies that evaluated impact of sentence length, although the early-release home detention curfew research (Dodgson et al., 2001) gave an indication that early release under this scheme did not impact on reconviction rates.

A number of studies included cost and benefits information, but these were in the minority. However, it is encouraging to note that some authors routinely include cost–benefit information. This is of value to both researchers and policy makers in making decisions on resource allocation, based on the best value for money.

Research is needed to answer some methodological questions, such as the validity of reconviction data compared with self-report of offending, the predictive validity of interim outcome measures, and the appropriate follow-up periods for different types of offender and offence.

RECOMMENDATIONS FROM THE UK EFFECTIVENESS REVIEW

- The gaps in research knowledge need to be filled; for example, more studies are required on interventions with specific groups of offenders, and on the impact of education and vocational training on reducing offending. Information is required on sentencing and what works, with whom.
- There is a need for a common standard of research design and analysis. It is recognised that 'gold standard' randomised controlled trial (RCT)

methodologies cannot always be implemented in operational settings, but where these are not possible there should be agreement on the appropriate statistical controls required to reduce bias.

- Where possible, researchers should be supported, by those commissioning research, in implementing rigorous research designs with RCTs or matched control groups.
- Quality checklists should be adopted to ensure good research practice is followed.
- Research studies need to include costs and benefits information on interventions.
- Research should identify and validate interim and longer-term outcome measures.
- Follow-up periods should be appropriate to the offence and offender type.

IMPLICATIONS FOR FUTURE DEVELOPMENT

It may seem discouraging that so many properly conducted systematic reviews in criminal justice end with the conclusion that comparatively few studies have been identified, and that a majority of studies are not sufficiently rigorous to allow firm conclusions to be drawn. There is an ongoing debate as to whether, therefore, the 'bar should be lowered' in order to include more studies, and indeed some of the authors who have contributed to this book hold that view. However, the counter-argument is that lowering the bar would be a premature and unsatisfactory solution. The Campbell Collaboration is still a relatively young organisation (founded in February 2000) and is currently laying the foundations of knowledge for future research. Although at present systematic reviews need to cover many years of research, only to find there is little in the way of firm evidence to report, this need not be a long-term problem. Once the foundations of knowledge have been laid, it will not be such a lengthy process to continually update systematic reviews, which is a prime Campbell Collaboration goal. Now that quality standards are being firmly proposed, it can be expected that updates of systematic reviews will in future have access to more rigorous research.

Although it can be argued that it is as easy to conduct good-quality research as poor research, the authors would not agree with this statement. In 'real world' research and evaluation there are many practical obstacles to setting up rigorous research, in particular RCTs (Farrington et al., 2002), even though there are firm intentions at the outset. Operational managers have practical considerations to take into account, pressure to provide interventions to reduce crime, targets to meet, and an impetus to implement new ideas. It is not easy to make a case for 'no treatment' control groups against these considerations. Quality research needs extra data collection, which can be time consuming and costly. When research evidence is required quickly and at minimum cost, these are formidable obstacles. However, rigorous research and evaluation is unlikely to become an accepted step in the process of implementation of interventions until such quality research produces results.

The case for quality research has been championed by the Campbell Collaboration and by the Jerry Lee Center in the US, along with the ground-breaking review for the National Institute of Justice (Sherman et al., 1997). There is evidence that the messages about quality research are being heard more widely and adopted within governments. The research strategy for the developing National Offender Management Service (NOMS) in the UK, bringing together prison and probation services, pledges to base its policies on the highest-quality research evidence, 'moving to adopt more powerful and more appropriate research designs, e.g. randomised controlled trials' (NOMS, 2004); and RCTs are beginning to be commissioned, as in the case of evaluation of restorative justice in the UK. It is for researchers to meet this challenge and to provide the quality research that will lay the foundations for effective criminal justice interventions.

REFERENCES

Allam, J. (1998). *Effective Practice in Work with Sex Offenders. A Reconviction Study Comparing Treated and Untreated Offenders*. West Midlands: Probation Service Sex Offender Unit.

Anderson, D., Chenery, S. & Pease, K. (1995). Biting Back: Tackling Repeat Burglary and Car Crime. *Crime Detection and Prevention Series Paper 58*. London: Home Office.

Armitage, R., Smyth, G., & Pease, K. (1999). Burnley CCTV evaluation. In: Painter K. & Tilley, N. (Eds.). *Surveillance of Public Space: CCTV, Street Lighting and Crime Prevention. Crime Prevention Studies* (Volume 10). Monsey, NY: Criminal Justice Press.

Armitage, R. (2000). An evaluation of secure by design housing within West Yorkshire. *Home Office Briefing Note 7/00*. London: Home Office.

Baldwin, S., Heather, N., Lawson, A., Ward, M., Robb, E., Williams, A., Greer, C., Gamba, S. & Robertson, I. (1991). Effectiveness of pre-release alcohol education courses for young offenders in a penal institution. *Behavioural Psychotherapy*, **19**, 321–31.

Barton, A. (2000). A tale of two projects: The growth and development of two neighbourhood watch schemes in South Wales. *Crime Prevention and Community Safety: An International Journal*, **2**(3), 7–16.

Bennett, T.H. (1990). *Evaluating Neighbourhood Watch*. Vermont: Gower.

Bonta, J., Wallace-Capretta, S. & Rooney, J. (2000) A quasi-experimental evaluation of an intensive rehabilitation supervision programme. *Criminal Justice and Behaviour*, **27**(3), 312–29.

Bottoms, A.E. (1995). *Intensive Community Supervision for Young Offenders: Outcomes, Process and Cost.* Cambridge: Institute of Criminology.

Bowers, K.J. (2001). Small business crime: The evaluation of a crime prevention initiative. *Crime Prevention and Community Safety: An International Journal,* **7**, 23–42.

Bowers, K.J., Shane, D. Johnson, S.D. & Hirschfield, A.F.G (2004). The measurement of crime prevention intensity and its impact on levels of crime. *British Journal of Criminology,* **44**(3), 419–40.

Brown, B. (1995). CCTV in Town Centres: Three Case Studies. *Crime Detection and Prevention Series Paper 68.* London: Home Office.

Burnside, J., Adler, J., Loucks, N. & Rose, G. (2001). Kainos programme evaluation. *Executive Summary 17.* London: Home Office.

Burrows, J.N. (1980). The impact of closed circuit television on crime in the London Underground. In: Mayhew, P., Clarke, R.V.G., Burrows, J.N., Hough, J.M. & Winchester, S.W.C. (Eds.). Crime in Public View. *Home Office Research Study 49.* London: HMSO.

Cann, J., Falshaw, L., Nugent, F. & Friendship, C. (2003). Understanding what works: Accredited cognitive skills programmes for adult men and young offenders. *Home Office Research Findings 226.* London: Home Office.

Chenery, S., Holt, J. & Pease, K. (1997). Biting back II: Reducing repeat victimization in Huddersfield. *Crime Detection and Prevention Series Paper 82.* London: Home Office.

Coid, J., Carvell, A., Kittler, Z., Healey, A. & Henderson, J. (2000). The impact of methadone treatment on drug misuse and crime. *Home Office Research Findings 120.* London: Home Office.

Cooke, D.J. (1991). Treatment as an alternative to prosecution: offenders diverted for treatment. *British Journal of Psychiatry,* **158**, 785–91.

Deering, J., Thurston, R. & Vanstone, M. (1996). Individual supervision: An experimental programme in Pontypridd. *Probation Journal,* **43**(2), 70–76.

Ditton, J. & Short, E. (1999). Yes, it works, no, it doesn't: Comparing the effects of open-street CCTV in two adjacent Scottish town centres. In K. Painter & N. Tilley (eds), *Surveillance of Public Space: CCTV, Street Lighting and Crime Prevention. Crime Prevention Studies* (Vol. 10). Monsey, NY: Criminal Justice Press.

Dobash, R., Cavanagh, K. & Lewis, R. (1996). Changing violent men. *Probation Journal,* **43**(4), 217–18.

Dobash, R. & Dobash, E.R. (1996). *Re-Education Programmes for Violent Men: An Evaluation.* London: HMSO.

Dobash, R., Dobash, E.R., Cavanagh, K. & Lewis, R. (1999). A research evaluation of British programmes for violent men. *Journal of Social Policy,* **28**(2), 205–33.

Dodgson, K., Goodwin, P., Howard, P., Llewellyn-Thomas, S., Mortimer, E., Russell, N. & Weiner, M. (2001). Electronic monitoring of released prisoners: An evaluation of the Home Detention Curfew Scheme. *Home Office Research Study 222.* London: Home Office.

Ekblom, P. (1996). Safer cities and residential burglary: A summary of evaluation results. *European Journal on Criminal Policy and Research,* **4**, 22–52.

Ekblom, P., Law, H. & Sutton, M. (1996). Safer cities and domestic burglary. *Home Office Research Study 164.* London: Home Office.

Falshaw, L., Friendship, C., Travers, R. & Nugent, F. (2003). Searching for 'what works': An evaluation of cognitive skills programmes. *Home Office Research Findings 206.* London: Home Office.

Falshaw, L., Friendship, C., Travers, R. & Nugent, F. (2004). Searching for 'What Works': HM Prison Service Accredited Cognitive Skills Programmes. *British Journal of Forensic Practice*, **6**(2), 3–11.

Farrington, D.P., Bennett, T.H. & Welsh, B.C. (2002). Rigorous evaluations of the effects of CCTV on crime. Unpublished manuscript. Cambridge: Institute of Criminology, University of Cambridge.

Farrington, D., Bowen, S., Buckle, A., Burns-Howell, T., Burrows, J. and Speed, M. (1993). An experiment on the prevention of shoplifting. *Crime Prevention Studies* (Vol. 1). New York: Criminal Justice Press.

Farrington, D.P., Ditchfield, J., Hancock, G., Howard, P., Jolliffe, D., Livingston, M.S. & Painter, K.A. (2002). Evaluation of two intensive regimes for young offenders. *Home Office Research Findings 239*. London: Home Office.

Farrington, D.P., Hancock, G., Livingston, M.S., Painter, K.A. & Towl, G. (2000). Evaluation of intensive regimes for young offenders. *Home Office Research Findings 121*. London: Home Office.

Farrington, D.P. & Welsh, B.C. (2002). Effects of improved street lighting on crime: A systematic review. *Home Office Research Study 251*. London: Home Office.

Forrester D., Frenz S., O'Connor M. & Pease K. (1990). The Kirkholt Burglary Prevention Project: Phase II. *Crime Prevention Unit Paper 23*. London: Home Office.

Foster, J. & Hope, T. (1993). Housing, community and crime: The impact of the Priority Estates Project. *Home Office Research Study 131*. London: Home Office.

Friendship, C., Blud, L., Erikson, M. & Travers, R. (2002). An evaluation of cognitive behavioural treatment for prisoners. *Home Office Research Findings 161*. London: Home Office.

Friendship, C., Mann, R. & Beech, A. (2003a). The prison-based Sex Offender Treatment Programme: An evaluation. *Home Office Research Findings 205*. London: Home Office.

Friendship, C., Mann, R.E. & Beech, A.R. (2003b). An evaluation of a national prison-based treatment program for sexual offenders in England and Wales. *Journal of Interpersonal Violence*, **18**, 744–59.

Haynes, P. (1998). Drug using offenders in south London: Trends and outcomes. *Journal of Substance Abuse Treatment*, **15**, 449–56.

Hedderman, C. & Sugg, D. (1996). Does treating sex offenders reduce reoffending? *Home Office Research Findings 45*. London: Home Office.

Hine, J. & Celnick, A. (2001). A one-year reconviction study of final warnings. London: Home Office. (www.homeoffice.gov.uk/rds/pdfs/reconvictstudywarn.pdf).

Hirschfield, A. (2004). The impact of the Reducing Burglary Initiative. *Home Office Online Report 40/04*. London: Home Office.

Hollin, C., Palmer, E., McGuire, J., Hounsome, J., Hatcher, R., Bilby, C. & Clark, C. (2004). Pathfinder programmes in the probation service: A retrospective analysis. *Home Office Online Report 66/04*. London: Home Office.

Home Office (1993). Reconvictions of those given probation and community service orders in 1987. *Home Office Statistical Bulletin 18/93*. London: Home Office.

Honess, T., Maguire, M. & Chapman, E. (1993). Vehicle watch and car theft: An evaluation. *Police Research Group Crime Prevention Unit Series Paper 50*. London: Police Research Group Crime Prevention Unit.

Hope, T., Bryan, J., Crawley, E., Crawley, P., Russell, N. & Trickett, A. (2004). Strategic Development Projects in the Yorkshire and the Humber, East Midlands and Eastern regions. *Home Office Online Report 41/04*. London: Home Office.

Hough, M., Clancy, A., McSweeney, T. & Turnbull, P.J. (2003). The impact of drug treatment and testing orders on offending: two-year reconviction results. *Home Office Research Findings 184*. London: Home Office.

James, D., Farnham, F., Moorey, H., Lloyd, H., Hill, K., Blizard, R. & Barnes, T.R.E. (2002). Outcome of psychiatric admission through the courts. *RDS Occasional Paper 79*. London: Home Office.

Keen, J., Rowse, G., Mathers, N., Campbell, M. & Seivewright, N. (2000). Can methadone maintenance for heroin-dependent patients retained in general practice reduce criminal conviction rates and time spent in prison? *British Journal of General Practice*, **50**, 48–9.

Latimer, J. & Kleinknecht, S. (2000) *The Effects of Restorative Justice Programming: A Review of the Empirical Research Reports*. Canada: Department of Justice, Research and Statistics Division.

Laycock, G. (1991). Operation identification or the power of publicity? *Security Journal*, **2**(2), 67–72.

Lees, J., Manning, N. & Rawlings, B. (1999). Therapeutic community effectiveness. *NHS CRD Report Number 17*. York: University of York.

Lloyd, C., Mair, G. & Hough, M. (1994). Explaining reconviction rates: A critical analysis. *Research, Development & Statistics, Research Findings 12*. London: Home Office.

MacKenzie, D.L. (2002). Reducing the criminal activities of known offenders and delinquents. Crime prevention in the courts and corrections. In L.W. Sherman, D.P. Farrington, B.C. Welsh & D.L. MacKenzie (eds), *Evidence-Based Crime Prevention*, pp. 330–404. London: Routledge.

MacKenzie, D.L., Wilson, D.B. & Kiders, B. (2001). Effects of correctional boot camps on offending. *The Annals of the American Association for Political and Social Sciences*, **578**, 126–43.

Mallender, J., Roberts, E. & Sedden, T. (2002). Evaluation of drug testing in the Criminal Justice System in three pilot areas. *Home Office Research Findings 176*. London: Home Office.

Marshall, P. (1997). A reconviction study of HMP Grendon therapeutic community. *Home Office Research Findings 53*, 1–4. London: Home Office.

Martin, C. & Player, E. (2000). *Drug Treatment in Prison: An Evaluation of the RAPt Treatment Programme*. Winchester: Waterside Press.

May, C. (1999a). Explaining reconviction following a community sentence: The role of social factors. *Home Office Research Study 192*. London: Home Office.

May, C. (1999b). The role of social factors in predicting reconviction for offenders on community penalties. *Home Office Research Findings 97*. London: Home Office.

May, C. & Wadwell, J. (2001). Enforcing community penalties: The relationship between enforcement and reconviction. *Home Office Research Findings 155*, 1–4. London: Home Office.

McCulloch, H. (1996). Shop theft: Improving the police response. *Crime Detection & Prevention Series Paper 76*. London: Home Office.

McCusker, C. & Davies, M. (1996). Prescribing drug of choice to illicit heroin users: The experience of a UK community drug team. *Journal of Substance Abuse Treatment*, **13**, 521–31.

McMurran, M. & Boyle, M. (1990). Evaluation of a self-help manual for young offenders who drink. *British Journal of Clinical Psychology*, **29**, 117–19.

Metrebian, N., Shanahan, W., Stimson, G.V., Small, C., Lee, M., Mtutu, V. & Wells, B. (2001). Prescribing drug of choice to opiate dependent drug users: A comparison of clients receiving heroin with those receiving injectable methadone at a West London drug clinic. *Drug and Alcohol Review*, **20**, 267–76.

Miers, D., Maguire, M., Goldie, S., Sharpe, K. & Hale, C. (2001). Exploratory evaluation of restorative justice schemes. *Crime Reduction Research Paper 9*, 113. London: Home Office.

Millie, A. & Hough, M. (2004). Assessing the impact of the Reducing Burglary Initiative in southern England and Wales. *Home Office Online Report 42/04*. London: Home Office.

National Probation Service (2002). Reducing reconviction rates. *Service Briefing. National Probation Service Issue 4*. London: National Probation Service.

NOMS (2004). Review of 'What Works' Evidence Base and the Juvenile and Adult Reconviction Results. *Home Office Briefing, Issue 2*. (www.probation. homeoffice.gov.uk/output/page27.asp)

Oldfield, M. (1997). What worked? A five year study of probation reconvictions. *Probation Journal*, **44**(1), 2–10.

Painter, K. & Farrington, D.P. (1997). The crime reducing effect of improved street lighting: The Dudley project. In R.V.G Clarke (ed.), *Situational Crime Prevention: Successful Case Studies* (2nd edn). Guilderland, NY: Harrow and Heston.

Painter, K.A. & Farrington, D.P. (1999a) Street lighting and crime: Diffusion of benefits in the Stoke-on Trent project. In K.A. Painter & N. Tilley (eds), *Surveillance of Public Space: CCTV, Street Lighting and Crime Prevention: Crime Prevention Studies* (pp 77–122). Monsey, NY: Criminal Justice Press.

Painter, K.A. & Farrington, D.P. (1999b). Improved street lighting: Crime reducing effects and cost–benefit analysis. *Security Journal*, **12**(4), 17–32.

Painter, K.A. & Farrington D.P. (2001a). Evaluating situational crime prevention using a young people's survey. *British Journal of Criminology*, **41**(2), 266–84.

Painter, K.A. & Farrington, D.P. (2001b). The financial benefits of improved street lighting, based on crime reduction. *Lighting Research Technology*, **331**(1), 3–12.

Parker, H. & Kirby, P. (1996). Methadone maintenance and crime reduction on Merseyside. *Police Research Group, Crime Detection and Prevention Series, Paper 72*. London: Home Office.

Patterson, D.G., Macpherson, J. & Brady, N.M. (1997). Community psychiatric nurse aftercare for alcoholics: A five-year follow-up study. *Addiction*, **92**, 459–68.

Pearson, F.S., Lipton, D.S., Cleland, C.M. & Yee, D.S. (2002). The effects of behavioural/cognitive-behavioural programs on recidivism. *Crime & Delinquency*, **4**(3), 476–96.

Pease, K. (1992). Situational crime prevention: Preventing burglary on a British public housing estate. In R.V.G Clarke (ed.), *Successful Case Studies*. New York: Harrow & Heston.

Pease, K. (1999). A review of street lighting evaluations: Crime reduction effects. In K. Painter & N. Tilley (eds), *Surveillance of Public Space: CCTV, Street Lighting and Crime Prevention* (pp 47–76). Monsey, NY: Criminal Justice Press.

Poyner, B. (1991). Situational crime prevention in two parking facilities. *Security Journal*, **2**, 96–101.

Proctor, E. (1994). Sex offender programmes: Do they work? *Probation Journal*, **41**(1), 31–2.

Rix, B. & Kock, E. (1997) A review of police trials of the CS aerosol incapacitant. *Police Research Series Paper 21*. London: Home Office.

Sallybanks, J. (2001). Assessing the police use of decoy vehicles. *Police Research Series Paper 137*, 1–38. London: Home Office.

Sarno, C. (1995). Impact of CCTV on Crime. In M. Bulos (ed.) *Towards a Safer Sutton? Impact of Closed Circuit Television on Sutton Town Centre*. London: London Borough of Sutton.

Sarno, C. (1996). The impact of closed circuit television on crime in Sutton town centre. In M. Bulos & D. Grant (eds), *Towards a Safer Sutton? CCTV One Year On*. London: London Borough of Sutton.

Sarno, C., Hearnden, I. & Hedderman, C. (2001). From offending to employment: A study of two probation schemes in inner London. *Home Office Research Findings 135*, 1–4. London: Home Office.

Sarno, C., Hearnden, I., Hedderman, C., Hough, M., Nee, C. & Herrington, V. (2000). Working their way out of offending: An evaluation of two probation employment schemes. *Home Office Research Study 218*. London: Home Office.

Sherman, L. & Eck, J. (2002). Policing for crime prevention. In L. Sherman, D. Farrington, B. Welsh & D. MacKenzie (eds), *Evidence-Based Crime Prevention* London: Routledge.

Sherman L.W., Gottfredson, D., Mackenzie, D., Eck, J., Reuler, P. & Bushay, S. (1997). *Preventing Crime: What Works, What Doesn't, What's Promising: A Report to the United States Congress*. (www.cjcentral.com/sherman/sherman.htm).

Short, E. & Ditton, J. (1995). Does Closed Circuit Television Prevent Crime? An Evaluation of the Use of CCTV Surveillance Cameras in Airdrie Town Centre. The Scottish Office Central Research Findings. (www.scotland.gov.uk/cru).

Singer, L.R. (1991). A non-punitive paradigm of probation practice: Some sobering thoughts. *British Journal of Social Work*, **21**, 611–26.

Skinns, D. (1998). Crime reduction, diffusion and displacement: evaluating the effectiveness of CCTV. In C. Norris, J. Moran & G. Armstrong (eds), *Surveillance, Closed Circuit Television and Social Control*. Aldershot: Ashgate.

Squires, P. (2002). *Independent Evaluation of the Battle Town Centre CCTV System*. Brighton, UK: Health and Social Policy Research Centre, University of Brighton.

Stewart-Ong, G., Harsent, L., Roberts, C., Burnett, R. & Al-Attar, Z. (2004). *Think first prospective research study: effectiveness and reducing attrition*. What Works NPD Programme Evaluation Findings June 2004. (National Probation Service). London: Home Office.

Taylor, R. (2000). Seven-year reconviction study of HMP Grendon therapeutic community. *Research Findings 115*, 1–4. London: Home Office.

Tilley, N. (1993). Understanding car parks, crime and CCTV: Evaluation lessons from safer cities. *Crime Prevention Unit Series Paper 42*. London: Home Office.

Tilley, N. & Hopkins, M. (1998). Business as usual: An evaluation of the Small Business and Crime initiative. *Policy Research Series Paper 95*. London: Home Office.

Webb, B. & Laycock, G. (1992). Reducing crime on the London Underground: An evaluation of three pilot projects. *Crime Prevention Unit Paper 30*. London: Home Office.

Welsh, B.C. & Farrington, D.P. (2002). Crime prevention effects of closed circuit television: A systematic review. *Home Office Research Study 252*. London: Home Office.

Williams, B. & Creamer, A. (1997). Evaluating Scottish special probation schemes: In G. Mair (ed.), *Evaluating the Effectiveness of Community Penalties*. Aldershot: Avery.

Wilkinson, J.M. (1995). Ilderton motor project. *Probation Journal*, **42**(3), 162–63.

Wilkinson, J.M. (1997). The impact of Ilderton motor project on motor vehicle crime and offending. *British Journal of Criminology*, **37**(4), 568–851.

Wilkinson, J.M. & Morgan, D. (1995). *The Impact of Ilderton Motor Project on Motor Vehicle Crime and Offending.* A report for the inner London probation service.

Willner, P., Hart, K., Binmore, J., Cavendish, M. & Dunphy, E. (2000). Alcohol sales to underage adolescents: An unobtrusive observational field study and evaluation of a police intervention. *Addiction*, **95**(9), 1373–88.

Index